Wiley Study Guide for 2018 Level I CFA Exam

Volume 2: Economics

Thousands of candidates from more than 100 countries have relied on these Study Guides to pass the CFA® Exam. Covering every Learning Outcome Statement (LOS) on the exam, these review materials are an invaluable tool for anyone who wants a deep-dive review of all the concepts, formulas, and topics required to pass.

Wiley study materials are produced by expert CFA charterholders, CFA Institute members, and investment professionals from around the globe. For more information, contact us at info@efficientlearning.com.

Wiley Study Guide for 2018 Level I CFA Exam

Volume 2: Economics

WILEY

Contents

ABOUT THE AUTHORS

Wiley's Study Guides are written by a team of highly qualified CFA charterholders and leading CFA instructors from around the globe. Our team of CFA experts work collaboratively to produce the best study materials for CFA candidates available today.

Wiley's expert team of contributing authors and instructors is led by Content Director Basit Shajani, CFA. Basit founded online education start-up Élan Guides in 2009 to help address CFA candidates' need for better study materials. As lead writer, lecturer, and curriculum developer, Basit's unique ability to break down complex topics helped the company grow organically to be a leading global provider of CFA Exam prep materials. In January 2014, Élan Guides was acquired by John Wiley & Sons, Inc., where Basit continues his work as Director of CFA Content. Basit graduated magna cum laude from the Wharton School of Business at the University of Pennsylvania with majors in finance and legal studies. He went on to obtain his CFA charter in 2006, passing all three levels on the first attempt. Prior to Élan Guides, Basit ran his own private wealth management business. He is a past president of the Pakistani CFA Society.

There are many more expert CFA charterholders who contribute to the creation of Wiley materials. We are thankful for their invaluable expertise and diligent work. To learn more about Wiley's team of subject matter experts, please visit: www.efficientlearning.com/cfa/why-wiley/.

STUDY SESSION 4: MICROECONOMICS AND MACROECONOMICS

READING 14: TOPICS IN DEMAND AND SUPPLY ANALYSIS

LESSON 1: DEMAND ANALYSIS: THE CONSUMER

Please note that this reading has three prerequisite readings that are not included in the curriculum or our study guides. You can find our coverage of the prerequisite readings and associated videos in the Resources section of www.efficientlearning.com/cfa.

LOS 14a: Calculate and interpret price, income, and cross-price elasticities of demand and describe factors that affect each measure. Vol 2, pp 6–18

LOS 14b: Compare substitution and income effects. Vol 2, pp 18–23

LOS 14c: Distinguish between normal goods and inferior goods. Vol 2, pp 18–23

Demand Analysis: The Consumer

Demand Concepts

Demand is defined as the willingness and ability of consumers to purchase a given amount of a good or a service at a particular price. The quantity that consumers are willing to purchase depends on several factors, the most important being the product's own-price. The law of demand states that as the price of a product increases (decreases), consumers will be willing and able to purchase less (more) of it (i.e., price and quantity demanded are inversely related). Other factors that influence the ability and willingness of consumers to purchase a good include income levels, tastes, and preferences, and prices and availability of substitutes and complements. The demand function captures the effect of all these factors on demand for a good.

Note that the law of demand need not hold in all circumstances.

$$\text{Demand function: } QD_x = f(P_x, I, P_y, \ldots) \quad \ldots \text{(Equation 1)}$$

Equation 1 is read as "the quantity demanded of Good X (QD_X) depends on the price of Good X (P_X), consumers' incomes (I), and the price of Good Y (P_Y), etc."

A hypothetical example of a demand function is the following equation, which links the per-household quantity of gasoline demanded per week (in gallons), **QD_G**, to the price (in terms of dollars per gallon) of gasoline, **P_G**, per-household annual income (in thousands of dollars), **I**, and the average price of an automobile (in thousands of dollars), **P_A**.

Economists use the term own-price when referring to the price of the good that is the focus of analysis. In Equation 2, P_G (price of gasoline) represents own-price.

$$\text{Demand equation: } QD_G = 7.5 - 0.5P_G + 0.1I - 0.05P_A \quad \ldots \text{(Equation 2)}$$

From the demand equation, notice that:

We shall learn about cross-price elasticity later in the reading. Complements are goods with negative cross-price elasticity, while substitutes exhibit positive cross-price elasticity.

- The sign on the coefficient of gasoline price is negative. An increase (decrease) in the price of gasoline results in a decrease (increase) in quantity demanded. Note that this relationship conforms to the law of demand.
- The sign on consumers' income is positive. An increase (decrease) in income results in an increase (decrease) in demand for gasoline.
- The sign on the price of automobiles is negative. An increase (decrease) in the price of automobiles results in a decrease (increase) in demand for gasoline. This suggests that gasoline and automobiles are complements.

The Latin phrase *ceteris paribus* is used widely in economics textbooks. It literally stands for "all other things being equal." In this reading, we will use the phrase "holding all other things constant" to stand for the same thing.

Note that income and the price of automobiles are not ignored in this equation. They are only assumed constant and their impact on demand for gasoline is incorporated in the new constant term (12).

Notice that we have used three independent variables in our example (own-price, consumers' income, and the price of automobiles). Economists typically concentrate on the relationship between quantity demanded and the product's **own-price** (which makes it easier to represent the relationship on a two-dimensional graph) and assume that all other independent variables that impact demand are constant when expressing the demand equation.

Let us now assume that the values of consumers' income (I) and the price of automobiles (P_A) are constant at 60 (or $60,000 per year) and 30 (or $30,000) respectively. Inserting these values in our demand equation allows us to express the relationship between the quantity of gasoline demanded and gasoline prices as:

$$QD_G = 7.5 - 0.5P_G + 0.1(60) - 0.05(30) = 12 - 0.5P_G \quad \text{... (Equation 3)}$$

Note that Equation 3 presents quantity demanded as the dependent variable and price as the independent variable. However, economists prefer to present demand curves with quantity on the x-axis and price on the y-axis. To come up with an equation in line with these preferences, we need to invert the demand function, which basically requires us to make price the subject of the demand equation. The inverse demand function in our example is determined as follows:

$$QD_G = 12 - 0.5P_G \Rightarrow P_G = 24 - 2QD_G \quad \text{... (Equation 4)}$$

Figure 1-1 presents the graph of our inverse demand function, which is called the demand curve. Note that we need to restrict the value of QD_G in Equation 4 to 12 so that price is not negative.

Figure 1-1: Demand Curve for Gasoline

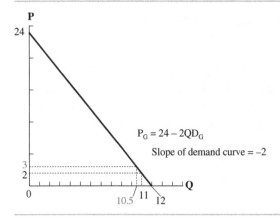

Note the following regarding the demand curve:

- The demand curve is drawn with quantity on the x-axis and price on the y-axis.
- The demand curve shows the maximum quantity of gasoline demanded at every given price (e.g., at a price of $2/gallon, an individual household would be willing and able to buy 11 gallons of gasoline every week).
- Alternatively, one could also interpret the demand curve as showing the highest price a household is willing and able to pay for every given quantity of gasoline (e.g., the highest price a household would be willing and able to pay for 11 gallons of gasoline every week is $2/gallon).

- If the price of gasoline were to rise by $1/gallon to $3/gallon, the quantity of gasoline a household would be able and willing to purchase would fall to 10.5 gallons per week.
- The slope of the demand curve is calculated as the change in price divided by the change in quantity demanded ($\Delta P / \Delta QD$). For our demand curve, the slope equals $(\$3 - \$2)/(10.5 - 11) = -2$.

It is very important for us to understand that the demand curve is drawn up based on the inverse demand function (which makes price the subject), not the demand function (which makes quantity demanded the subject). The slope of the demand curve is therefore not the coefficient on own-price (P_G) in the demand function; instead it equals the coefficient on quantity demanded (QD_G) in the inverse-demand function. Note that the slope of the demand curve is also the reciprocal of the coefficient on own-price (P_G) in the demand function ($1/-0.5 = -2$).

Demand Elasticities

Own-Price Elasticity of Demand

A firm's total revenue equals quantity sold times price. Given that price and quantity demanded are negatively related, a firm needs to know how sensitive quantity demanded is to changes in price to determine the overall impact of a price change on total revenue. For example, if prices were increased, a firm would need to analyze how much quantity demanded would fall and how total revenue would be affected. If the percentage increase in price is greater than the percentage decrease in quantity demanded, total revenue will increase. If the percentage increase in price is lower than the percentage decrease in quantity demanded, total revenue will decline.

Assume that the following equation represents the market demand function:

$$Q_{DG} = 12,000 - 500_{PG} \quad \text{... (Equation 5)}$$

One measure of the sensitivity of quantity demanded to changes in price is the slope of the demand function. Equation 5 tells us that for a one-unit change in price, quantity demanded moves by 500 units in the other direction. Unfortunately, this measure is dependent on the units in which we measure QD and P. As a result, economists prefer to use elasticity as a measure of sensitivity. Elasticity uses percentage changes in the variables and is independent of the units used to measure the variables.

The own-price elasticity of demand is calculated as:

$$ED_{Px} = \frac{\% \Delta QD_x}{\% \Delta P_x} \quad \text{... (Equation 6)}$$

If we express the percentage change in X as the change in X divided by the value of X, Equation 6 can be expanded to the following form:

Slope of demand function

Coefficient on own-price in market demand function

$$ED_{Px} = \frac{\% \Delta QD_x}{\% \Delta P_x} = \frac{\Delta QD_x / QD_x}{\Delta P_x / P_x} = \left(\frac{\Delta QD_x}{\Delta P_x} \right) \left(\frac{P_x}{QD_x} \right) \quad \text{... (Equation 7)}$$

$TR = Q \times P$

The expression that is Equation 7 tells us that we can compute the own-price elasticity of demand by multiplying the slope (−500) of the demand function, $\Delta QD_x/\Delta P_x$ (or the inverse of the slope of the demand curve, $1/[\Delta QD_x/\Delta P_x]$), by the ratio of price to quantity, P_x/QD_x. At a price of \$2 per gallon, using the equation for the market demand for gasoline ($QD_G = 12{,}000 - 500\,P_G = 11{,}000$), we can compute the own-price elasticity of demand for gasoline as:

$$ED_{PG} = -500 \times (2/11{,}000) = -0.09091$$

We usually look at the absolute value of own-price elasticity of demand when classifying how sensitive quantity demanded is to changes in price:

- If own-price elasticity of demand equals 1 (percentage change in quantity demanded is the same as the percentage change in price), demand is said to be unit elastic (see Figure 1-2a).
- If own-price elasticity of demand equals 0 (quantity demanded does not change at all in response to a change in price), demand is said to be perfectly inelastic (see Figure 1-2b).
- If own-price elasticity of demand equals ∞ (quantity demanded changes by an infinitely large percentage in response to even the slightest change in price), demand is said to be perfectly elastic (see Figure 1-2c).
- If the absolute value of price elasticity of demand lies between 0 and 1, demand is said to be relatively inelastic.
- If the absolute value of price elasticity of demand is greater than 1, demand is said to be relatively elastic.

[handwritten margin note: Know these definitions]

Figure 1-2: Price Elasticity of Demand

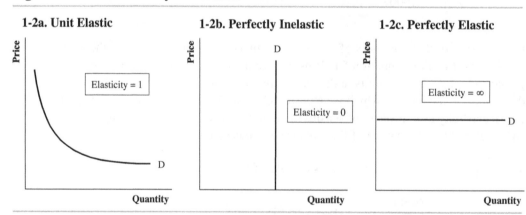

1-2a. Unit Elastic   1-2b. Perfectly Inelastic   1-2c. Perfectly Elastic

In our example, demand for gasoline appears to be relatively inelastic, as the absolute value of own-price elasticity lies between 0 and 1.

An important thing to note is that while the slope of the demand curve remains constant along a downward-sloping linear demand curve, the ratio of price to quantity is different at each point along the demand curve (unless the demand curve is perfectly elastic or perfectly inelastic), as shown in Figure 1-3.

Figure 1-3: The Elasticity of a Linear Demand Curve

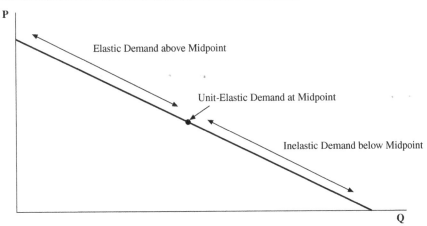

Note: For all negatively sloped linear demand curves, elasticity varies depending on where it is calculated.

At relatively low prices (relatively high quantities), the ratio of price to quantity is relatively low, so own-price elasticity of demand (absolute value of ED_P) is low and demand is relatively inelastic.

At relatively high prices (relatively low quantities), the ratio of price to quantity is relatively high, so own-price elasticity of demand (absolute value of ED_P) is high and demand is relatively elastic.

Demand is unit elastic at the midpoint of the demand curve, relatively elastic above the midpoint, and relatively inelastic below the midpoint.

Predicting Demand Elasticity

Availability of Close Substitutes

If a consumer can easily switch away from a good, her ability to respond to a price increase (by reducing consumption of the good) is high, and demand for that product would be relatively elastic. Generally speaking, the demand curve faced by an individual producer is relatively more elastic than the demand curve for the entire market. For example, demand for Nike® shoes is more elastic than demand faced by the shoe industry as a whole, as there are more substitutes for Nike shoes (e.g., Reebok®, Adidas®, etc.) than for shoes in general.

Proportion of Income Spent on the Good

If a relatively small proportion of a consumer's income is spent on a good (e.g., soap), she will not significantly cut down on consumption if prices increase. Demand for such a good will be relatively inelastic. However, if consumption of the good takes up a larger proportion of her income (e.g., automobiles), she might be forced to reduce quantity demanded significantly when the price of the good increases. Demand for such a good will be relatively elastic.

Time Elapsed since Price Change

The longer the time that has elapsed since the price change, the more elastic demand will be. For example, if the price of gasoline goes up, we may not be able to immediately reduce the quantity we consume because we cannot make radical changes to our modes of transportation, housing, and work location. Therefore, short-run demand for gasoline will be relatively inelastic. However, in the long term, if the price of gasoline remains high, we may use a different mode of transportation or reduce the distance of our commute. Therefore, long-run demand for gasoline will be relatively elastic.

Note, however, that durable goods tend to behave differently. If the prices of refrigerators were to fall, we might react quickly and make a purchase if we have an old machine that we know will need replacing soon. However, if the prices of refrigerators were to stay low for an extended period of time, it is unlikely that we would buy more refrigerators over a lifetime.

The Extent to Which the Good Is Viewed as Necessary or Optional

The more the good is seen as being necessary (or non-discretionary), the less elastic its demand is likely to be. The more the good is seen as being optional (or discretionary), the more elastic its demand is likely to be. For example, demand for milk (a non-discretionary item) is less elastic than demand for opera tickets (a discretionary item).

Own-Price Elasticity of Demand and Total Expenditure

We established earlier that own-price elasticity changes along the demand curve. Now let's look into how total expenditure on a good changes as its price fluctuates.

Total expenditure (and revenue) equals price times quantity purchased (sold). If prices are *reduced* to stimulate sales, total revenue will only increase if the percentage *increase* in demand (sales) is *greater* than the percentage *decrease* in prices.

The relationship between total expenditure and price depends on price elasticity of demand:

- If demand is relatively elastic (elasticity greater than 1), a 5% *decrease* in price will result in an *increase* in quantity demanded of *more* than 5%. Therefore, total expenditure will *increase*.
- If demand is relatively inelastic (elasticity less than 1), a 5% *decrease* in price will result in an *increase* in quantity demanded of *less* than 5%. Therefore, total expenditure will *decrease*.
- If demand is unit elastic, a 5% *decrease* in price will result in an *increase* in quantity demanded of exactly 5%. Therefore, total expenditure will *not change*.

> When price elasticity is greater than one (relatively elastic), the numerator MUST be greater than the denominator. If the denominator changes by 5%, the numerator HAS to change by more than 5%. The effect of a decrease in prices will be outweighed by the effect of the increase in quantity demanded and total expenditure will rise.

The total expenditure (revenue) test gauges price elasticity by looking at the direction of the change in total revenue in response to a change in price:

- If the price cut *increases* total revenue, demand is relatively elastic.
- If the price cut *decreases* total revenue, demand is relatively inelastic.
- If the price cut *does not change* total revenue, demand is unit elastic.

The values in Table 1-1 are used to construct the demand and total revenue curves in Figure 1-4.

Table 1-1: Price, Demand, Total Revenue, and Elasticity

Price $	Quantity units	Total Revenue $	Elasticity
1	50	50	
			–0.16
2	45	90	
			–0.29
3	40	120	
			–0.47
4	35	140	
			–0.69
5	30	150	
			–1
6	25	150	
			–1.44
7	20	140	
			–2.14
8	15	120	
			–3.4
9	10	90	
			–6.33
10	5	50	

Note that we have used the arc elasticity formula to calculate the elasticities in this table.

Just FYI: Arc elasticity of demand is calculated using the formula below:

$$E_P = \frac{\frac{(Q_0 - Q_1)}{(Q_0 + Q_1)/2} \times 100}{\frac{(P_0 - P_1)}{(P_0 + P_1)/2} \times 100}$$

You do NOT need to know this formula or how to perform these calculations. We have just provided them here to illustrate an important concept with numbers.

Figure 1-4: Elasticity and Total Expenditure

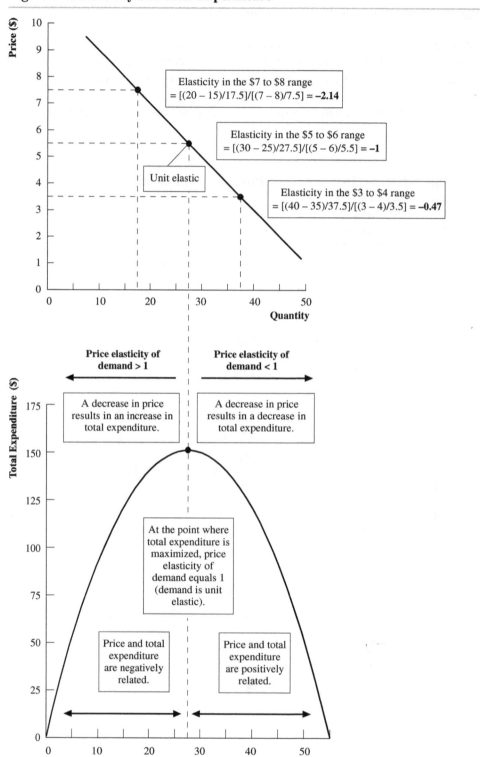

Total Revenue and Price Elasticity

Looking at things from a producer's perspective, the change in the total amount of money earned from sales also depends on sensitivity of quantity demanded to changes in price.

- If the demand curve facing a producer is relatively elastic, an *increase* in price will *decrease* total revenue.
- If the demand curve facing a producer is relatively inelastic, an *increase* in price will *increase* total revenue.
- If the demand curve facing a producer is unit elastic, an *increase* in price will not change total revenue.

Note that if a producer is currently charging a price that lies in the inelastic region of the demand curve, she can increase total revenue by increasing her prices. The benefit of higher prices would outweigh the negative impact of lower quantities sold. Further, since a lower quantity is being sold (and produced), total costs would also fall, which implies a certain boost in profitability. Therefore, no producer would knowingly set a price that falls in the inelastic region of the demand curve.

Income Elasticity of Demand

Income elasticity of demand measures the responsiveness of demand for a particular good to a change in income, holding all other things constant.

$$ED_I = \frac{\%\Delta QD_x}{\%\Delta I} = \frac{\Delta QD_x / QD_x}{\Delta I / I} = \left(\frac{\Delta QD_x}{\Delta I}\right)\left(\frac{I}{QD_x}\right) \quad \text{... (Equation 8)}$$

Same as coefficient on I in market demand function

$$E_I = \frac{\% \text{ change in quantity demanded}}{\% \text{ change in income}}$$

Income elasticity of demand can be positive, negative, or zero. Products are classified along the following lines:

If income elasticity is *greater* than 1, demand is income elastic, and the product is classified as a normal good.

$E_I > 1 \Rightarrow$ Normal good (income elastic)

- As income *rises*, the percentage increase in demand *exceeds* the percentage change in income.
- As income *increases*, a consumer spends a *higher proportion* of her income on the product.

$0 < E_I < 1 \Rightarrow$ Normal good (income inelastic)

If income elasticity lies *between* zero and 1, demand is income inelastic, but the product is still classified as a normal good.

$E_I < 0 \Rightarrow$ Inferior good

- As income *rises*, the percentage *increase* in demand is *less* than the percentage increase in income.
- As income *increases*, a consumer spends a *lower proportion* of her income on the product.

If income elasticity is *less than zero (negative)*, the product is classified as an inferior good.

- As income *rises*, there is a *negative* change in demand.
- The *amount* spent on the good *decreases* as income *rises*.

For some goods, in some income ranges, income may have no impact on demand for the good. For these goods, income elasticity of demand equals 0.

Note that when income changes, there is a shift in the demand curve (change in demand). An increase in income results in an increase in demand (shift in demand curve to the right) for normal goods, and a decrease in demand (shift in demand curve to the left) for inferior goods. Further, an income elasticity of demand of 0.5 for a particular good means that whenever income increases by 1%, the quantity demanded **at each price** would rise by 0.5%.

Cross-Price Elasticity of Demand

Cross elasticity of demand measures the responsiveness of demand for a particular good to a change in price of *another* good, holding all other things constant.

Same as coefficient on P_Y in market demand function (Equation 11)

$$ED_{Py} = \frac{\%\Delta QD_x}{\%\Delta P_y} = \frac{\Delta QD_x / QD_x}{\Delta P_y / P_y} = \left(\frac{\Delta QD_x}{\Delta P_y}\right)\left(\frac{P_y}{QD_x}\right) \quad \text{... (Equation 9)}$$

$$E_C = \frac{\% \text{ change in quantity demanded}}{\% \text{ change in price of substitute or complement}}$$

Substitutes

If the price of Burger King®'s burgers were to go up, what would be the effect on demand for McDonald's® burgers?

$E_C > 0 \Rightarrow$ substitutes

$E_C < 0 \Rightarrow$ complements

For most people, these are close *substitutes* for each other. An increase in price of Burger King®'s burgers will result in a significant increase in demand for McDonald's® burgers as consumers switch to the relatively lower priced substitute.

The magnitude of the cross elasticity figure tells us how closely the two products serve as substitutes for each other. A *high* value indicates that the products are very *close* substitutes (i.e., if the price of one rises by only a small amount, demand for the other will rise significantly). For substitutes, the numerator and denominator of the cross-elasticity formula head in the *same* direction. Therefore cross-price elasticity of demand for substitutes is *positive*. Note that two products are classified as substitutes if the cross-price elasticity of demand is positive, regardless of whether they would actually be considered similar.

Complements

If the price of playing a round of golf on a golf course were to rise, what would be the effect on demand for golf balls?

Since playing a game of golf is impossible without golf balls, these products are *complements* for each other. An *increase* in price of using a golf course will reduce the number of rounds of golf played, and bring about a *decrease* in demand for golf balls.

For complements, the numerator and denominator of the cross-elasticity formula head in *opposite* directions. Therefore, the cross elasticity of demand for complements is *negative*. Note that two products are classified as complements if the cross-price elasticity of demand is negative, regardless of whether they are typically consumed as a pair.

The *absolute value* of the cross-elasticity figure tells us how closely consumption of the two products is tied together and how closely they serve as complements for each other. A *high* absolute number indicates very *close* complements. If the price of one *rises,* consumers will *significantly reduce* their demand for the other.

Also note that for substitutes, an increase in the price of another good results in an increase in demand (shift in demand to the right), while for complements, an increase in price of another good results in a decrease in demand (shift in demand to the left).

Calculating Demand Elasticities from Demand Functions

Given Equations 7, 8, and 9, we can easily calculate the own-price, cross-price, and income elasticities of demand for gasoline. Assume that the market demand function for gasoline is given by:

$$QD_G = 7{,}500 - 500P_G + 100I - 50P_A$$

Let's calculate the own-price, income, and cross-price elasticities of demand assuming that $P_G = \$3/\text{gallon}$, $I = \$60{,}000/\text{year}$, and $P_A = \$30{,}000$. The first step is to determine quantity demanded given the above values for the independent variables:

$QD_G = 7{,}500 - 500(3) + 100(60) - 50(30) = 10{,}500$ gallons. Given the quantity demanded, we calculate the different elasticities by simply plugging numbers into the elasticity formulas:

$$ED_{Px} = \frac{\%\Delta QD_x}{\%\Delta P_x} = \frac{\Delta QD_x/QD_x}{\Delta P_x/P_x} = (-500)\left(\frac{3}{10{,}500}\right) = -0.143$$

Coefficient on own-price in market demand function

$$ED_I = \frac{\%\Delta QD_x}{\%\Delta I} = \frac{\Delta QD_x/QD_x}{\Delta I/I} = (100)\left(\frac{60}{10{,}500}\right) = 0.571$$

Same as coefficient on I in market demand function

$$ED_{Py} = \frac{\%\Delta QD_x}{\%\Delta P_y} = \frac{\Delta QD_x/QD_x}{\Delta P_y/P_y} = (-50)\left(\frac{30}{10{,}500}\right) = -0.143$$

Same as coefficient on P_Y in market demand function

- Since the absolute value of own-price elasticity lies between 0 and 1, we conclude that demand is relatively inelastic at a price of $3/gallon.
- Since income elasticity is positive and lies between 0 and 1, we conclude that gasoline is a normal good.
- Since cross-price elasticity is negative, we conclude that gasoline and automobiles are complements.

Substitution and Income Effects

The law of demand states that when the price of a good falls, quantity demanded increases, and when the price of a good rises, quantity demanded decreases. There are two main reasons for this:

1. The substitution effect: The good becomes relatively cheaper compared to other goods, so more of the good gets substituted for other goods in the consumer's consumption basket. For example, when the price of beef falls, it becomes relatively cheaper compared to chicken. As a result, the typical consumer will purchase a little more beef and a little less chicken than before.
2. The income effect: The consumer's real income increases (in terms of the quantity of goods and services that can be purchased with the same dollar income), which leads to an increase in quantity of the good purchased. For example, if the price of beef were to fall, the typical consumer would purchase more beef (and other goods, as well) because of the increase in her real income.

Normal and Inferior Goods

We introduced the concepts of normal and inferior goods earlier when we described income elasticity of demand.

- For normal goods, an increase in income causes consumers to buy more of those goods.
- For inferior goods, an increase in income causes consumers to buy less of those goods.

We know that there are two effects at play when there is a change in the price of a good: the substitution effect and the income effect.

Normal Goods

If a good is normal, a decrease in price will result in the consumer buying more of that good. Both the substitution effect and the income effect are at play here:

- A decrease in price tends to cause consumers to buy more of this good in place of other goods.
- The increase in real income resulting from the decline in this good's price causes people to buy even more of this good.

Essentially, for normal goods (e.g., restaurant meals, which most people tend to buy more of when their incomes rise), the substitution and the income effects reinforce one another.

Inferior Goods

If a good is an inferior good:

- The substitution effect of a change in price will be the same as for a normal good (i.e., a decrease in price of the good will cause the consumer to buy more of the good).
- However, the income effect will be the opposite of what it is for a normal good. For an inferior good, the increase in real income resulting from a decline in the good's price will cause the consumer to buy **less** of this good.

Overall, for an inferior good (e.g., margarine, which most people buy less of as their incomes rise), the income effect mitigates the substitution effect of a price change.

Note the following:

- "Inferior" does not imply that the good is of poor quality; it is just a term that is used to refer to a good that some people tend to buy less of if they have an increase in income.
- The same good can be a normal good to some consumers and an inferior good to others. For example, fast-food meals may be a normal good for the very low-income segment of the population, but an inferior good for high-income groups.

To conclude:

- The substitution effect of a change in price will always go in the direction opposite to that of the price change. If the price increases, less will be consumed, and if the price decreases, more will be consumed.
- The income effect of that same price change, however, depends on whether the good is normal or inferior.
  - For a normal good, the income effect reinforces the substitution effect, both leading to a negatively sloped demand curve.
  - For an inferior good, the income effect and the substitution effect work in opposite directions.

Giffen and Veblen Goods

For Giffen goods and Veblen goods, the demand curve is actually upward sloping. An increase in price results in an increase in quantity demanded, and a decrease in price results in a decrease in quantity demanded. However, the reasons behind this anomalous shape of the demand curve are different for these two types of goods.

Giffen Goods

A Giffen good is a special case of an inferior good where the negative income effect of a decrease in price of the good is so strong that it outweighs the positive substitution effect. Therefore, for a Giffen good, quantity demanded actually falls when there is a decrease in price, which makes the demand curve upward sloping.

Note the following:

- All Giffen goods are inferior goods because the income effect and substitution effect work in opposite directions.
- However, not all inferior goods are Giffen goods.
  - For inferior goods, the income effect partially mitigates or offsets the substitution effect.
  - For Giffen goods, the income effect outweighs the substitution effect.

Veblen Goods

Sometimes, the price tag of a good itself determines its desirability for consumers. For example, with status goods such as expensive jewelry, the high price itself adds to the utility from the good, such that the consumer values the item more if it has a higher price. Such goods are known as Veblen goods, and it is argued that their demand curves are also upward sloping just like Giffen goods. However, there remains a fundamental difference between the two:

- Giffen goods are inferior goods. They are not status goods. An increase in income would reduce demand for them (due to negative income elasticity of demand).
- Veblen goods are not inferior goods. An increase in income would not lead to a decrease in demand.

LESSON 2: SUPPLY ANALYSIS: THE FIRM

LOS 14d: Describe the phenomenon of diminishing marginal returns. Vol 2, pp 23–43

LOS 14e: Determine and interpret breakeven and shutdown points of production. Vol 2, pp 39–43

LOS 14f: Describe how economies of scale and diseconomies of scale affect costs. Vol 2, pp 43–48

Productivity

In the short run, at least one factor of production is fixed. Usually we assume that labor is the only variable factor of production in the short run. Therefore, the only way that a firm can respond to changing market conditions in the short run is by changing the quantity of labor that it employs. In hard times, firms lay off labor, and in good times, firms employ more labor. However, the quantities of capital and land employed remain fixed. A firm cannot increase output in the short run by acquiring more machinery or equipment.

In the long run, quantities of all factors of production can be varied. Output can be increased by employing more labor, acquiring more machinery, or even buying a whole new plant. However, once a long-run decision has been made (e.g., the acquisition of a new plant), it cannot be easily reversed.

The analyses in the sections that follow pertain to the short run.

Marginal Returns and Productivity

The cost of producing a given level of output can fall as a result of:

- A decline in the cost of inputs, and/or
- An increase in input productivity. An improvement in labor productivity occurs when, given a fixed amount of capital, fewer units of labor are required to produce the same output.

Productivity is important because a firm that lags behind the industry in productivity is at a competitive disadvantage and is likely to face decreases in future earnings and shareholder wealth.

Total, Average, and Marginal Product of Labor

In Table 2-1 we assume that in the short run, the firm invests in 2 units of capital, which comprise its fixed costs. The only factor of production whose quantities it can vary is labor. As more units of labor are employed to work with 2 units of capital, total output increases.

Table 2-1: Total Product, Marginal Product, and Average Product

Quantity of Labor (Q_L)	Quantity of Capital (Q_K)	Total Product (TP)	Marginal Product (MP) $\dfrac{\text{Change in TP}}{\text{Change in } Q_L}$	Average Product (AP) $\dfrac{\text{TP}}{Q_L}$
0	2	0		
1	2	5	5	5.00
2	2	12	7	6.00
3	2	17	5	5.67
4	2	20	3	5.00
5	2	22	2	4.4
6	2	21	−1	3.5

Total product (TP) is the maximum output that a given quantity of labor can produce when working with a fixed quantity of capital units. While TP provides an insight into the company's size relative to the overall industry, it does not show how efficient the firm is in producing its output.

Marginal product (MP) (also known as marginal return) equals the increase in total product brought about by hiring one more unit of labor, while holding quantities of all other factors of production constant. MP measures the productivity of the individual additional unit of labor.

Average product (AP) equals total product of labor divided by the quantity of labor units employed. AP is a measure of overall labor productivity. The higher a firm's AP, the more efficient it is.

AP and MP provide valuable insights into labor productivity. However, when individual worker productivity is difficult to monitor, (e.g., when tasks are performed collectively) AP is the preferred measure of labor productivity.

From Table 2-1, notice that TP continues to increase until the 6th unit of labor is employed. The firm would obviously not hire a unit with negative productivity, so only the first 5 units of labor are considered for employment.

Figure 2-1 illustrates the firm's total product (TP) curve. In the initial stages (as the first and second units of labor are employed), total product *increases at an increasing rate*. The slope of the total product curve is relatively *steep* at this stage. Later, as more units of labor are employed to work with the fixed 2 units of capital, total output *increases at a decreasing rate*, and the slope of the TP curve becomes *flatter*.

Figure 2-1: Total Product

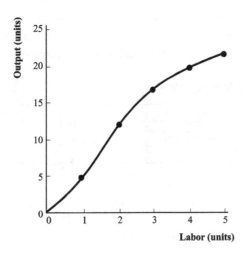

The marginal product (MP) curve (see Figure 2-2) shows the change in total product from hiring one additional unit of labor. The MP curve is simply the slope of the TP curve. Recall that MP is calculated as the change in TP (change on y-axis) divided by the change in labor units (change on x-axis). The MP curve rises initially, (over the first two units of labor when TP is increasing at an increasing rate) and then falls (as the 3rd, 4th, and 5th units of labor are employed and TP increases at a decreasing rate). If the 6th unit is employed, MP turns negative and TP falls.

The firm benefits from increasing marginal returns over the first two units of labor (as MP increases) and then suffers from decreasing (or diminishing) marginal returns over the next four units of labor (as MP decreases). Increasing marginal returns occur because of specialization and division of labor, while decreasing marginal returns set in because of inefficiency, over-crowdedness, and underemployment of some units of labor given the fixed amount of capital.

> Diminishing marginal returns may also set in as the most productive units of labor are hired initially, and then as the firm seeks to increase production, less competent units of labor must be employed.

The average product (AP) curve (see Figure 2-2) shows output per worker, which equals total product divided by total quantity of labor. Observe two important relationships from the AP and MP curves:

1. MP intersects AP from *above* through the *maximum point* of AP.
2. When MP is *above* AP, AP *rises*, and when MP is *below* AP, AP falls.

An interesting way to remember the relationship stated in Point 2 is by analyzing the historical returns earned by a fund manager. If her 5-year average return is 10%, and she earns 15% this year (marginal return), her average would rise. If however, she were to earn only 5% this year, her average would fall.

Figure 2-2: Average and Marginal Product Curves

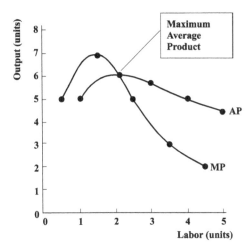

Note the following:

- Total product is simply an indication of a firm's output volume and potential market share.
- Average product and marginal product are better measures of productivity, as they can reveal competitive advantage through production efficiency.
- Average product is the preferred measure of productivity when workers perform tasks collectively, as individual worker productivity is not easily measurable.

Breakeven and Shutdown Analysis

Accounting Profit versus Economic Profit

Accounting Profit
Accounting profit (also known as net profit, net income, and net earnings) equals revenue less all accounting (or explicit) costs. Accounting costs are payments to non-owner parties for goods and services supplied to the firm, and do not necessarily require a cash outlay.

Accounting profit (loss) = Total revenue − Total accounting costs

Economic Profit and Normal Profit
Economic profit (also known as abnormal profit or supernormal profit) is calculated as revenue less all economic costs. Economic costs equal the sum of total accounting costs and implicit opportunity costs. The opportunity cost of any particular decision refers to the benefit forgone by not implementing the next best alternative. Alternatively, economic profit can be calculated as accounting profit less all implicit opportunity costs that are not included in total accounting costs.

Economic profit = Total revenue − Total economic costs

Economic profit = Total revenue − (Explicit costs + Implicit costs)

Economic profit = Accounting profit − Total implicit opportunity costs

Example 2-1: Economic Profit, Accounting Profit, and Normal Profit

Consider two companies, a startup, SU, and a public limited company, PLC. The following table includes revenue and cost information for the two companies:

	Start-Up (SU) $	Public Limited Company (PLC) $
Total revenue	4,500,000	60,000,000
Total accounting costs	4,100,000	57,000,000

The owner of SU takes a salary reduction of $50,000 relative to the job he gave up to work on the start-up. He also invested $2,000,000 in the business on which he could expect to earn $350,000 annually if he had invested the money in a similar-risk investment. PLC has equity investment worth $25,000,000 on which shareholders require a return of 7%.

Given that there are no other identifiable implicit opportunity costs for either firm, calculate accounting and economic profits for both the companies for 2011.

Solution:

Accounting profit (loss) = Total revenue − Total accounting costs

Accounting profit (SU) = $4,500,000 − $4,100,000 = $400,000
Accounting profit (PLC) = $60,000,000 − $57,000,000 = $3,000,000

Economic profit (loss) = Accounting profit (loss) − Total implicit opportunity costs

The salary cut taken by SU's owner relative to his previous job ($50,000) and the investment income forgone on the money invested in SU ($350,000) are both implicit opportunity costs that must be deducted from SU's accounting profit to determine its economic profit.

Economic profit (SU) = $400,000 − ($50,000 + $350,000) = 0

The cost of equity capital is an implicit opportunity cost for PLC. Therefore, economic profit is calculated as:

Economic profit (PLC) = $3,000,000 − ($25,000,000 × 0.07) = $1,250,000

Notice that for SU, economic profit equals 0 as total revenues and total economic costs are equal. Since it just meets its opportunity costs, we can state that SU is earning normal profit of $400,000. Normal profit is the level of accounting profit that is required to cover the implicit opportunity costs that are not included in accounting costs. PLC's normal profit equals $1,750,000 (dollar cost of equity).

Accounting profit, economic profit, and normal profit are linked by the following equation:

Accounting profit = Economic profit + Normal profit

Notice that:

- When accounting profit equals normal profit, economic profit equals 0 (as is the case with SU).
- When accounting profit is greater than normal profit, economic profit is positive (as is the case with PLC).
- When accounting profit is less than normal profit, economic profit is negative. The firm incurs an economic loss.

Economic Costs versus Accounting Costs Example: Depreciation

Accounting depreciation distributes the historical cost of fixed capital among units of production for financial reporting purposes. The historical cost of fixed capital is typically a sunk cost. **Sunk costs** refer to expenses that cannot be altered, and therefore have no role to play in making optimal forward-looking decisions.

Economic depreciation considers opportunity costs of using the plant and equipment (which have already been paid for) for one more period of time to produce output. It specifically asks the question: What else could be done with that fixed capital if it were not used to produce our output?

Note that economic depreciation is forward looking, while accounting depreciation is backward looking. While both are useful—one for making operating decisions and the other for reporting and tax purposes—there isn't necessarily a direct link between the two.

Total, Average, and Marginal Revenue

Table 2-2 lists the formulas for calculating different revenue items:

Table 2-2: Summary of Revenue Terms[1]

Revenue	Calculation
Total revenue (TR)	Price times quantity (P × Q), or the sum of individual units sold times their respective prices; $\Sigma(P_i \times Q_i)$
Average revenue (AR)	Total revenue divided by quantity; (TR/Q)
Marginal revenue (MR)	Change in total revenue divided by change in quantity; ($\Delta TR/\Delta Q$)

We will study the various market structures in detail in the next reading. For the purposes of illustrating the different revenue terms we introduce perfect competition and imperfect competition at this point:

- In perfect competition, each individual firm faces a perfectly elastic demand curve (i.e., it can sell as many units of output as it desires at the given market price). The firm has no impact on market price, and is referred to as a price-taker.
- In imperfect competition, the firm has at least some control over the price at which it sells its output. The demand curve facing the firm is downward sloping so in order to increase units sold, the firm must lower its price. Stated differently, price and quantity demanded are inversely related. Firms operating in imperfect competition are referred to as price-searchers.

1 - Exhibit 3, Volume 2, CFA Program Curriculum 2018

Total, Average, and Marginal Revenue Under Perfect Competition

Table 2-3 presents total, average, and marginal revenue for a firm that is a price-taker at each quantity of output (faces a perfectly elastic demand curve).

Table 2-3: TR, AR, and MR in Perfect Competition

	Perfect Competition			
Qty.	Price	TR	MR	AR
0	8	0	0	–
1	8	8	8	8
2	8	16	8	8
3	8	24	8	8
4	8	32	8	8
5	8	40	8	8
6	8	48	8	8
7	8	56	8	8

Note that since the firm is a price-taker, price is fixed at $8 at all quantities of output sold.

Note: Under perfect competition, MR = Price. Therefore, the MR curve is the same as the demand curve.

Prices are determined by demand and supply in the market. Once market price is determined, a firm in perfect competition can sell as many units of output as it desires at this price.

From Table 2-3 notice the following:

- Total revenue (TR) simply equals price times quantity sold. TR at 4 units is calculated as $4 \times \$8 = \$32$.
- Marginal revenue (MR) is defined as the increase in total revenue from selling one more unit. It is calculated as the change in total revenue divided by the change in quantity sold. MR from selling Unit 4 is calculated as $(\$32 – \$24)/(4 – 3) = \$8$.
- Average revenue (AR) equals total revenue divided by quantity sold. AR at 4 units of output is calculated as $\$32/4 = \$8$.

For any firm that sells all its output at a uniform price, average revenue will equal price regardless of the shape of the demand curve.

Important takeaways: In a perfectly competitive environment (where price is constant regardless of the quantity sold by the firm):

- MR always equals AR, and they both equal market price.
- If there is an increase in market demand, the market price increases, which results in both MR and AR shifting up (to MR_1 and AR_1 in Figure 2-2) and TR pivoting upward (to TR_1 in Figure 2-2).

Figure 2-2: TR, MR, and AR Under Perfect Competition

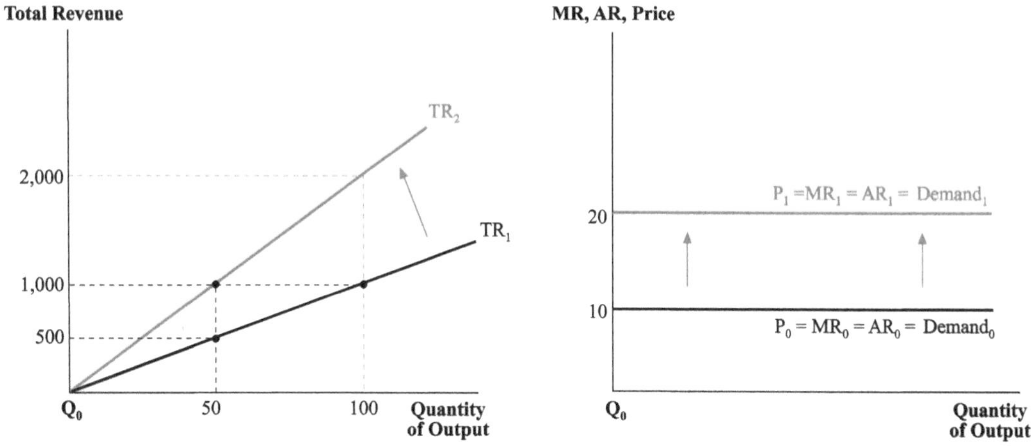

Total, Average, and Marginal Revenue under Imperfect Competition

Table 2-4 presents total, average, and marginal revenue for a firm that is a price-searcher at each quantity of units sold (faces a downward-sloping demand curve).

Table 2-4: TR, AR, and MR in Imperfect Competition

Price Searcher				
Qty.	**Price**	**TR**	**MR**	**AR**
0	0	0	0	–
1	15	15	15	15
2	13	26	11	13
3	11	33	7	11
4	9	36	3	9
5	7	35	−1	7
6	5	30	−5	5
7	3	21	−9	3

Note: Under imperfect competition, MR does not equal price. The MR curve has a steeper slope than the demand curve.

- Total revenue (TR) simply equals price times quantity sold. TR at 4 units is calculated as $4 \times \$9 = \$36$.
- Marginal revenue (MR) is defined as the increase in total revenue from selling one more unit. It is calculated as the change in total revenue divided by the change in quantity sold. MR from selling Unit 4 is calculated as $(\$36 - \$33)/(4 - 3) = \$3$. Under imperfect competition, in order to sell the 4th unit, the firm must entice further consumption by reducing its price to $9. Moreover, not only does the buyer of the 4th unit pay a reduced price of $9, but the 3 previous consumers also benefit from reduced prices and now only pay $9 instead of $11. On one hand, revenue increases by selling a larger quantity (4th unit sells for $9 resulting in an increase in TR of $9). On the other hand, revenue falls (from selling the first three units

Note that since the firm is a price-searcher, price and quantity are inversely related.

We mentioned earlier that for a firm that sells at a uniform price, average revenue will equal price. In Table 2-4 we have assumed that in order to increase quantity demanded and sold from 3 to 4 units, the firm must bring down its price from $11 to $9. The lower price ($9) is applicable not only on the additional unit sold (the 4th unit) but also on all units that were previously selling for $11. Only if the firm were a perfect monopolist would it be able to charge $11 each for the first 3 units sold and $9 for the 4th unit.

at the new lower market price) by ($11 − $9) × 3 = $6. The net increase in total revenue from selling the 4th unit equals $9 − $6 = $3.

- Average revenue (AR) equals total revenue divided by quantity sold. AR at 4 units of output is calculated as $36/4 = $9.

Figure 2-3 illustrates TR, MR, and AR for a firm in imperfect competition.

Figure 2-3: TR, AR, and MR Under Imperfect Competition

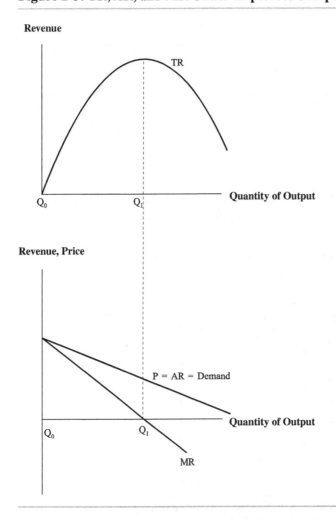

Through some algebra, we can prove that MR equals price plus Q multiplied by the slope of the demand curve.

$$MR = P + Q(\Delta P/\Delta Q) \text{ or } MR = P + Q * \text{Slope of demand curve}$$

- Under perfect competition, the slope of the demand curve is zero. Therefore, MR = P.
- Under imperfect competition, the slope of the demand curve is negative. As a result, MR is less than price.

Important takeaways: In imperfect competition (where price and quantity are inversely related):

- As quantity increases, the rate of increase in TR (as measured by MR) decreases.
- AR equals price at each output level.
- MR is also downward sloping with a slope that is steeper than that of AR (demand).
- TR reaches its maximum point when MR equals 0.

Total, Average, Marginal, Fixed, and Variable Costs

Table 2-5 summarizes various cost terms.

Table 2-5: Summary of Cost Terms[2]

Costs	Calculation
Total fixed cost (TFC)	Sum of all fixed expenses; here defined to include all opportunity costs
Total variable cost (TVC)	Sum of all variable expenses, or per unit variable cost times quantity; (per unit VC × Q)
Total costs (TC)	Total fixed cost plus total variable cost; (TFC + TVC)
Average fixed cost (AFC)	Total fixed cost divided by quantity; (TFC/Q)
Average variable cost (AVC)	Total variable cost divided by quantity; (TVC/Q)
Average total cost (ATC)	Total cost divided by quantity; (TC/Q) or (AFC + AVC)
Marginal cost (MC)	Change in total cost divided by change in quantity; ($\Delta TC/\Delta Q$)

> In this section we discuss the cost curve relationships in the short run (with labor as the only variable factor of production). In the long run all factors of production including technology, plant size, and physical capital are variable.

Table 2-6 presents total costs, average costs, and marginal costs for a hypothetical company. We assume that the firm has rented 2 units of capital (Q_K) in the short run at $20 per unit. Labor is the only variable factor of production and the firm pays a wage of $10 per unit of labor employed. Even if the firm shuts down in the short run, it will still have to pay its total fixed costs (TFC), and if it wants to increase production in the short run, only total variable costs (TVC) will rise.

2 - Exhibit 13, Volume 2, CFA Program Curriculum 2018

2-6: Total Cost, Average Cost, and Marginal Cost

Q_L	Q_K	TP	TFC	TVC	TC	AFC $\left(\dfrac{TFC}{TP}\right)$	AVC	ATC $\left(\dfrac{TC}{TP}\right)$	MC
0	2	0	40	0	40				
1	2	5	40	10	50	8	2	10	2
2	2	12	40	20	60	3.33	1.67	5	1.43
3	2	17	40	30	70	2.35	1.76	4.12	2
4	2	20	40	40	80	2	2	4	3.33
5	2	22	40	50	90	1.82	2.27	4.09	5

AVC = $\dfrac{TVC}{TP}$ MC = $\dfrac{\text{Change in TC}}{\text{Change in TP}}$

...y is
...n output
...n quantity of
labor can produce
when working
with a given
quantity of capital
units. Product
terms (including
total product) are
discussed in detail
later in the reading.

Total costs (TC) equal total fixed costs (TFC) plus total variable costs (TVC). Initially TC increases at a decreasing rate (green portion of TC curve in Figure 2-4). As production approaches full capacity TC increases at an increasing rate (gray portion of TC curve in Figure 2-4). At zero production, TC equals TFC as TVC equals 0.

Total fixed costs (TFC) equal the sum of all expenses that remain constant regardless of production levels. Since they cannot be arbitrarily reduced when production falls, fixed costs are the last expenses to be trimmed when a firm considers downsizing. Note that normal profit is also included in fixed cost.

Total variable costs (TVC) are the sum of all variable costs. TVC is directly related to quantity produced (TP), and the shape of the TVC curve mirrors that of the TC curve. Whenever a firm looks to downsize or cut costs, its variable costs are the first to be considered for reduction as they vary directly with output.

Fixed costs include sunk costs. They also include quasi-fixed costs (e.g., utilities) that remain the same over a particular range of production, but move to another constant level outside of that range of production.

Figure 2-4: Cost Curves

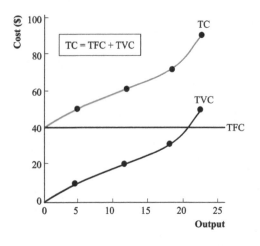

Notice in Figure 2-4 that the TC and TVC increase at a decreasing rate at low levels of output, and increase at an increasing rate at higher levels of output. The difference between TC and TVC equals TFC.

Average total cost (ATC) is simply total cost (TC) divided by total product (TP).

Average fixed cost (AFC) equals TFC divided by TP.

Average variable cost (AVC) equals TVC divided by TP.

Marginal cost (MC) equals the increase in total costs brought about by the production of one more unit of output. It equals change in total costs divided by the change in output (TP). Since TFC is fixed, MC can also be calculated as the change in TVC divided by the change in TP. Though not clearly visible from Figure 2-5, we should emphasize that the MC curve is shaped like a "J."

Figure 2-5: Marginal and Average Cost Curves

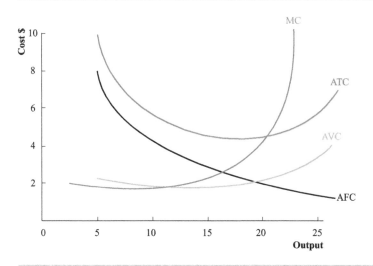

A firm's MC is the increase in total cost from producing the last unit of output. For example, when output increases from 12 to 17 units (Table 2-6), TC increases by $10, to $70. The MC of any of these 5 units (the 13th to 17th units) equals $10 divided by 5, or $2.

It is important to bear in mind that MC illustrates the slope of the TC curve at a particular level of output. MC initially decreases (see Figure 2-5) because of the benefits from *specialization*. However, MC eventually increases because of *diminishing marginal returns*. To produce more output given the same amount of capital, more and more units of labor must be employed because each additional unit of labor is less productive than the previous one. Since more workers are required to produce one more unit of output, the cost of producing that additional unit (the marginal cost) increases.

From Figure 2-5, also notice that:

- As output levels rise, total fixed costs are spread over more and more units and AFC continues to fall at a decreasing rate.
- The average total cost curve is U-shaped. It falls initially as fixed costs are spread over an increasing number of units. Later, however, the effect of falling AFC is offset by diminishing marginal returns so ATC starts rising.

- The vertical distance between the AVC and ATC curves equals AFC. This vertical distance between the AVC and ATC curves gets smaller as output increases because AFC decreases as output expands.
- The minimum point of the AVC does not correspond to the minimum point of ATC. The firm's profit-maximizing quantity does not necessarily occur at the point where ATC is minimized, even though profit per unit may be maximized at this point.

Important Relationships between Average and Marginal Cost Curves

- MC intersects ATC and AVC from *below* at their respective *minimum* points.
- When MC is below AVC, AVC falls, and when MC is above AVC, AVC rises.
- When MC is below ATC, ATC falls, and when MC is above ATC, ATC rises.

Economists distinguish between short-run marginal cost (SMC) and long-run marginal cost (LMC).

- SMC is the additional cost of the variable input, labor, that must be incurred to increase the level of output by one unit.
- LMC is the additional cost of all inputs necessary to increase the level of output, allowing the firm the flexibility of changing both labor and capital inputs in a way that maximizes efficiency.

Figure 2-6 illustrates important relationships between costs and product curves.

Figure 2-6: Cost and Product Curves

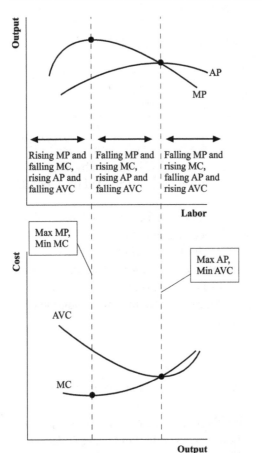

- A firm's MP curve is linked to its MC curve. Initially, as more labor is hired, MP rises and MC falls.
- At the point where MP reaches its maximum, MC stands at its minimum.
- As output expands further, MP falls and MC rises.

- A firm's AP curve is linked to its AVC curve. Initially, as the firm hires more labor, AP rises and AVC falls.
- At the point where AP reaches its maximum, AVC is at its minimum.
- As the firm increases output further, AP falls and AVC rises.

Costs are directly related to input prices and inversely related to productivity.

- If the wage rate were to rise, costs would also rise, but if labor productivity were to improve, costs would fall. This relationship can be captured by the expression: $MC = w/MP_L$.
- Similarly, if wages rise, AVC also rises, but if labor productivity were to improve, AVC would fall. Therefore, $AVC = w/AP_L$.
- As the firm benefits from increasing marginal returns, MP_L increases and MC declines. However, as more and more labor is added to a fixed amount of capital, diminishing marginal returns set in and MP_L falls, causing MC to rise.

Marginal Revenue, Marginal Cost, and Profit Maximization

When we talk about profit maximization, note that we are referring to economic profit. Profits are maximized when the difference between TR and TC is at its highest. The level of output at which this occurs is the point where (1) marginal revenue equals marginal cost (MC = MR) and (2) MC is not falling.

- When MR > MC, the firm should increase production, as the last unit produced added more to revenue that it did to costs.
- When MR < MC, the firm should reduce production, as the last unit produced added more to costs than it did to revenue.
- Recall that $MC = w/MP_L$, so if MC is falling, MP would be rising. If an additional unit of labor causes MC to fall, the firm would want to add that unit of labor until MC is upward sloping.

Profit-Maximization, Breakeven, and Shutdown Points of Production

Perfect Competition

Figure 2-7: Perfect Competition[3]

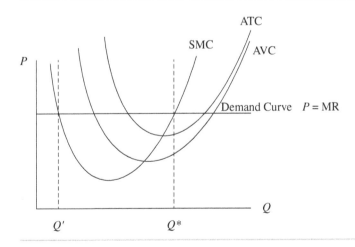

Analysis (see Figure 2-7):

- The firm's profit-maximizing quantity is Q*, where:
  - MR (which equals P and AR) equals MC.
  - MC is rising.
- Q is not the profit-maximizing level of production, because MC is still falling at that stage.
- If P were to rise, the firm's demand and MR curves would shift higher, and the new profit-maximizing level of output would lie to the right of Q*.
- If P were to fall, the firm's demand and MR curves would move lower, and the new profit-maximizing level of output would lie to the left of Q*.
- At Q*, the firm is earning positive economic profits because P exceeds ATC. Economic profits are possible only in perfect competition in the short run. In the long run, more firms will enter the industry, taking market prices down to a level where they equal ATC.

Monopoly

Figure 2-8: Monopoly[4]

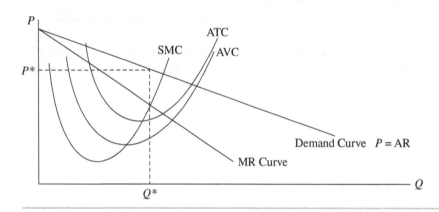

Analysis (see Figure 2-8):

- A monopoly faces a downward-sloping demand curve. As a result, the MR and demand curves are not identical.
- The profit-maximizing level of output occurs at the point where MC equals MR. This point is denoted by Q*.
- Once the profit-maximizing level of output has been determined, the optimal price is obtained from the demand curve at P*.
- The monopolist is earning positive economic profit, as P is greater than ATC. Further, the monopolist can continue to earn positive economic profits in the long run due to high barriers to entry.

Breakeven Analysis

A firm is said to break even if its TR equals its TC. At the breakeven quantity of production, price (or AR) equals ATC. This is true under perfect and imperfect competition. Breaking even implies that the firm is covering all of its economic costs

---

4 - Exhibit 18, Volume 2, CFA Curriculum 2018

(total accounting costs and implicit opportunity costs), so while it is not earning positive economic profits, the firm is at least covering the opportunity cost of all of its factors of production, including capital. In other words, the firm is earning normal profit.

Figure 2-9 illustrates the breakeven point for a firm under perfect competition and a firm that is a monopolist. At the profit-maximizing level of output (where MC = MR), price equals ATC. Economic profits, therefore, equal zero, and the firms earn normal profits.

Figure 2-9: Breakeven under Perfect Competition and Monopoly[5]

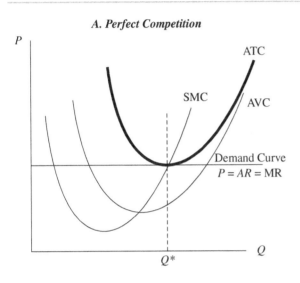

A. Perfect Competition

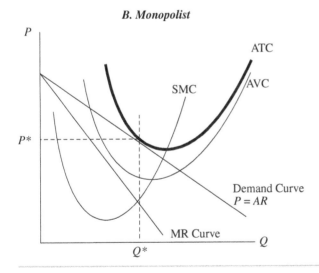

B. Monopolist

The Shutdown Decision

In the long run, a firm will continue to operate in the industry only if it earns at least a normal profit or zero economic profits. In the short run, it may choose to continue to operate even if it does not earn a normal profit (and makes an economic loss), as we will now see.

In the short run, a firm incurs fixed and variable costs of production. If the firm decides to shut down, it will still incur fixed costs (that are sunk costs) in the short run and make a loss equal to total fixed cost. This loss can be reduced by continuing production and earning revenues that are greater than the variable costs of production. This surplus (excess of revenues over variable costs) would serve to meet some of the fixed costs that the firm is stuck with in the short run. A firm should shut down immediately if it does not expect revenues to exceed variable costs of production. If the firm continues to operate in such an environment, it would suffer a loss greater than just total fixed cost. (See Figure 2-10.)

Figure 2-10: Shutdown and Breakeven Points under Perfect Competition

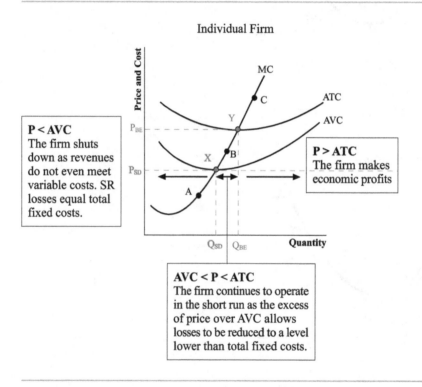

- At price levels below AVC (e.g., Point A where P < AVC), the firm will not be willing to produce, as continued production would only extend losses beyond simply total fixed costs. Any quantity to the left of Point X (with quantity Q_{SD}) would define a shutdown point for the firm.
- When price lies between AVC and ATC (e.g., Point B where AVC < P < ATC), the firm will remain in production in the short run as it meets all variable costs and covers a portion of its fixed costs.

- To remain in business in the long run, the firm must break even or cover all costs (revenues should meet total costs). Therefore, Point Y defines the firm's breakeven point. In the long run, at any price lower than P_{BE}, the firm will exit the industry.
- Once prices exceed ATC (e.g., Point C where P > ATC), the firm makes economic profits.

Table 2-7 presents the decisions to operate, shut down, or exit the market in both the short run and the long run.

Table 2-7: Short Run and Long Run Operating Decisions

Revenue-Cost Relationship	SR Decision	LR Decision
TR = TC	Continue to operate	Continue to operate
TR = TVC but TR < TC	Continue to operate	Exit market
TR < TVC	Shut down	Exit market

Understanding Economies and Diseconomies of Scale

Short Run and Long Run Production Functions

We defined the short run and long run in the previous section. Stated briefly, at least one factor of production is fixed in the short run, while no factors of production are fixed in the long run. Table 2-8 illustrates a company's production function, which shows how different quantities of labor and capital affect total product. In our short-run scenario, different quantities of labor were combined with fixed quantities of capital (2 units). Now we explore the effects of varying capital quantities (Q_K) as well (note: no factor of production is fixed, so we are basically working with the long-run scenario here). Plant 1 has 2 units of capital (the SR scenario that we analyzed earlier), Plant 2 has 4 units of capital, Plant 3 has 6 units of capital, and Plant 4 has 8 units of capital.

Table 2-8: A Firm's Production Function

Units of Labor	Plant 1 $Q_K = 2$	Plant 2 $Q_K = 4$	Plant 3 $Q_K = 6$	Plant 4 $Q_K = 8$
1	5	11	15	18
2	12	25	34	39
3	17	36	48	56
4	20	42	57	67
5	22	45	59	68

Diminishing Marginal Returns to Labor

Diminishing Marginal Returns to Capital

The effect of diminishing marginal returns to labor is obvious. Marginal product declines as more and more units of labor are added to each plant (move down the columns in Table 2-8). But now, we also see diminishing marginal returns to capital (see Table 2-9, and move right along the rows in Table 2-8). For example, with 3 units of labor, moving from Plant 1 to Plant 2 (increasing quantity of capital by 2 units) increases production by 19 units from 17 to 36 (MP of capital = change in output/change in quantity of capital = 19/2 = 9.5). Adding a further 2 units of capital and moving to Plant 3 increases production by only 12 units from 36 to 48 (MP of capital = change in output/change in quantity of capital = 12/2 = 6). Finally, adding another 2 units of capital and moving to Plant 4 and holding quantity of labor constant at 3 units increases output only by 8 units (MP of capital = 4).

Table 2-9: Diminishing Marginal Returns to Capital

	Units of Capital Combined with 3 Units of Labor	Total Product when $Q_L = 3$	Marginal Product	
Plant 1	2	17	8.5	
Plant 2	4	36	9.5	Diminishing Marginal Returns to Capital
Plant 3	6	48	6	
Plant 4	8	56	4	

When we map the average cost curves for all 4 plants on one graph (see Figure 2-11), notice that:

- Short-run ATC curves are U-shaped.
- The larger the plant, the greater the output at which short-run ATC is at its minimum.

Figure 2-11: Average Cost Curves for Different Plant Sizes

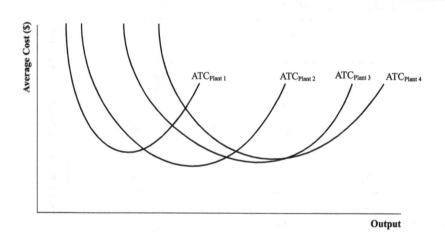

The optimal output level for each plant is when its ATC curve is at its minimum. The long-run average cost (LRAC) curve illustrates the relationship between the lowest attainable average total cost and output when all factors of production are variable. The LRAC curve is also known as a planning curve because it shows the expected per-unit cost of producing various levels of output using different combinations of factors of production.

Economies and Diseconomies of Scale

Economies and diseconomies of scale are long-run concepts. They relate to conditions of production when all factors of production are variable. In contrast, increasing and diminishing marginal returns are short-run concepts, applicable only when the firm has one variable factor of production.

Economies of scale or increasing returns to scale refer to reductions in the firm's average costs that are associated with the use of larger plant sizes to produce large quantities of output. They are present over the range of output when the LRAC curve is falling. Economies of scale occur because mass production is more economical, the specialization of labor and equipment improves productivity, and costs such as advertising can be spread across more units of output. Other reasons include discounted prices as a result of bulk purchasing of resources and the ability to adopt more expensive but more efficient technology. When a firm is operating in the economies of scale region of the LRAC curve (see Figure 2-11), it should aim to expand capacity to enhance competitiveness and efficiency.

> Economies and diseconomies of scale can occur at the same time. The impact on long-run average total cost (LRAC) depends on which dominates.

Diseconomies of scale or decreasing returns to scale occur in the upward-sloping region of the LRAC curve. A typical reason for an increase in average costs as output levels rise is an increase in bureaucratic inefficiencies as effective management, supervision, and communication become difficult in large organizations. Other reasons include duplication of business functions and product lines, and high resource prices due to supply constraints. When a firm is operating in the diseconomies of scale region of the LRAC curve (see Figure 2-12), it should aim to downsize and reduce costs to increase competitiveness.

Figure 2-12: The Planning Curve

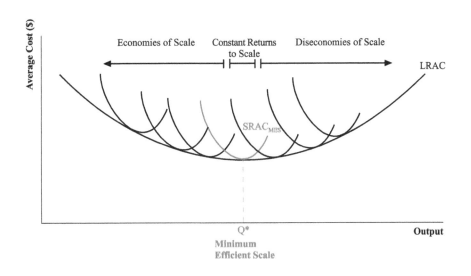

In the horizontal portion of the LRAC curve, when an increase in output does not result in any change in average costs, a firm realizes constant returns to scale.

Aside from the shape illustrated in Figure 2-11, the LRAC curve may also take one of the shapes described in Figure 2-13.

Figure 2-13: Types of LRAC Curves

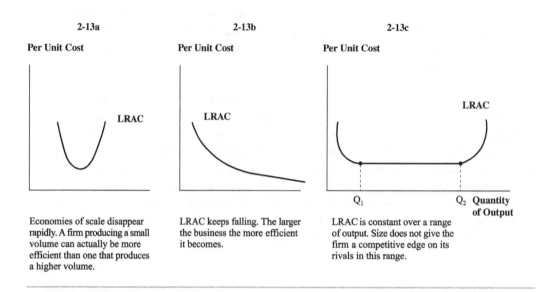

2-13a	2-13b	2-13c
Per Unit Cost	Per Unit Cost	Per Unit Cost
LRAC	LRAC	LRAC
Economies of scale disappear rapidly. A firm producing a small volume can actually be more efficient than one that produces a higher volume.	LRAC keeps falling. The larger the business the more efficient it becomes.	LRAC is constant over a range of output. Size does not give the firm a competitive edge on its rivals in this range.

Under perfect competition, given the different SRAC options available to the firm, $SRAC_{MES}$ embodies the optimal combination of technology, plant capacity, capital, and labor that minimizes the firm's average costs in the long run. The lowest point on the LRAC curve is called the firm's minimum efficient scale. In the long run, all firms in perfect competition operate at their minimum efficient scale as price equals minimum average cost (see next section).

READING 15: THE FIRM AND MARKET STRUCTURES

LESSON 1: MARKET STRUCTURE 1: PERFECT COMPETITION

LOS 15a: Describe characteristics of perfect competition, monopolistic competition, oligopoly, and pure monopoly. Vol 2, pp 64–83

LOS 15b: Explain relationships between price, marginal revenue, marginal cost, economic profit, and the elasticity of demand under each market structure. Vol 2, pp 64–83

LOS 15c: Describe a firm's supply function under each market structure. Vol 2, pp 64–83

LOS 15d: Describe and determine the optimal price and output for firms under each market structure. Vol 2, pp 64–83

LOS 15e: Explain factors affecting long-run equilibrium under each market structure. Vol 2, pp 64–83

LOS 15f: Describe pricing strategy under each market structure. Vol 2, pp 64–83

LOS 15h: Identify the type of market structure within which a firm operates. Vol 2, pp 64–83

Perfect Competition

Characteristics
- There are a large number of buyers and sellers.
- Each seller offers an identical product for sale.
- There are minimal barriers to entry.
- Sellers have no pricing power.
- There is no nonprice competition in the market.

Demand in a Perfectly Competitive Market

The market demand curve is downward sloping (due to the income and substitution effects). Let's assume that the market demand curve is given by the following equation:

$$P = 20 - 0.5Q_D$$

Since total revenue (TR) equals price (P) times quantity (Q), the market's total revenue equation is:

$$TR = PQ_D = (20 - 0.5Q_D)Q_D = 20Q_D - 0.5Q_D^2$$

Average revenue (AR) is calculated as total revenue divided by quantity. Therefore:

$$AR = TR/Q_D = (20Q_D - 0.5Q_D^2)/Q_D = 20 - 0.5Q_D$$

> Marginal revenue is the derivative of total revenue with respect to quantity demanded.

Notice that the average revenue curve is the same as the demand curve. Average revenue equals price. Bear in mind that we are assuming that:

- The relationship between quantity demanded and price is linear.
- Own-price is the only determinant of quantity demanded.

Marginal revenue (MR) is the change in total revenue brought about by selling an additional unit of output.

$$MR = \Delta TR / \Delta Q_D = 20 - Q_D$$

Elasticity of Demand

> Price elasticity is typically presented as an absolute value. We follow this convention in this reading.

Price Elasticity of Demand

Price elasticity of demand measures the percentage change in quantity demanded given the percentage change in price of a product.

Price elasticity $= E_P = - (\%\Delta Q_D)/(\%\Delta P)$

- If $E_P > 1 \Rightarrow$ Demand is elastic
- If $E_P = 1 \Rightarrow$ Demand is unitary elastic
- If $E_P < 1 \Rightarrow$ Demand is inelastic
- If $E_P = 0 \Rightarrow$ Demand is perfectly inelastic and the demand curve is vertical
- If $E_P = \infty \Rightarrow$ Demand is perfectly elastic and the demand curve is horizontal

Factors Affecting Price Elasticity of Demand
- Price elasticity will be higher if there are many close substitutes for the product.
- Price elasticity will be higher if a greater share of the consumer's income is spent on the good.
- Price elasticity will be higher in the long run.
- Along the demand curve, price elasticity is higher (lower) at higher (lower) prices

Price Elasticity, Marginal Revenue, and Total Revenue
- If $E_P > 1 \Rightarrow$ Demand is elastic   If $P\uparrow \Rightarrow TR\downarrow$ and if $P\downarrow \Rightarrow TR\uparrow$
- If $E_P = 1 \Rightarrow$ Demand is unitary elastic   If $P\updownarrow \Rightarrow$ No change in TR
- If $E_P < 1 \Rightarrow$ Demand is inelastic   If $P\uparrow \Rightarrow TR\uparrow$ and if $P\downarrow \Rightarrow TR\downarrow$

Understanding price elasticity of demand is very important.

- If a company is operating in the relatively inelastic portion of the demand curve, *increasing* price would result in an increase in total revenue.
- If a company is operating in the relatively elastic portion of the demand curve, *decreasing* price would result in an increase in total revenue.

The relationship between MR and price elasticity can be expressed as:

$$MR = P[1 - (1/E_P)]$$

If producers know the price and price elasticities of demand for different products, they can use the relationship defined in the equation above to determine marginal revenue and use the information to decide which product to supply.

- The higher the price and marginal revenue of a product, the greater the incentive to supply that particular product.

Income Elasticity of Demand

Income elasticity of demand measures the responsiveness of demand to changes in income.

Income elasticity = $E_I = (\%\Delta Q_D)/(\%\Delta I)$

- If $E_I > 0 \Rightarrow$ Normal good
- If $E_I > 1 \Rightarrow$ Luxury good
- If $E_I < 0 \Rightarrow$ Inferior good

Cross Elasticity of Demand

Cross elasticity of demand measures the responsiveness of demand for a product to a change in the price of another product.

Cross elasticity = $E_X = (\%\Delta Q_{DA})/(\%\Delta P_B)$

- If $E_X > 0 \Rightarrow$ The two products are substitutes
- If $E_X < 0 \Rightarrow$ The two products are complements

The more numerous and the closer the substitutes available for a product, the lower the pricing power of firms selling that product.

- A very important thing for you to understand is that the demand adjustment for price elasticity occurs along the demand curve.
- For income and cross elasticity, the demand adjustment is represented by a shift in the demand curve.

Consumer Surplus: Value Minus Expenditure
- The area under the demand curve (to the left of quantity purchased) represents the total value (utility) derived by the consumer from consuming her chosen quantity of a product.
- Quantity purchased times the market price equals the consumer's total expenditure on the product.
- The difference between the total value derived from quantity purchased and the total cost of the purchase equals consumer surplus. Alternatively, consumer surplus may be defined as the difference between the amount that a consumer was willing and able to spend on a given product and the amount she actually spends to purchase the given quantity of the product.

Supply Analysis in Perfectly Competitive Markets
- As prices increase, firms are willing and able to supply greater quantities of the product.
- Economic profit equals total revenue minus explicit and implicit (opportunity) costs.
- Accounting profit does not account for opportunity costs. It only reflects explicit payments for resources and depreciation.

Optimal Price and Output in Perfectly Competitive Markets

Equilibrium price and output are determined at the intersection point of the market demand and supply curves.

- The market demand curve is downward sloping, while the market supply curve is upward sloping.

Each firm in perfect competition is very small compared to the size of the overall market. The actions of any firm do not impact market equilibrium. Each firm can sell as much output as it desires at the equilibrium market price.

- Therefore, the demand curve faced by an individual firm is perfectly elastic (horizontal).
- A firm will not sell any output if it raises prices above the equilibrium market price (as all other sellers are willing and able to supply at the market price).
- A firm would not be willing to sell its output at a price lower than the market price (since it can sell as much as it wants to at the market price anyway).

Average revenue equals price and marginal revenue. AR = P = MR

- Earlier in the reading we proved that the average revenue curve equals the demand curve, so average revenue equals price.
- Marginal revenue also equals price (since the demand curve is perfectly elastic).

The law of diminishing marginal returns dictates the "U" shape of SR cost curves.

- Average cost (AC) equals total cost divided by quantity produced.
- Marginal cost (MC) equals the change in total cost divided by the change in quantity produced.
- Since fixed costs do not vary with output, marginal cost only reflects changes in variable costs.
- MC intersects AC from below through minimum AC.

Firms always maximize profits at the point where MC equals MR.

- Total revenue equals price times quantity sold.
- Total cost equals AC times quantity sold.
- The positive (negative) difference between the two equals economic profit (loss).
- If the two are equal, the firm only makes normal profit.

In the short run, a firm in perfect competition can make economic profits, economic losses, or normal profit.

- In each scenario, the firm produces the output level at which MC equals MR.
- Whether it makes a profit or a loss depends on the position of the demand curve relative to its average cost at the profit-maximizing quantity.
- If P > AC ⇒ Economic profit
- If P = AC ⇒ Normal profit
- If P < AC ⇒ Economic loss

In the long run (LR), all firms in perfect competition will only make normal profit.

- If firms were making economic profits in the short run (SR), over time more firms will enter the industry, raising industry supply. This would force prices lower until only normal profits are made by all firms.

- If firms were making economic losses in the SR, over time some firms will leave the industry, reducing industry supply. This would force prices upward until normal profits are made by all remaining firms.
- Price will equal minimum average cost and there are zero economic profits in the long run.
- Firms will still produce the output level where MC equals MR and constantly strive to lower their costs.
- Therefore, in the LR, MC = MR = P = AR = min AC

Changes in Plant Size

In an earlier reading, we learned that when plant size is increased, initially firms realize economies of scale (falling average costs), and later suffer from diseconomies of scale. A firm already operating at its minimum short-run average cost in a perfectly competitive environment would make zero economic profits. However, there is always the incentive to increase plant size, move onto another (lower) short-run average cost curve, which would give the firm a chance to earn economic profits. Firms will continue to increase plant size in the long run till they operate on the short-run average cost (SRAC) curve whose minimum point coincides with the minimum point of the long-run average cost (LRAC) curve (Point M in Figure 1-1). There is no point in expanding beyond this size, as diseconomies of scale would set in and actually increase the firm's average costs.

Figure 1-1: Plant Size and LR Equilibrium

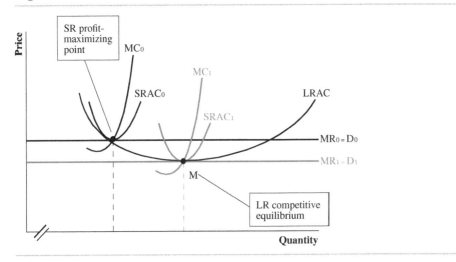

Each SRAC curve has an associated marginal cost curve, which intersects it from below through its minimum point. If a firm moves from $SRAC_0$ to $SRAC_1$, it will also move from MC_0 to MC_1. Because the MC curve defines an individual firm's supply curve, the firm's move to MC_1 implies a rightward shift (increase) in individual firm supply. As more firms expand and move to their respective $SRAC_1$s, the market supply curve also shifts to the right. Consequently, prices fall to the level where $SRAC_1$ is at its minimum (P_1), and once again, economic profits are eliminated.

Conclusion: A firm might increase plant size to reduce average costs and realize economic profits, but its ability to do so will be limited because as more firms increase their respective plant sizes, industry supply will increase and prices will fall to the level where they equal the firm's new minimum average cost.

If firms in perfect competition are incurring economic losses some will exit the industry. Others, who can reduce average costs by cutting down production, will choose to downsize. Each of these actions will reduce industry supply to a point where economic losses are eliminated and replaced by normal profits for the firms remaining in the industry.

Permanent Decrease in Demand for a Product

A permanent reduction in demand results in lower prices. Perfectly competitive firms that were previously making normal profits will now suffer economic losses. Lower prices force each firm to reduce output to point Q_{PM1} (see Figure 1-2), where its marginal cost curve intersects the new (lower) marginal revenue curve. The reduction in each firm's output results in a decrease in quantity supplied from Q_0 to Q_1.

Economic losses prompt some firms to exit the industry. Their exit reduces market supply to S_1 and boosts prices for all remaining firms back to P_0. These firms see an upward shift in their individual demand curves and now once again produce at their original profit-maximizing levels, Q_{PM0}, where they earn normal profits.

Figure 1-2: Permanent Decrease in Demand for a Product

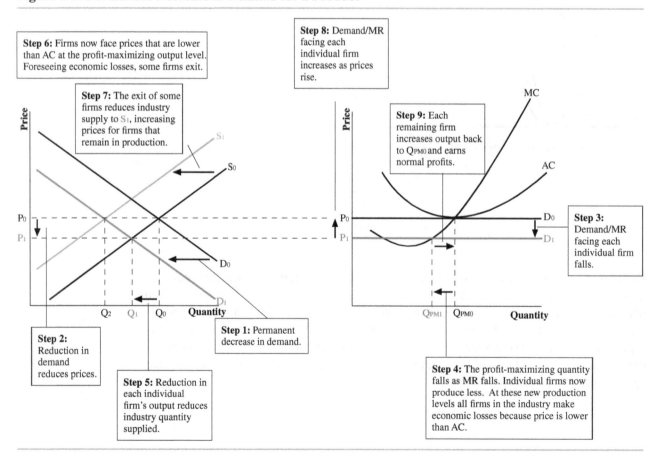

Schumpeter's Take on Perfect Competition

Joseph Schumpeter suggested that perfect competition is more of a long-run type of market structure. In the short run, companies develop new products or processes that give them an edge over competitors. During this period innovative firms see their profits soar. However, what follows is a "swarming" stage in which other firms follow the innovative company and try to copy its idea. What happens eventually is that the innovation is no longer new as all firms have adopted it. Since no company has an edge, perfect competition prevails, and we have long-run equilibrium until someone comes up with a new innovative product or process.

LESSON 2: MARKET STRUCTURE 2: MONOPOLY

LOS 15a: Describe characteristics of perfect competition, monopolistic competition, oligopoly, and pure monopoly. Vol 2, pp 97–105

LOS 15b: Explain relationships between price, marginal revenue, marginal cost, economic profit, and the elasticity of demand under each market structure. Vol 2, pp 97–105

LOS 15c: Describe a firm's supply function under each market structure. Vol 2, pp 97–105

LOS 15d: Describe and determine the optimal price and output for firms under each market structure. Vol 2, pp 97–105

LOS 15e: Explain factors affecting long-run equilibrium under each market structure. Vol 2, pp 97–105

LOS 15f: Describe pricing strategy under each market structure. Vol 2, pp 97–105

LOS 15h: Identify the type of market structure within which a firm operates. Vol 2, pp 97–105

Monopoly

Characteristics
- There is a single seller of a highly differentiated product, which has no close substitutes.
- There are high barriers to entry.
- The firm has considerable pricing power.
- The product is differentiated through nonprice strategies (e.g., advertising).

Factors that Give Rise to Monopolies
- Control over critical sources of production (e.g., De Beers in the diamond-mining industry)
- Patents or copyrights
- Nonprice differentiation leading to pricing-power (e.g., Rolex watches)
- Network effects, which result from synergies related to increasing market penetration (e.g., firms use Microsoft Word because there is no need to train employees as everyone knows how to use it)
- Government-controlled authorization (e.g., natural monopolies)

Demand Analysis in Monopoly Markets

The demand curve faced by the monopoly is effectively the industry demand curve. It is downward sloping.

- The AR curve is the same as the demand curve.
- The MR curve and the demand curve have the same y-intercept.
- The slope of the MR curve is two times the slope of the demand curve.
- The x-intercept of the MR curve is half of that of the demand curve.
- The MR curve is the derivative of the TR curve with respect to quantity sold.

Supply Analysis in Monopoly Markets

- The monopolist does not have a well-defined supply function that determines optimal price and output.
- The profit-maximizing output level occurs at the point where MR = MC (see Figure 2-1).
- The price is determined from the demand curve (based on the profit-maximizing quantity).

Figure 2-1: Analysis of Single Price Monopoly

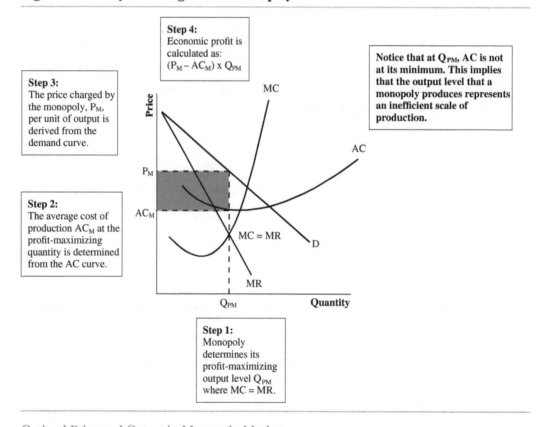

Step 4:
Economic profit is calculated as:
$(P_M - AC_M) \times Q_{PM}$

Notice that at Q_{PM}, AC is not at its minimum. This implies that the output level that a monopoly produces represents an inefficient scale of production.

Step 3:
The price charged by the monopoly, P_M, per unit of output is derived from the demand curve.

Step 2:
The average cost of production AC_M at the profit-maximizing quantity is determined from the AC curve.

Step 1:
Monopoly determines its profit-maximizing output level Q_{PM} where MC = MR.

Optimal Price and Output in Monopoly Markets

The profit-maximizing output level equals the quantity at which:

- MC = MR
- Profit is unaffected by changes in quantity: $\Delta\pi/\Delta Q_D = 0$

The profit-maximizing level of output always occurs in the relatively elastic portion of the demand curve. This is because MC and MR will always intersect where MR is positive. We stated earlier that the relationship between MR and price elasticity is given as:

$$MR = P[1 - (1/E_P)]$$

In a monopoly, MC = MR so:

$$P[1 - (1/E_P)] = MC$$

The monopoly can use this relationship to determine the profit-maximizing price if it knows its cost structure and price elasticity of demand. For example, if MC is constant at $100 and market analysis indicates that E_P equals 1.25, the optimal price will be:

$$100 / [1 - (1/1.25)] = \$500$$

Natural Monopolies

A natural monopoly is an industry where the supplier's average cost is still falling, even when it satisfies total market demand entirely on its own. A natural monopoly has high fixed costs, but low and relatively constant marginal costs. Therefore, it is able to reduce its average costs significantly through economies of scale. The higher the quantity sold by a natural monopoly, the lower its average cost of production. If two firms were sharing the market, each would produce a lower output and incur higher average costs. Therefore, governments allow only one firm to continue to dominate the industry, and find it more effective to regulate it.

An example of a natural monopoly is a power-distribution company. The cost of providing electricity to one more house is just the little bit of additional wiring and labor required (low marginal cost). The distribution company has already incurred the high initial fixed costs (setting up the grid). As the number of users increases, power-distribution companies see their average costs fall and their scale of production becomes more efficient.

Regulation of Natural Monopolies

The profit maximizing output for a monopoly occurs where MC equals MR. (See Figure 2-2.) At this output level, monopolies charge a relatively high price (P_{PM}) and earn economic profits.

Governments can regulate a natural monopoly and force it to charge a price equal to its marginal cost. This is known as **efficient regulation**. At this point, allocative efficiency is reached as marginal benefit equals marginal cost (demand equals supply). At P_{MCP}, the entire surplus goes to consumers, as they benefit from lower prices and increased output (Q_{MCP}). However, under marginal cost pricing, the monopoly will suffer economic losses (as P < LRAC), and will cease operations if it does not foresee a favorable change in government policy. In order to convince the monopoly to remain in production, the government might have to offer a subsidy that at least covers the monopoly's economic loss. The government could also allow the natural monopoly to price discriminate or to charge two-part prices to enable it to make normal profits.

Another option available to the government is to restrict prices to average cost (P_{ACP}). In this situation, the monopolist makes a normal profit, where it covers opportunity costs, and is not tempted to exit the industry.

Figure 2-2: Regulating a Natural Monopoly

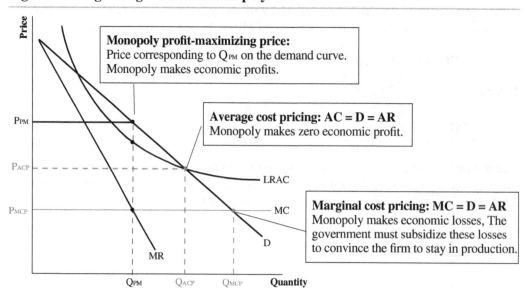

Price Discrimination and Consumer Surplus

First-degree price discrimination occurs when a monopolist is able to charge each individual consumer the highest price that she is willing and able to pay.

This is best explained through an example. Suppose that a monopolist produces a good that has 7 potential buyers. The individual buyer's marginal benefit from consuming the good is reflected in the demand curve (Table 2-1). The first buyer is willing to pay $10 for the good, while the 7th one is willing to pay only $4. Table 2-1 also lists the firm's marginal cost at various levels of output.

Table 2-1: Monopoly's Price and Output Decision

Q	P	TR	MR	MC
1	10	10	10	0.5
2	9	18	8	1.25
3	8	24	6	2.10
4	7	28	4	4
5	6	30	2	6
6	5	30	0	9
7	4	28	−2	13

The profit-maximizing output level for a single-price (nondiscriminating) monopoly occurs at 4 units where marginal cost ($4) equals marginal revenue ($4).

The firm will have an opportunity to discriminate on prices if the first user (the user who is willing to pay $10) can be separated from the others and charged the price that she is willing and able to pay for that unit ($10). The advantage to the monopolist would be that it would earn revenue of $10 from her, and $7 from each of the other 3 consumers. This will increase total revenue from $28 to $31 [($7×3) + ($10×1)]. The first user's consumer surplus of $3 (the difference between the maximum price she is willing to pay and the market price) has now been captured by the monopolist (see Figure 2-3).

Remember that this practice will only be possible if the monopolist knows that the first user is willing and able to pay $10 for the product. Further, the consumers who purchase the product for $7 cannot resell it to the first user.

Figure 2-3: Price Discrimination

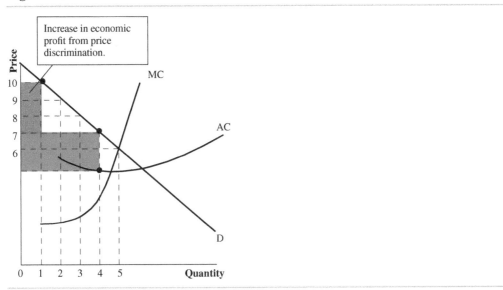

Under perfect price discrimination, each consumer who incurs the benefit of consumer surplus from the existence of a single market price is charged the maximum she is willing and able to pay for the good. In this extreme scenario, the first user will pay $10; the second, $9; the third, $8; the fourth, $7; and so on. The monopolist is able to capture all of the consumer surplus and increase its economic profit. Also notice that under perfect price discrimination, the monopolist's marginal revenue curve is the same as the demand curve (see Figure 2-3). In order to increase sales, prices do not have to be brought down for all previous consumers. Each consumer pays the maximum she is willing to pay, and the beneficiary of a price reduction is only the last buyer. The increase in revenue (marginal revenue) from the last unit of output equals the price that is paid by the purchaser of the last unit. Effectively, under perfect price discrimination the MR curve equals the demand curve.

Since the MR curve equals the demand curve for a monopoly that is able to engage in perfect price discrimination, the profit-maximizing level of output increases. The entire consumer surplus is eaten up by the producer, and there is no deadweight loss as output expands to 5 units (see Figure 2-4). This is because MC ($6, which also equals price) now equals MR ($6) at 5 units of output. Therefore, with perfect price discrimination, allocative efficiency is reached as the sum of consumer and producer surplus is maximized, and marginal benefit equals marginal cost. The more perfectly a monopolist can price discriminate, the more "efficient" the outcome.

Figure 2-4: Perfect Price Discrimination

Note that not every consumer is worse off with perfect price discrimination. The consumer of Unit 5 for example, is charged a price ($6) that is lower than the previously existing market price ($7).

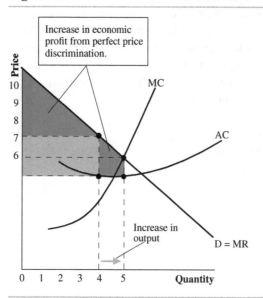

In second-degree price discrimination the monopolist uses the quantity purchased to determine whether the consumer values the product highly (and is therefore willing to pay a higher price per unit to purchase a larger quantity) or not so highly (and is therefore only willing to pay the lower price for a small quantity). The monopolist would then sell small quantities at the marginal price and large quantities at a higher price.

Third-degree price discrimination can occur when customers can be separated by geographical or other traits. One set of customers is charged a higher price, while the other is charged a lower price (e.g., airlines charge higher fares on one-day roundtrip tickets as they are more likely to be purchased by business people).

Factors Affecting Long Run Equilibrium in Monopoly Markets

An unregulated monopoly can earn economic profits in the long run as it is protected by substantial barriers to entry.

For regulated monopolies, such as natural monopolies, there are various solutions:

Economies of scale and regulation may make monopolies more "efficient" than perfect competition.

- A marginal cost pricing structure. However, the firm must be provided a subsidy in this scenario.
- An average cost pricing structure.
- National ownership of the monopoly.
- Franchising the monopoly via a bidding war (e.g., selling retail space at railway stations and airports).

LESSON 3: MARKET STRUCTURE 3: MONOPOLISTIC COMPETITION

LOS 15a: Describe characteristics of perfect competition, monopolistic competition, oligopoly, and pure monopoly. Vol 2, pp 83–87

LOS 15b: Explain relationships between price, marginal revenue, marginal cost, economic profit, and the elasticity of demand under each market structure. Vol 2, pp 83–87

LOS 15c: Describe a firm's supply function under each market structure. Vol 2, pp 83–87

LOS 15d: Describe and determine the optimal price and output for firms under each market structure. Vol 2, pp 83–87

LOS 15e: Explain factors affecting long-run equilibrium under each market structure. Vol 2, pp 83–87

LOS 15f: Describe pricing strategy under each market structure. Vol 2, pp 83–87

LOS 15h: Identify the type of market structure within which a firm operates. Vol 2, pp 83–87

Monopolistic Competition

Characteristics
- There are a large number of buyers and sellers.
- The products offered by each seller are similar, but not identical. They serve as close substitutes to each other.
- Firms try to differentiate their product from the competition through advertising and other nonprice strategies.
- There are low barriers to entry and exit.
- Firms have some degree of pricing power.

A firm can establish significant pricing power in monopolistic competition if it is able to build brand loyalty (e.g., Apple® customers pay premium prices on its iPhone® and iPad® devices). However, in the long run competition will result in falling prices and an equilibrium position that resembles (but is not identical to) perfect competition.

Demand and Supply Analysis in Monopolistically Competitive Markets

Demand
- Each firm faces a downward-sloping demand curve.
- Demand is relatively elastic at higher prices and relatively inelastic at lower prices.

Supply
- There is no well-defined supply function.
- Neither the MC nor the AC curve represent the firm's supply curve.
- The firm will always produce at the output level where MC = MR.
- The price that is charged is derived from the market demand curve.

In the short run, a firm operating in monopolistic competition will make its price and output decision just like a monopoly does. It will produce at the output level where MC equals MR, and earn economic profits equal to the shaded region in Figure 3-1.

Figure 3-1: Economic Profit in the Short Run

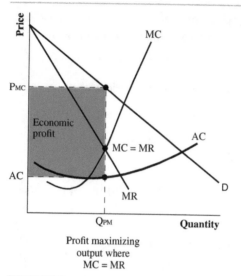

Profit maximizing
output where
MC = MR

However, it is also possible for a firm in monopolistic competition to face relatively low demand for its product. In this situation, the firm's average cost curve will lie above its demand curve and the firm will suffer economic losses in the short run. See Figure 3-2.

Figure 3-2: Economic Loss in the Short Run

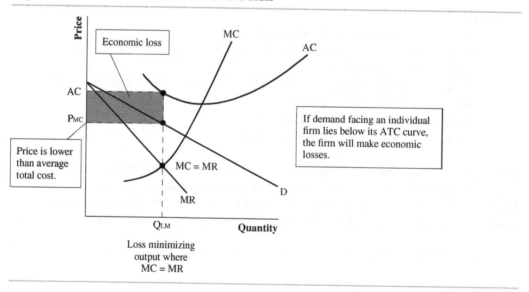

If demand facing an individual firm lies below its ATC curve, the firm will make economic losses.

Loss minimizing
output where
MC = MR

In the short run, a firm in monopolistic competition operates in a very similar manner to how a monopoly operates. It produces the output level where MC equals MR, and charges the maximum possible price that buyers are willing to pay for its product (determined by the demand curve). The key difference between the two industry structures lies in what happens in the long run in response to short-run economic profits and losses.

Factors Affecting Long-Run Equilibrium in Monopolistically Competitive Markets

If firms in monopolistic competition are making economic profits in the short run, new firms will try to move into the industry. As there are low barriers to entry, new firms will make similar products and successfully capture some market share in the industry. This eventually reduces demand faced by each individual firm to a level where demand is tangent to the average cost curve. No economic profits or losses are made (only normal profits are made) and the industry reaches long run equilibrium (see Figure 3-3).

Figure 3-3: Long-Run Equilibrium

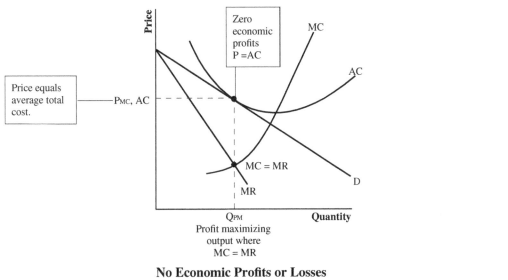

No Economic Profits or Losses

If demand is lower than average cost, firms make economic losses in the short run, and some firms will exit the industry. This will result in an increase in demand faced by each remaining firm. Eventually, firms in the industry make normal profits and, in long-run equilibrium, there is no incentive for new firms to enter or for existing firms to exit the industry.

Monopolistic Competition versus Perfect Competition

A firm in monopolistic competition generally produces lower output and charges a higher price than a firm in perfect competition. Significantly, the price charged under monopolistic competition is higher than the marginal cost of production, which implies that the outcome is not allocatively efficient. Recall that allocative efficiency is reached when price (marginal benefit) equals marginal cost.

In perfect competition, price *equals* marginal cost, while in monopolistic competition, price *exceeds* marginal cost (see Figures 3-4a and 3-4b). This excess of price over marginal cost is known as markup. In monopolistic competition, consumers pay a price that is *higher* than the price they would pay under perfect competition.

In the long run, firms in perfect competition and monopolistic competition both produce at levels where marginal cost equals marginal revenue (see Figures 3-4a and 3-4b). For a firm in monopolistic competition, this output level occurs where demand is tangent to the average cost curve, but at a stage where average costs are *still falling*. In perfect competition, all firms produce an output level where average cost is at its *minimum* or at the efficient scale of production. Firms in monopolistic competition therefore have excess

Figure 3-4: Excess Capacity and Markup

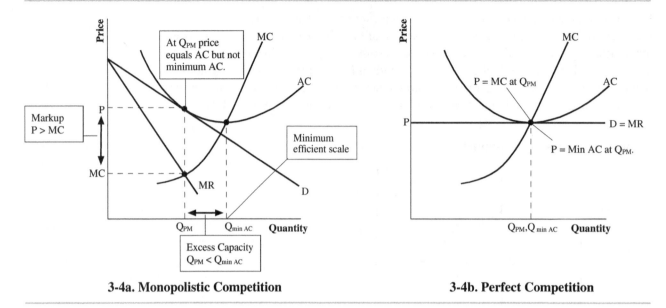

3-4a. Monopolistic Competition   **3-4b. Perfect Competition**

capacity. Excess capacity is a situation where a firm produces an output level that is short of its minimum efficient scale.

However, monopolistic competition has its supporters. Monopolistic competition offers consumers variety and gives them options to choose from.

LESSON 4: MARKET STRUCTURE 4: OLIGOPOLY

LOS 15a: Describe characteristics of perfect competition, monopolistic competition, oligopoly, and pure monopoly. Vol 2, pp 87–96

LOS 15b: Explain relationships between price, marginal revenue, marginal cost, economic profit, and the elasticity of demand under each market structure. Vol 2, pp 87–96

LOS 15c: Describe a firm's supply function under each market structure. Vol 2, pp 87–96

LOS 15d: Describe and determine the optimal price and output for firms under each market structure. Vol 2, pp 87–96

LOS 15e: Explain factors affecting long-run equilibrium under each market structure. Vol 2, pp 87–96

LOS 15f: Describe pricing strategy under each market structure. Vol 2, pp 87–96

LOS 15h: Identify the type of market structure within which a firm operates. Vol 2, pp 87–96

Oligopoly

Characteristics

- There are a small number of sellers.
- The products offered by sellers are close substitutes for each other. Products may be differentiated by brand (e.g., Coke® and Pepsi®) or be homogenous (e.g., oil).

- There are high costs of entry and significant barriers to competition.
- Firms enjoy substantial pricing power.
- Products are often differentiated on the basis of quality, features, marketing, and other nonprice strategies.

The fact that there are such few firms in an oligopoly means that they have significant pricing power. Further, there is always an incentive for price collusion to increase profits further. In some oligopoly markets, the dominant firm may become the price-maker even without price collusion.

Demand Analysis and Pricing Strategies in Oligopoly Markets

There are three basic pricing strategies in oligopoly markets:

Pricing interdependence (kinked demand curve model) is when there are "price wars" between the firms in the industry (e.g., the commercial airline industry). The kinked demand curve model assumes that if a firm operating in an oligopoly increases its price, others will not follow suit so the firm will suffer a large decrease in quantity demanded (elastic demand). However, if the firm were to reduce its price, competitors would follow its lead, and the increase in quantity demanded for the firm would not be significant (inelastic demand). These two contrasting shapes of the demand curve (i.e., relatively elastic above current prices, and relatively inelastic below current prices) result in a kink in the firm's demand curve and a break in its marginal revenue curve (see Figure 4-1).

Figure 4-1: Kinked Demand Curve Model

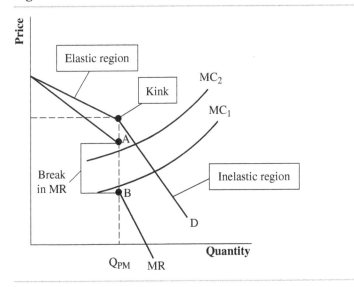

The break in the marginal revenue curve (between Points A and B) implies that if an increase in cost of production were to shift the marginal cost curve from MC_1 to MC_2, the firm would still produce the same level of output. It would take a significant change in costs of production (one that forces the MC curve to shift outside the range between Points A and B) to change the firm's profit-maximizing output level.

The kinked demand theory is useful, as it explains why stable prices have been seen in oligopoly markets. However, since it does not discuss how the original price is determined (the price at which the demand curve kinks), it is considered an incomplete analysis.

The second price strategy is based on the Cournot assumption, which asserts that each firm determines its profit-maximizing level assuming that other firms' output will not change. In equilibrium, no firm has an incentive to change output. In the long run, prices and output are stable—there is no possible change in output or price that would make any firm better off. Example 4-1 illustrates how the Cournot assumption works in a duopoly (an oligopoly market with only two sellers) and contrasts the long-run equilibrium for a duopoly (under Cournot's assumption) with long-run equilibrium under a monopoly and perfect competition.

Example 4-1

The market demand curve is given as: $QD = 400 – P$. There are only two firms in the industry and the supply curve for each firm is represented by its marginal cost, which is constant at \$40.

1. Determine equilibrium price and output in the long run under Cournot's assumption.
2. Determine long-run equilibrium price and output under perfect competition.
3. Determine long-run equilibrium price and output under a monopoly.

Solutions:

1. Market demand (QD) equals q_1 plus q_2 (the quantities produced by the two firms in the industry). Therefore:

    $$P = 400 – Q_D = 400 – q_1 – q_2$$

    Total revenue equals price times quantity, so total revenue for the two firms is presented by the following expressions:

    $$TR_1 = P \times q_1 = (400 – q_1 – q_2)\, q_1 = 400q_1 – q_1^2 – q_1q_2$$
    $$TR_2 = P \times q_2 = (400 – q_1 – q_2)\, q_2 = 400q_1 – q_1q_2 – q_2^2$$

    Marginal revenue is the derivative of the TR expression with respect to quantity. Therefore, MR for the two firms equals:

    $$MR_1 = 400 – 2q_1 – q_2$$
    $$MR_2 = 400 – q_1 – 2q_2$$

    Both firms will aim to maximize profits. The profit-maximizing level of output occurs where MC = MR. Since both firms have constant MR of \$40, and q_1 equals q_2 (under Cournot's assumption), we can solve for q_1 as:

    $$400 – 2q_1 – q_1 = 40$$
    $$q_1 = 120$$
    $$q_2 = 120$$
    $$Q_D = 240$$
    $$P = 400 – Q_D = \$160$$

    In the Cournot strategic-pricing solution, equilibrium price will be \$160 and equilibrium market quantity will be 240 units.

2. In perfect competition, price equals MR equals MC.

    $$P = MR = MC \Rightarrow 400 – Q_D = \$40$$
    Therefore, $Q_D = 360$ and $P = \$40$

---

3. In a monopoly, equilibrium is established where MR = MC.

Industry and monopolist's TR = $P \times Q_D = (400 - Q_D)Q_D = 400Q_D - Q_D^2$
MR = $400 - 2Q_D$

MR = MC implies that $400 - 2Q_D = 40$
Therefore, $Q_D = 180$ and P = \$220

Note the following:

- The monopoly charges the highest price and produces the lowest output.
- Perfect competition results in the lowest price and the highest output.
- The Cournot solution falls between competitive and monopoly equilibrium.
- As the number of firms in the industry increases (from the two that we assumed in this example), industry equilibrium approaches competitive equilibrium.

The third pricing strategy is based on game theory. Nash equilibrium is achieved when none of the firms in an oligopoly market can increase profits by unilaterally changing its price. Each firm tries to maximize its own profits given the responses of its rivals. Each firm anticipates how its rival will respond to a change in its strategy and tries to maximize its profits under the forecasted scenario. As a result, the firms in the market are interdependent, but their actions are noncooperative: firms do not collude to maximize profits.

Figure 4-2 illustrates the duopoly in Nash equilibrium. Company A and Company B are the only two firms in the industry. Each of them can either charge a high price (HP) or a low price (LP). The market outcomes under 4 different scenarios are illustrated in the figure.

Figure 4-2: Nash Equilibrium in Duopoly Market

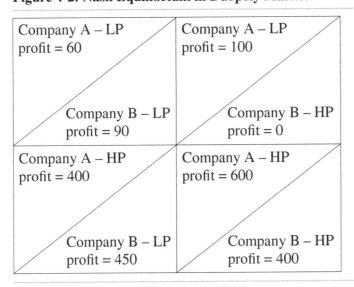

Note:

- Maximum joint profits occur when both firms charge HP.
- However, B will be able to increase its profits (from \$400 to \$450) if it charges LP when A charges HP.
- A can only maximize its profits if B agrees to charge HP. In order to incentivize B to charge HP, A must pay B at least \$51. Such behavior is known as collusion and is unlawful in most countries. When collusive agreements are made openly and formally, the firms involved are said to have formed a cartel (e.g., OPEC).

Factors Affecting Chances of Successful Collusion

The chances of successful collusion improve when:

- There are fewer firms in the industry or if one firm is dominant. Collusion becomes difficult as competition between firms in the industry increases.
- The firms produce similar products.
- The firms have similar cost structures.
- Order size is small and orders are received more frequently.
- There is minimal threat of retaliation from other firms in the industry.
- There is minimal external competition.

> The leader can increase production (lower prices) to eliminate weaker opponents. This approach is known as the top dog strategy.

Another decision-making strategy in oligopoly markets is known as the Stackelberg model (also known as the dominant firm model). In contrast to the Cournot model (which assumes that decision-making is simultaneous) this model assumes that decision-making is sequential. The leader or dominant firm determines its profit-maximizing level of output, the price is determined from the demand curve for its product (the dominant firm is the price-maker), and then each of the follower firms determine their quantities based on the given market price (they are price-takers). (See Figure 4-3.)

Figure 4-3: Dominant Firm Pricing Leadership

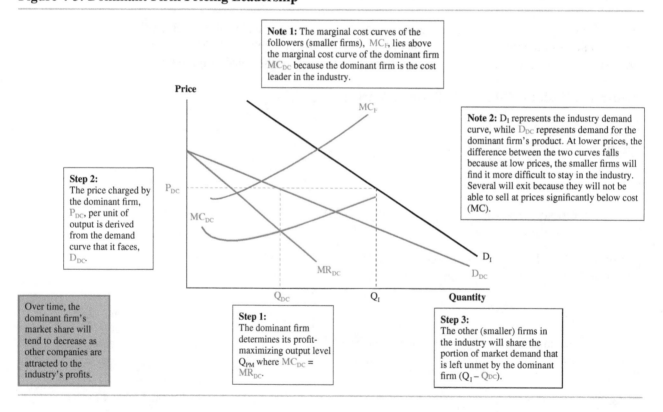

Note 1: The marginal cost curves of the followers (smaller firms), MC_F, lies above the marginal cost curve of the dominant firm MC_{DC} because the dominant firm is the cost leader in the industry.

Note 2: D_I represents the industry demand curve, while D_{DC} represents demand for the dominant firm's product. At lower prices, the difference between the two curves falls because at low prices, the smaller firms will find it more difficult to stay in the industry. Several will exit because they will not be able to sell at prices significantly below cost (MC).

Step 2:
The price charged by the dominant firm, P_{DC}, per unit of output is derived from the demand curve that it faces, D_{DC}.

Step 1:
The dominant firm determines its profit-maximizing output level Q_{PM} where $MC_{DC} = MR_{DC}$.

Step 3:
The other (smaller) firms in the industry will share the portion of market demand that is left unmet by the dominant firm ($Q_I - Q_{DC}$).

> Over time, the dominant firm's market share will tend to decrease as other companies are attracted to the industry's profits.

Supply Analysis in Oligopoly Markets

- The supply function for a firm in an oligopoly is not well defined because optimal quantity and price depend on the actions of rival firms.
- The firm produces where MC = MR.
- Equilibrium price comes from the demand curve.

Optimal Price and Output in Oligopoly Markets

There is no single optimal price and output that fits all oligopoly market situations.

- In the kinked demand curve model, the optimal price is the prevailing price (at which the demand curve kinks).
- In the dominant firm model, the leader produces an output level where MC = MR. Followers have little or no power to influence price.
- In Cournot's assumption, each firm assumes that rivals will have no response to any actions on their part. Each firm produces where MC = MR.
- In Nash equilibrium, firms continue to respond to changing circumstances with the aim of maximizing their own profit. Since there is significant interdependence between firms, there is no certainty regarding an individual firm's price and output.

Factors Affecting Long-Run Equilibrium in Oligopoly Markets

Firms in oligopolies can make economic profits in the long run. Sometimes, as more firms enter the industry in the long run (and adopt more efficient technologies), they can displace the dominant firm over time. In the long run, optimal pricing decisions must be made in light of the reactions of rivals. History has shown that pricing wars should be avoided because any gains in market share arising from them are temporary. Innovation however, can lead to sustained market leadership.

Characteristics of Market Structure

Market Structure	Number of Sellers	Degree of Product Differentiation	Barriers to Entry	Pricing Power of Firm	Nonprice Competition
Perfect Competition	Many	Homogeneous/ Standardized	Very low	None	None
Monopolistic Competition	Many	Differentiated	Low	Some	Advertising and product differentiation
Oligopoly	Few	Homogeneous/ Standardized	High	Some or considerable	Advertising and product differentiation
Monopoly	One	Unique product	Very high	Considerable	Advertising

LESSON 5: IDENTIFICATION OF MARKET STRUCTURE

LOS 15g: Describe the use and limitations of concentration measures in identifying market structure. Vol 2, pp 105–108

Identification of Market Structure

Econometric Approaches

Estimate the price elasticity of market demand:
- If demand is relatively elastic, the market is probably close to perfect competition.
- If demand is relatively inelastic, supplying firms may enjoy pricing power.

Limitation
- Problem of endogeneity: Observed prices and quantities are equilibrium prices and quantities (which are determined through the interaction of demand and supply). The entire demand and supply curves cannot be observed and therefore must be estimated.

Time Series Analysis
- Compute price elasticity using historical sales and market price data.

Limitations
- A large number of observations are required.
- There is always the possibility that the market structure and elasticities have changed over the sample period (e.g., mergers may cause the supply curve to change).

Cross Sectional Regression Analysis
- Examine sales made by different companies in the market over a specific period.
- Look at single transactions from different buyers.

Limitations
- It is very complicated.
- Obtaining data can be difficult.

Other Measures

N-firm concentration ratio: Simply computes the aggregate market share of the N largest firms in the industry. The ratio will equal 0 for perfect competition and 100 for a monopoly. While it is very easy to calculate, it has two disadvantages:

- It does not quantify market power. For example, a monopoly may currently enjoy a 100% market share, but if barriers to entry are insignificant, it will not have any pricing power and will likely behave like a firm in perfect competition to remain competitive and keep potential rivals from entering the market.
- It is unaffected by mergers in the top tier. For example, if the two largest firms in the market were to merge, the pricing power of the combined entity would have improved, but the ratio will not have significantly changed.

Herfindahl-Hirschman Index (HHI): Adds up the squares of the market shares of each of the largest N companies in the market. The HHI equals 1 for a monopoly. If there are M firms in the industry with equal market shares, the HHI will equal 1/M.

- Just like the concentration ratio, the HHI does not account for the possibility of entry, nor does it consider the elasticity of demand. However, as the following example illustrates, it is more useful than the concentration ratio.

Example 5-1: Calculating HHI and the Concentration Ratio

There are 7 producers of a certain good in an economy whose market shares are given in the following table:

Firm	Market Share
1	30%
2	25%
3	15%
4	12%
5	8%
6	5%
7	5%
Total	**100%**

1. Calculate:
   a. The four-firm concentration ratio
   b. HHI of the four largest firms
2. Now suppose that the two largest firms merge. Based on the new market shares, calculate
   a. The four-firm concentration ratio
   b. HHI of the four largest firms
3. Comment on the change in the two ratios before and after the merger.

Solutions:

1. Before the merger:
   a. Four-firm concentration ratio = $0.3 + 0.25 + 0.15 + 0.12 = 82\%$
   b. HHI = $0.3^2 + 0.25^2 + 0.15^2 + 0.12^2 = 0.1894$
2. After the merger:
   a. Four-firm concentration ratio = $0.55 + 0.15 + 0.12 + 0.03 = 90\%$
   b. HHI = $0.55^2 + 0.15^2 + 0.12^2 + 0.08^2 = 0.3458$
3. Notice that after the merger, the four-firm concentration ratio rises by only a small amount (10%) even though now there is a large entity that dominates the market (controls 55%). The HHI on the other hand, rises by a substantial amount (by almost 83%), which indicates that there has been a significant change in market structure.

READING 16: AGGREGATE OUTPUT, PRICES, AND ECONOMIC GROWTH

LESSON 1: AGGREGATE OUTPUT AND INCOME

In contrast to microeconomics, which is the study of the activity and behavior of individual economic units (e.g., a household or a company), macroeconomics focuses on *aggregates* (e.g., total consumption of all households or total business investment in an economy).

GDP

LOS 16a: Calculate and explain gross domestic product (GDP) using expenditure and income approaches. Vol 2, pp 119–127

Aggregate output refers to the total value of all the goods and services produced in an economy over a period of time.

Aggregate income refers to the total value of all payments earned by the suppliers of factors of production in an economy over a period of time. Since the value of output produced in the economy flows through to the factors of production, aggregate output and aggregate income are equal. Aggregate income is composed of:

- Employee compensation including wages and benefits.
- Rent for the use of property.
- Interest earned on funds loaned out.
- Profits earned by businesses.

Aggregate expenditure refers to the total amount spent on the goods and services produced in the domestic economy over a period of time.

Aggregate output, aggregate income, and aggregate expenditure basically represent different ways of breaking down the same quantity. For example, households supply labor and capital (factors of production) to businesses in return for wages and interest (income). Businesses use the services of factors of production to produce goods and services (output) that are sold to households (expenditure). Figure 1-1 illustrates the flow of output, expenditure, and income in a simple economy.

> Although businesses own much of the property and physical capital in an economy, households (through their ownership of businesses) are the ultimate owners of these assets and recipients of profits.

Figure 1-1: Output, Income, and Expenditure in a Simple Economy[1]

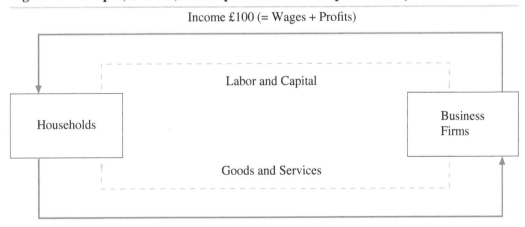

1 - Exhibit 1, Volume 2, CFA Program Curriculum 2018

Note that the (rather simplistic) scenario illustrated in Figure 1-1 rarely holds in practice because:

- Households may spend on foreign goods (imports).
- Households may save a portion of their income.
- Household incomes may be reduced by taxes.
- Businesses may sell goods to foreigners (exports).
- Businesses may reinvest funds in the business instead of distributing profits to shareholders.

These discrepancies often lead to differences between aggregate output, aggregate income, and aggregate expenditure (which we ignore for the time being, but add to the analysis later in the reading as statistical discrepancies).

Gross Domestic Product (GDP)

GDP may be defined in two ways:

- Output definition: GDP is the market value of all final goods and services produced within an economy over a period of time.
- Income definition: GDP is the aggregate income earned by all households, companies, and the government in an economy over a period of time.

Based on these two definitions, GDP may either be calculated using the expenditure approach (total amount spent on goods and services produced in the economy), or the income approach (total amount earned by households and companies in the economy). For the economy as a whole, total income must equal total expenditure, so GDP can be calculated using either of these approaches.

In order to ensure consistency in the method used to calculate GDP in different countries, the following criteria are applied:

- Only goods and services produced *during* the measurement period are included.
  - Transfer payments from the government to individuals (e.g., unemployment compensation) are excluded.
  - Income from capital gains is excluded.
- Only goods and services whose value can be determined by being sold in the market are included.
  - The value of labor used in activities that are not sold in the market (e.g., gardening or cooking for one's own benefit) is excluded.
  - By-products of production processes which have no explicit market value are not included.
  - Activities in the underground economy (e.g., illegal drug trading and undocumented laborers being paid "off-the-books") are not included.
  - Barter transactions (e.g., a person raking a neighbor's lawn in exchange for help in repairing her fence) are not included.
- Only the value of *final* goods and services is included in the calculation of GDP. The value of intermediate goods (that are resold to produce another good) is excluded because the entire value added during the production process is reflected in the selling price of the final good produced (value-of-final-output). GDP can also be measured by summing the value added at each stage of the production and distribution processes (sum-of-value-added).

Some economists measure the flow of income using GNP (instead of GDP). GDP accounts for all production within a country's borders regardless of whether the factors of production are owned domestically or by foreigners. GNP measures output produced by domestically owned factors of production regardless of whether production occurs within the economy's boundaries or outside.

Note that owner-occupied housing and government services are included in the calculation (based on imputed values) of GDP even though they are not "sold in the marketplace." No rent is actually paid if the homeowner lives in the house herself so an estimate of owner-occupied rent is used. The value of services provided by the government (e.g., police officers) is included in the calculation of GDP at cost (wages paid).

The reliability of official GDP data varies considerably across countries because there are estimates involved in the calculation of GDP and underground economies vary in size. Other potential problems include poor data collection practices and use of unreliable statistical methods.

LOS 16b: Compare the sum-of-value-added and value-of-final-output methods of calculating GDP. Vol 2, pp 121–123

> "Final goods" should not be confused with so-called final sales, and "intermediate goods" should not be confused with inventories. GDP includes both final sales to customers and increases in companies' inventories. If sales exceed current production, then GDP is less than final sales by the amount of goods sold out of inventory.

Example 1-1: Value of Final Output

A farmer sells wheat to a miller for $0.30. The miller grinds the wheat into flour and sells it to a baker for $0.85. The baker makes bread and sells it to a retailer for $1.45, who sells it on to the final customer for $2. What is the value of the contribution of all these economic agents to the GDP of the economy?

Solution:

For the purposes of calculating a product's contribution to GDP, we can either include the value of the final product (i.e., $2 for the bread), *or* we can sum the value added at each step of the production process. We will not include the value of wheat or flour in the calculation of GDP as these are "intermediate products" whose values are reflected in the "final value" of bread. The value added at each stage is calculated below:

	Selling Price at Each Stage ($)	Value Added at Each Stage ($)	
Wheat sold by farmer to the miller	0.30	0.30	Value added by the farmer
Flour sold by miller to the baker	0.85	0.55	Value added by the miller
Bread sold by baker to the retailer	1.45	0.60	Value added by the baker
Bread sold by retailer to the final customer	2.00	0.55	Value added by the retailer as a distributor
	2.00	**2.00**	
	Value of final output	Total value added	

The value of GDP using either of the two methods is the same. Note that if some of the inputs were imported into the economy, the value added would be reduced by the amount paid for the inputs. For example, if the miller were to import the wheat for $0.30, the contribution of the bread-making activity to GDP would be $2.00 − $0.30 = $1.70.

LOS 16c: Compare nominal and real GDP and calculate and interpret the GDP deflator. Vol 2, pp 124–127

The average standard of living in a country is evaluated on the basis of per capita real GDP (real GDP divided by the size of the population).

Nominal GDP refers to the value of goods and services included in GDP measured at **current prices**.

$$\text{Nominal GDP} = \text{Quantity produced in Year t} \times \text{Prices in Year t}$$

Since it is based on current prices, nominal GDP includes the effects of inflation. Analysts usually remove the effect of changes in the price level on GDP by measuring GDP at base-year prices. This measure is known as **real GDP**.

It is important to remove the effects of inflation on GDP because higher (lower) income driven by higher price levels does not indicate higher (lower) levels of economic activity.

$$\text{Real GDP} = \text{Quantity produced in Year t} \times \text{Base-year prices}$$

Example 1-2: Nominal and Real GDP

An analyst gathered the following information regarding the production of cars in an economy:

	2007	2008	2009
No. of cars manufactured	500,000	500,000	520,000
Average market price ($)	20,500	22,140	23,247

What is the contribution of the automobile industry toward nominal and real GDP in each of the three years? Comment on your answers.

Solution:

2007:
Nominal GDP = 500,000 × 20,500 = $10,250,000,000
Real GDP = 500,000 × 20,500 = $10,250,000,000

2008:
Nominal GDP = 500,000 × 22,140 = $11,070,000,000
Real GDP = 500,000 × 20,500 = $10,250,000,000

2009:
Nominal GDP = 520,000 × 23,247 = $12,088,440,000
Real GDP = 520,000 × 20,500 = $10,660,000,000

The quantity of cars manufactured in 2008 was the same as that in 2007, so real GDP did not change. On the other hand, nominal GDP grew by 11,070,000,000/10,250,000,000 – 1 = 8% in 2008. Note that the increase in nominal GDP in 2008 is simply due to the increase in car prices: (22,140 / 20,500) – 1 = 8%.

Comparing 2009 to 2008, we see an increase in prices and in the number of cars manufactured. Therefore, both nominal and real GDP increased. Prices increased by 23,247/22,140 − 1 = 5%, while the number of cars manufactured increased by 520,000/500,000 − 1 = 4%. As a result, nominal GDP increased by (1.05 × 1.04) − 1 = 9.2%, while real GDP only grew by 4%. The real GDP growth rate is more informative, as it effectively captures the growth in actual output in the economy over the period.

GDP Deflator

The GDP deflator broadly measures the aggregate change in prices across the overall economy. Changes in the GDP deflator provide a useful measure of inflation.

$$\text{GDP deflator} = \frac{\text{Value of current year output at current year prices}}{\text{Value of current year output at base year prices}} \times 100$$

$$\text{GDP deflator} = \frac{\text{Nominal GDP}}{\text{Real GDP}} \times 100$$

Rearranging the above equation gives us:

$$\text{Real GDP} = \frac{\text{Nominal GDP}}{\text{GDP deflator}} \times 100$$

Therefore, we can say that the effects of changes in price can be removed from nominal GDP by dividing it by the GDP deflator.

Example 1-3: GDP Deflator

Given the values of real and nominal GDP in Example 1-2, calculate the GDP deflator for each of the three years.

Solution:

GDP Deflator (2007) = (10,250,000,000 / 10,250,000,000) × 100 = 100

GDP Deflator (2008) = (11,070,000,000 / 10,250,000,000) × 100 = 108

GDP Deflator (2009) = (12,088,440,000 / 10,660,000,000) × 100 = 113.4

The percentage change in the GDP deflator gives us a measure of the inflation rate. For example, the inflation rate for 2008 can be estimated as 108/100 − 1 = 8%, and that for 2009 can be estimated as 113.4/108 − 1 = 5%.

The Components of GDP

Based on the expenditure approach, GDP may be calculated as:

$$GDP = C + I + G + (X - M)$$

where:
C = Consumer spending on final goods and services
I = Gross private domestic investment, which includes business investment in capital goods (e.g., plant and equipment) and changes in inventory (inventory investment)
G = Government spending on final goods and services
X = Exports
M = Imports

The flow of expenditures, income, and financing among the four major sectors of the economy in the three principal markets is illustrated in Figure 1-2.

Figure 1-2: Output, Income, and Expenditure Flows[2]

Households:
- Spend on consumption (C) in the goods market. This amount goes back to businesses.
- Save (S) for future consumption. This amount may go to businesses or the government through the financial market.
- Pay taxes (T) to the government.

In the factor market:
- Services of labor, land, and capital flow to businesses.
- Income flows from businesses to households.

Businesses
- Use funds to make investments (I) (i.e., purchase capital goods from the goods market).
- Investment flows from and to firms in the goods market because businesses demand goods (physical capital) and produce goods.
- Investment spending is a very important determinant of the economy's long-term growth rate.
- Investment spending is also the most volatile component of AD (especially inventory). Changes in capital spending are one of the major causes of short-term economic fluctuations.

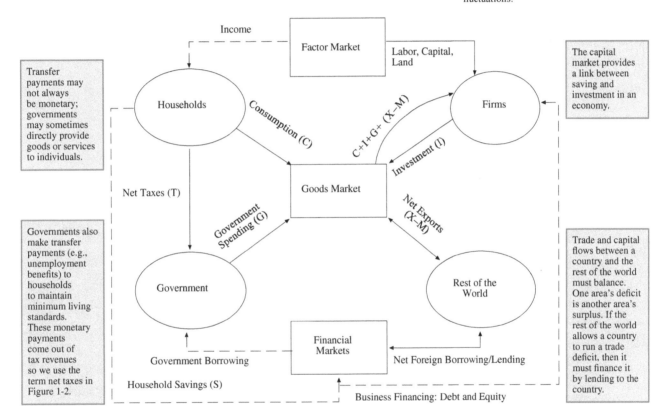

Government Sector
- Receives tax revenues from households and businesses and spends money (G) to purchase goods and services from the business sector (in the goods market). Please note that only taxes collected from the household sector are shown in the figure.
- Transfer payments are not included in government spending. The household spending (C) facilitated by transfer payments is included in GDP.
- A government has a fiscal deficit if its expenditure exceeds net taxes. To finance this deficit, it borrows from financial markets (or from the external sector). If the government runs a fiscal surplus, its savings are loaned out in the financial market.
- Government employment and corresponding income are not shown in the figure.

Foreign (External) Sector
- The external sector interacts with the domestic economy through purchases (exports from the domestic economy) and sales (imports into the domestic economy) in the goods market.
- An economy has a balance of trade deficit if imports exceed exports (i.e., the economy is spending more on foreign goods and services than foreign economies are spending on domestic goods and services). A trade deficit implies that the country is spending more than it produces. This may be the result of domestic savings not being adequate to finance domestic investment or the government's fiscal deficit.
- A trade deficit must be funded by borrowing from the rest of the world through the financial market. The rest of the world should be able to finance a country's trade deficit because it must have savings (as it must be running a corresponding trade surplus, which implies that it is spending less than it is producing).

2 - Exhibit 6, Volume 2, CFA Program Curriculum 2018

LOS 16d: Compare GDP, national income, personal income, and personal disposable income. Vol 2, pp 131–136

Theoretically, GDP measured under the expenditure and income approaches should be equal. Practically however, this is not the case due to statistical discrepancies.

Expenditure Approach

Under the expenditure approach, GDP at market prices may be calculated as:

This equation is just a breakdown of the expression for GDP we stated in the previous LOS [i.e., GDP = C + I + G + (X – M)].

GDP = Consumer spending on goods and services
+ Business gross fixed investment
+ Change in inventories
+ Government spending on goods and services
+ Government gross fixed investment
+ Exports – Imports
+ Statistical discrepancy

The following important points should be noted:

- In the above equation, we have separately classified a portion of government expenditures as "gross fixed investment." This distinction is not made by all countries.
- The "change in inventories" is included in expenditures to account for goods produced but not yet sold.

Income Approach

Under the income approach, GDP at market prices may be calculated as:

GDP = National income + Capital consumption allowance
+ Statistical discrepancy   ... (Equation) 1

National income equals the sum of incomes received by all factors of production used to generate final output. It includes:

- Employee compensation
- Corporate and government enterprise profits before taxes, which includes:
  - Dividends paid to households
  - Corporate profits retained by businesses
  - Corporate taxes paid to the government
- Interest income
- Rent and unincorporated business net income (proprietor's income): Amounts earned by unincorporated proprietors and farm operators who run their own businesses.
- Indirect business taxes less subsidies: This amount reflects taxes and subsidies that are included in the final price of a good or service, and therefore represents the portion of national income that is directly paid to the government.

The **capital consumption allowance (CCA)** accounts for the wear and tear or depreciation that occurs in capital stock during the production process. It represents the amount that must be reinvested by the company in the business to maintain current productivity levels. You should think of profits + CCA as the amount earned by capital.

Other GDP-Related Measures

Personal income measures the ability of households to make purchases and includes all income received by households, regardless of whether it is **earned** or **unearned**. It differs from national income in the following respects:

> Unearned income refers to transfer payments, which are not "earned" but can be spent by households.

- National income includes income that goes to businesses and the government (e.g., indirect business taxes, corporate income taxes, and retained earnings), which personal income does not.
- National income does not include household income that is not earned (e.g., transfer payments).

Personal income = National income
   − Indirect business taxes
   − Corporate income taxes
   − Undistributed corporate profits
   + Transfer payments   ... (Equation 2)

Personal disposable income measures the amount of income that households have left to spend or to save after paying taxes.

Personal disposable income = Personal income − Personal taxes   ... (Equation 3)

Personal disposable income = Household consumption − Household saving   ... (Equation 4)

Household saving = Personal disposable income
   − Consumption expenditures
   − Interest paid by consumers to businesses
   − Personal transfer payments to foreigners   ... (Equation 5)

Business sector saving = Undistributed corporate profits
   + Capital consumption allowance   ... (Equation 6)

LESSON 2: AGGREGATE DEMAND, AGGREGATE SUPPLY, AND EQUILIBRIUM: PART 1 (FUNDAMENTAL RELATIONSHIPS)

LOS 16e: Explain the fundamental relationship among saving, investment, the fiscal balance, and the trade balance. Vol 2, pp 136–138

We know that:

$$\text{GDP} = \text{National income} + \text{Capital consumption allowance} + \text{Statistical discrepancy} \quad \text{... (Equation 1)}$$

Make national income the subject in Equation 2:

$$\text{Personal income} = \text{National income} - \text{Indirect business taxes} - \text{Corporate income taxes} - \text{Undistributed corporate profits} + \text{Transfer payments} \quad \text{... (Equation 2)}$$

$$\text{National income} = \text{Personal income} + \text{Indirect business taxes} + \text{Corporate income taxes} + \text{Undistributed corporate profits} - \text{Transfer payments} \quad \text{... (Equation 2a)}$$

Insert Equation 2a in Equation 1 (replacing national income)

$$\text{GDP} = \text{Personal income} + \text{Indirect business taxes} + \text{Corporate income taxes} + \text{Undistributed corporate profits} - \text{Transfer payments} + \text{Capital consumption allowance} \quad \text{... (Equation 1a)}$$

Make personal income the subject in Equation 3:

$$\text{Personal disposable income} = \text{Personal income} - \text{Personal taxes} \quad \text{... (Equation 3)}$$

$$\text{Personal income} = \text{Personal disposable income} + \text{Personal taxes} \quad \text{... (Equation 3a)}$$

Insert Equation 3a in Equation 1a:

$$\text{GDP} = \text{Personal disposable income} + \text{Personal taxes} + \text{Indirect business taxes} + \text{Corporate income taxes} + \text{Undistributed corporate profits} - \text{Transfer payments} + \text{Capital consumption allowance} \quad \text{... (Equation 1b)}$$

Undistributed corporate profits plus the capital consumption allowance equals business sector saving (Equation 6). Therefore Equation 1b can be rewritten as:

$$\text{GDP} = \text{Personal disposable income} + \text{Personal taxes} + \text{Indirect business taxes} + \text{Corporate income taxes} + \text{Business sector saving} - \text{Transfer payments} \quad \text{... (Equation 1c)}$$

Grouping personal taxes, indirect business taxes, and corporate income taxes under one head (Direct and indirect taxes), we can rewrite Equation 1c as:

$$\text{GDP} = \text{Personal disposable income} + \text{Direct and indirect taxes} + \text{Business sector saving} - \text{Transfer payments} \quad \text{... (Equation 1d)}$$

Rearranging Equation 1d to make personal disposable income the subject:

Personal disposable income = GDP + Transfer payments − Direct and indirect taxes
− Business sector saving   ... (Equation 1e)

Personal disposable income is what households have left to spend or to save after paying taxes.

Personal disposable income = Household consumption + Household saving   ... (Equation 4)

Replacing personal disposable income on the left-hand side of Equation 1e with the expression on the right-hand side of Equation 4:

Household consumption + Household saving = GDP + Transfer payments − Direct and
indirect taxes − Business sector saving
... (Equation 1f)

Rearranging Equation 1f gives us:

GDP = Household consumption + Household saving + Business sector saving
+ Direct and indirect taxes − Transfer payments

Combining household saving and business sector saving gives us total private sector saving. Subtracting transfer payments from direct and indirect taxes gives us net taxes. Therefore,

> GDP = Household consumption + Total private sector saving + Net taxes

Denoting household consumption as C, total private sector saving as S, and net taxes as T, we get:

GDP = C + S + T

Earlier, we expressed GDP as:

GDP = C + I + G + (X − M)

Therefore,

C + S + T = C + I + G + (X − M)

$$S = I + (G - T) + (X - M)$$ ... (Equation 7)

This equation is referred to as the equality of expenditure and income. Based on this equation we can say that domestic private saving can be used for:

Admittedly, we have gone about this derivation in an extremely roundabout manner. For the purposes of the exam, just ensure that you know Equation 7 and its implications (below).

- Investment spending (I);
- Financing government deficits (G − T); and/or
- Building up financial claims against overseas economies by financing their trade deficits (lending the domestic economy's trade surplus, X − M).

Note that:

- If an economy has a negative trade balance, foreign savings will supplement domestic savings and foreigners will build up financial claims against the domestic economy.
- If the government runs a fiscal surplus, the surplus will add to domestic savings.

We can also evaluate the effects of government deficits and surpluses by rearranging Equation 19 as:

$$(G - T) = (S - I) - (X - M)$$

A fiscal deficit occurs when government expenditures exceed net taxes (i.e., $G - T > 0$). In order to finance a fiscal deficit:

- The private sector must save more than it invests ($S > I$); and/or
- The country's imports must exceed its exports ($M > X \Rightarrow$ trade deficit) with a corresponding inflow of foreign saving.

LESSON 3: AGGREGATE DEMAND, AGGREGATE SUPPLY, AND EQUILIBRIUM: PART 2 (IS-LM ANALYSIS AND THE AD CURVE)

LOS 16f: Explain the IS and LM curves and how they combine to generate the aggregate demand curve. Vol 2, pp 141–148

The **aggregate demand (AD)** curve shows the combinations of aggregate income and price level at which the following conditions are satisfied:

- Planned expenditures equal actual (or realized) income/output. This equality does not hold, for example, if businesses end up with more inventory than planned as that would mean that actual output exceeded planned expenditures and the difference resulted in unplanned business investment.
- There is equilibrium in the money market, that is, available real money supply equals demand for real money.

The first condition gives rise to the **IS curve**, while the second gives rise to the **LM curve**. By combining the IS and LM curves, we obtain the **aggregate demand curve**.

The IS Curve (Relationship Between Income and the Real Interest Rate)

In order to derive the relationship between income and the real interest rate, we look at the factors that influence each of the components of aggregate demand.

Consumption

The main determinant of consumption expenditure in an economy is disposable income.

Personal disposable income = GDP + Transfer payments − Direct and indirect taxes
− Business sector saving   ... (Equation 1e)

Direct and indirect taxes − Transfer payments = Net taxes.

Therefore:

$$\text{Disposable income} = \text{GDP} - \text{Business saving} - \text{Net taxes}$$

For simplicity, we ignore retained earnings and depreciation (business saving). Disposable income is then a function of GDP minus net taxes, and since consumption is, in turn, a function of disposable income, we can express consumption as a function of GDP minus taxes:

$$C = f(Y - T)$$

When households receive a unit of disposable income, they spend a portion and save the rest.

- The marginal propensity to consume (MPC) is the portion of an additional unit of disposable income that is consumed or spent.
- The marginal propensity to save (MPS) is the portion of an additional unit of disposable income that is saved (MPS = 1 – MPC).

More sophisticated models also incorporate the positive relation between wealth and consumption. Generally speaking, individuals tend to spend a higher proportion of their income as wealth increases.

Generally speaking, aggregate consumption spending (C) in an economy will increase (decrease) when there is an increase (decrease) in real income or a decrease (increase) in taxes. The effects of these variables on aggregate output vary depending on the economy's MPC. Consider two countries: Country A has an MPC of 0.725 and Country B has an MPC of 0.542. Since Country A has a higher MPC, a governmental policy that increases disposable income (e.g., lower taxes) would have a more significant impact on Country A's economy relative to Country B's.

Sometimes the average propensity to consumer (APC = C/Y) is used as a proxy for MPC in an economy.

Bottom Line: Consumption varies positively with income and negatively with taxes.

Investment

GDP includes gross investment (which refers to total investment including replacement of worn-out equipment) as opposed to net investment (which only reflects additions of new capacity). The two most important determinants of investment spending (I) in an economy are:

- The level of interest rates represents the cost of obtaining funds for investment. The higher the cost of obtaining funds, the lower the level of investment in an economy.
- The current level of aggregate output/income serves as an indicator of expected profitability of new investments. The higher the level of aggregate output/income, the higher the return expected on new investments.

Investment expenditure is a decreasing function of the real interest rate and positively related to the level of aggregate output.

$$I = f(r, Y)$$

Another important driver of investment expenditure is the availability of newer and better technology.

Bottom Line: Investment expenditure varies positively with income and negatively with real interest rates.

Government Expenditure

The government's fiscal balance can be represented as:

$$G - T = \bar{G} - t(Y)$$

- Government expenditure $(\bar{G})$ is treated as an exogenous policy variable that is not affected by the interest rates, exchange rates, and other economic factors.
- Net taxes (T) increase as aggregate income increases and decrease as aggregate income declines.
    - Taxes collected (e.g., income and valued added taxes) increase as aggregate income increases and vice versa.
    - Transfer payments (which are typically based on economic need) are inversely related to aggregate income. Unemployment benefits paid out decrease as unemployment falls and aggregate income rises.

Automatic
stabilizers are
described in detail
in a later reading.

Since G does not vary with aggregate income and T is positively related to aggregate income, overall the fiscal balance is inversely related to aggregate income (Y). This effect is known as an automatic stabilizer as it reduces the fluctuations in aggregate output.

Bottom Line: Government expenditure does not vary with income. Taxes vary positively with income. Therefore, the government's fiscal balance varies negatively with income.

Net Exports

Two of the most important factors that affect net exports (X – M) are:

- Relative incomes in the domestic country and in the rest of the world:
    - An increase in domestic income increases demand for imported goods, reducing net exports.
    - An increase in income in the rest of the world increases foreign demand for domestic goods, increasing domestic exports.
- Relative prices of domestic and foreign goods and services
    - An increase in prices of domestic goods increases demand for imports (as foreign goods become more competitive), reducing net exports.
    - An increase in foreign prices increases foreign demand for domestic goods, increasing net exports.

Bottom Line: Net exports vary negatively with income and negatively with domestic price levels.

To identify the
source of this
equation refer to the
earlier discussion
where we said that:

GDP(income) =
C + S + T

GDP(expenditure) =
C + I + G + (X – M)

We mentioned earlier that the IS curve assumes that planned expenditure equals actual (or realized) income/output. The equality of income and expenditure is expressed through the following equations that we derived earlier:

C + S + T = C + I + G + (X – M)

$$S - I = (G - T) + (X - M) \quad \ldots \text{(Derived from Equation 7)}$$

The right-hand side of this equation represents government's fiscal balance $(G - T)$ and the trade balance $(X - M)$. An increase in aggregate income results in:

- Higher net taxes (lowering the fiscal balance); and
- Higher imports (lowering the trade balance).

Therefore, the right-hand side of the equation **declines** as income rises. This **negative relationship** between income and the fiscal and trade balances combined $(G - T) + (X - M)$ is represented by the **downward-sloping line** in Figure 3-1.

Figure 3-1: Balancing Aggregate Income and Expenditure

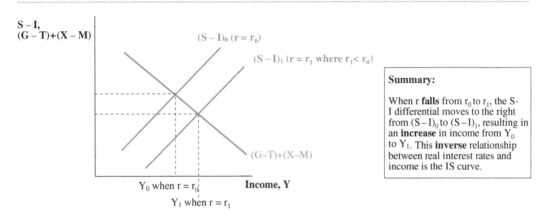

The summary box in the figure reads:

Summary:

When r **falls** from r_0 to r_1, the S-I differential moves to the right from $(S-I)_0$ to $(S-I)_1$, resulting in an **increase** in income from Y_0 to Y_1. This **inverse** relationship between real interest rates and income is the IS curve.

As for the left-hand side, the saving-investment differential $(S - I)$, **we assume that the direct effect of an increase in income on saving is greater than its impact on investment**. Therefore, this side of the equation **increases** as income increases. This **positive** relationship between income and the saving-investment differential $(S - I)$ is captured by the **upward-sloping line** in Figure 3-1.

Note that this line is drawn for a given level of real interest rate (r_0). **The explanatory variable when drawing up the $(S - I)$ line is income**. All other variables are assumed constant.

The point of intersection between these two lines defines the point where aggregate expenditure and aggregate income are equal.

- At higher levels of income (to the right of the point of intersection), the saving-investment differential is greater than fiscal and trade balances combined, which implies excess saving or insufficient expenditure.
- At lower levels of income (to the left of the point of intersection), the saving-investment differential is smaller than the fiscal and trade balances combined, which implies that expenditure exceeds income/output.

To derive this equation, we have simply subtracted I from both sides of Equation 7.

Think of it this way. The saving in the economy should be used either to fund the government's fiscal deficit $(G - T)$ or the rest of the world's trade deficit against the domestic economy $(X - M)$.

We mentioned earlier that the real interest rate is assumed constant when drawing up the S – I line.

Changes in the level of real interest rates (r) cause shifts in the line representing the saving-investment differential:

- If real interest rates were to fall, investment expenditure would rise. To maintain the saving-investment differential at the same level, there would need to be a similar increase in saving. This increase in saving would come about only if income were to rise. Therefore, with a lower real interest rate, in order to maintain the saving-investment differential at a particular level, income would need to be higher (so the S – I curve would shift to the right).

You should now be able to see that if the real interest rate falls (rises), the point of intersection between the two curves, "S – I" and "(G – T) + (X – M)," occurs at a higher (lower) level of income. Equilibrating income and expenditure implies an **inverse relationship between income and the real interest rate**. This relationship is referred to as the **IS curve** (see Figure 3-2) because investment and saving are the main components that adjust to maintain a balance between aggregate expenditure and income.

Figure 3-2: The IS Curve

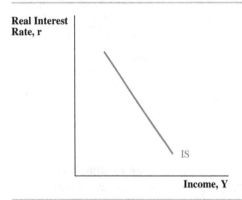

Example 3-1: The IS Curve

The following equations are given for a hypothetical economy:

Consumption function:	$C = 1,500 + 0.5(Y - T)$
Investment function:	$I = 300 + 0.1Y - 20r$
Government spending:	$G = 1,000$
Net export function:	$(X - M) = 1,200 - 0.2Y$
Tax function:	$T = -150 + 0.2Y$

1. Based on the above equations, find the equation that describes the IS curve.
2. Given a real interest rate of 5%, find:
   a. The level of GDP
   b. Tax receipts
   c. Consumption spending
   d. Investment spending
   e. Net exports

3. Find the new IS curve if the government increases its expenditure from 1,000 to 1,500.

4. Given a real interest rate of 5%, determine how the increased government spending is funded.

5. Given that the output level calculated in Question 2 is the most the economy can produce with the given resources and that the economy is operating at that level, what must happen to maintain the balance between expenditure and income if the government increases its expenditure from 1,000 to 1,500?

Solutions:

1. The IS curve illustrates the combinations of real interest rates (r) and income (Y) at which income and expenditure are equal (equilibrium in the goods market)

    Compute Y as the sum of the components of AD:

    $Y = C + I + G + (X - M)$
    $Y = 1,500 + 0.5(Y - T) + 300 + 0.1Y - 20r + 1,000 + 1,200 - 0.2Y$
    $Y = 4,000 + 0.5Y - 0.5T + 0.1Y - 20r - 0.2Y$
    $Y = 4,000 + 0.4Y - 0.5(-150 + 0.2Y) - 20r$ **Note : T = -150 + 0.2Y**
    $Y = 4,000 + 0.4Y + 75 - 0.1Y - 20r$
    $Y = 4,075 + 0.3Y - 20r$
    $Y = 5,821.43 - 28.57r$

2. If r = 5%, then:

    a. $Y = 5,821.43 - 28.57(5) = 5,678.58$
    b. $T = -150 + 0.2(5,678.58) = 985.72$
    c. $C = 1,500 + 0.5(5,678.58 - 985.72) = 3,846.43$
    d. $I = 300 + 0.1(5,678.58) - 20(5) = 767.86$
    e. $(X - M) = 1,200 - 0.2(5,678.58) = 64.28$

3. If the government increases its expenditure to 1,500, the new IS curve will be:

    $Y = 6,535.71 - 28.57r$ (performing the same steps as in Part 1, but with G = 1,500; not 1,000)

    When G rises by $500 (from $1,000 to $1,500), at any level of interest rates, income increases by $6,535.71 - 5,821.43 = 714.28$. This is $714.28/500 = 1.43$ times the increase in government spending. What this means is that the increase in government expenditure has a "multiplier effect" in the economy. As income rises (due to the increase in G), consumption and investment expenditure also rise, which leads to even further increases in income and more spending. Some of the higher income is saved. Some of the spending goes to imports and taxes.

    We know that $G = (S - I) + T + (M - X)$ … (Equation 7 rearranged)

    Therefore, an increase in government spending must be offset by:

    *   An increase in saving relative to investment.
    *   An increase in taxes.
    *   An increase in imports relative to exports.

Given the interest rate, an increase in each of the above aggregates must be induced by the increase in aggregate income.

$$S = Y - C - T$$
$$\Delta S = \Delta Y - \Delta C - \Delta T = \Delta Y - [0.5(\Delta Y - \Delta T)] - \Delta T$$
$$\Delta S = \Delta Y(1 - 0.5) + \Delta T(0.5 - 1) = 0.5\Delta Y - 0.5\Delta T \quad \textbf{Note: } \Delta C = \mathbf{0.5(\Delta Y - \Delta T)}$$
$$\Delta S = 0.5\Delta Y - 0.5(0.2\Delta Y) \quad \textbf{Note: } \Delta T = \mathbf{0.2\Delta Y}$$
$$\Delta S = 0.4\Delta Y$$

$$G = (S - I) + T + (M - X)$$
$$\Delta G = 0.4\Delta Y - 0.1\Delta Y + 0.2\Delta Y + 0.2\Delta Y \quad \textbf{Note: } \Delta(M - X) = -\Delta(X - M) = \mathbf{0.2\Delta Y}$$
$$\Delta G = 0.7\Delta Y$$
$$\Delta Y = 1.43\Delta G$$

Note that an additional unit of income increases saving by 0.4 but only increases investment by 0.1. The S − I differential is quite sensitive to changes in income. This implies that a relatively small change in income is required to restore income/expenditure balance when there is a change in spending.

4. Change in fiscal balance $= \Delta G - \Delta T = \Delta G - 0.2\Delta Y$
$$= \Delta G - 0.2(1.43\Delta G) = 0.714(\Delta G)$$
$$= 0.714(500) = 357 \quad \textbf{Note: } \Delta G = \mathbf{\$500}$$

The fiscal balance changed by $357. Given that the government increased its spending by $500, taxes collected rose by 500 − 357 = 143.

Change in trade balance $= \Delta(X - M) = -0.2\Delta Y$
$$= -0.2(1.43\Delta G)$$
$$= -0.286(500) = 143$$

Change in S − I differential $= \Delta(S - I) = 0.4\Delta Y - 0.1\Delta Y = 0.3\Delta Y$
$$= 0.3(1.43\Delta G) = 214$$

The increase in government spending is financed by an increase in taxes worth 143, an increase in borrowing from the rest of the world (to finance the trade deficit) worth 143, and an increase in private-sector saving of 214.

5. If the economy is operating at its potential output, the increase in government expenditure should be offset by a decrease in private expenditure to keep the amount of expenditure equal to output/income. In other words, the real interest rate must rise to a level such that the decrease in investment expenditure equals the increase in government expenditure (500). Equating the new IS curve (from Question 3: $Y = 6{,}535.71 - 28.57r$) to the original level of income (from Question 2: $Y = 5{,}678.58$) we solve for r:

$$6{,}535.71 - 28.57r = 5{,}678.58$$

$$r = 30\%$$

Therefore, real interest rates should rise to 30% to crowd out enough investment spending such that aggregate income remains the same despite the increase in government expenditure.

The LM Curve

The LM curve shows the combinations of interest rates and real income for which the money market is in equilibrium.

The quantity theory of money describes the relationship between nominal money supply (M), the price level (P), and real income/expenditure (Y). Velocity of circulation is the number of times a unit of currency changes hands annually to purchase goods and services. If a $20 bill is used by 10 people over the year, it would have been used to buy goods and services worth $M \times V = \$200$.

Quantity theory of money: $MV = PY$

To simplify things, velocity is assumed constant. The quantity theory of money then implies that money supply determines the value of nominal output (PY). An increase in money supply would increase nominal GDP, but note that we cannot still segregate the impact of the increase on real output (Y) and price levels (P). The quantity theory equation can also be written as:

Note that k also equals M_D/PY so we can think of k as the amount of money people want to hold for every currency unit of real income. M_D/P is referred to as real money demand.

> M/P and $M_D/P = kY$
>
> where:
> $k = I/V$
> M = Nominal money supply
> M_D = Nominal money demand
> M_D/P is referred to as real money demand and M/P is real money supply.

Demand for real money (RM_D or M_D/P) is a positive function of real income and a negative function of interest rates.

- The quantity theory equation above suggests that real money demand increases with real income (Y).
- Households choose to hold less money in favor of investing it in higher-yielding securities when interest rates rise. Therefore, demand for real money varies inversely with interest rates (r).

Equilibrium in the money market requires that money supply and money demand be equal.

Money market equilibrium: $M/P = RM_D$

RM_D is a function of r and Y. Given the real money supply (RM or M/P), an increase in real income (which would lead to an increase in real money demand) must be accompanied by an increase in interest rates (which would decrease real money demand) so that demand for real money remains the same and equilibrium in the money market is maintained. **Therefore, if real money supply is held constant, we can infer a positive relationship between real income (Y) and the real interest rate (r).**

This **positive** relationship between real income and the real interest rate is illustrated by the LM curve and is shown by the upward-sloping line in Figure 3-3.

Figure 3-3: The LM Curve

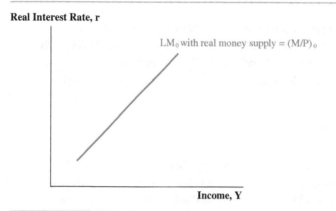

Real Interest Rate, r

LM_0 with real money supply = $(M/P)_0$

Income, Y

Changes in real money supply cause shifts in the LM curve. When real money supply is increased, real money demand would also have to increase in order to maintain equilibrium in the money market. For a higher real money demand, given the real interest rate, real income would have to be higher. **Therefore, if real money supply increases (decreases), the LM curve would shift to the right (left).**

The point where the IS and LM curves intersect defines the combination of real interest rates and real income where:

- Planned expenditures equal actual (or realized) income/output.
- There is equilibrium in the money market, that is, the available real money supply is equal to the demand for real money.

The Aggregate Demand Curve

VERY IMPORTANT: Also note that this analysis suggests a positive relationship between the price level and real interest rates.

If money supply (M) is held constant, then the only variable that affects real money supply (RM) is the price level (P). In Figure 3-4, a decrease in the price level (from P_0 to P_1) leads to an increase in real money supply (from RM_0 to RM_1). The increase in real money supply leads to a rightward shift in the LM curve (to LM_1) so the point of intersection of the IS and LM curves now occurs at a higher income (Y_1 versus Y_0) and lower real interest rate (r_1 versus r_0). The inverse relationship between the price level (P) and real income (Y) is captured by the aggregate demand curve (see Figure 3-5).

Figure 3-4: IS and LM Curves—Deriving the Aggregate Demand Curve

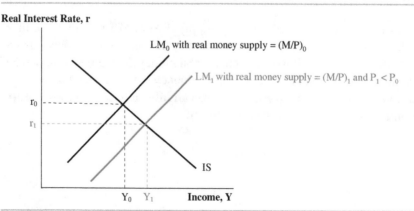

Real Interest Rate, r

LM_0 with real money supply = $(M/P)_0$

LM_1 with real money supply = $(M/P)_1$ and $P_1 < P_0$

r_0

r_1

IS

Y_0 Y_1 **Income, Y**

Figure 3-5: The Aggregate Demand Curve

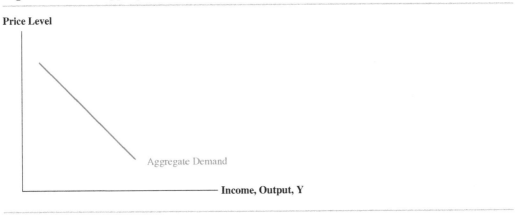

Other factors that explain the negative slope of the aggregate demand curve are:

- Higher prices reduce the purchasing power of those whose incomes are fixed in nominal terms.
- Higher prices reduce the real value of assets and decrease real wealth.
- Higher prices reduce the value of nominal assets like stocks and bonds.
- Higher prices make foreign goods more competitive and domestic goods less competitive so imports rise and exports fall.

Now let's look more closely at the slope of the AD curve. For simplicity, we assume that the fiscal and trade balances are fixed. **Therefore, in order to ensure that aggregate expenditure equals aggregate income, any change in investment must be matched by a similar change in private saving.**

- As the price level increases, real money supply (M/P) falls.
- To bring about an equivalent reduction in real money demand (to keep the money market in equilibrium), the real interest rate must rise (so that other assets are more attractive as investments) and income must fall (to reduce the need for money balances).
- The higher interest rate results in a decrease in investment spending, while a lower income results in a decrease in household saving.
- Therefore, the steepness of the slope of the AD curve depends on the relative sensitivities of investment, saving, and money demand to income and real interest rates.

The AD curve will be flatter (small changes in price cause relatively large changes in quantity demanded) if:

- Investment expenditure is highly sensitive to the interest rate: When prices rise, the real interest rate also rises. If investment is highly sensitive to changes in interest rates, the increase in interest rates would bring about a significant decrease in investment spending and a significant decrease in quantity demanded.
- Saving is insensitive to income: When prices rise, the real interest rate also rises, which reduces investment expenditure. Since the saving-investment differential must remain constant, the decrease in investment must be matched by an equivalent decrease in saving. In order to bring about the fall in saving, the decrease in income (Y) required would be greater the more insensitive saving is to income.

> The S – I differential is constant as we have assumed (and mentioned earlier) that the fiscal balance and trade balance do not change.

- Money demand is insensitive to interest rates: **When prices rise, real money supply falls. In order to maintain equilibrium in the money market, real money demand must also fall. If money demand is insensitive to interest rates, the increase in interest rates required to decrease money demand will be higher. This higher interest rate would decrease investment and reduce aggregate demand significantly.**
- Money demand is insensitive to income: **When prices rise, real money supply falls. In order to maintain equilibrium in the money market, real money demand must also fall. If money demand is insensitive to changes in income, the decrease in income required to reduce real money demand will be higher.**

We will learn about Monetary Policy in detail later in the reading.

Example 3-2: Aggregate Demand

The following equations are given for a hypothetical economy:

$M_D/P = -250 + 0.4Y - 35r$ Real money demand
$M/P = 1,800 / P$ Real money supply

1. Find the equation for the LM curve.
2. Using the IS curve from Question 1 of Example 3-1, find the equation of the AD curve.
3. Find the levels of GDP and the interest rate if $P = 1$.
4. What will happen to GDP and the interest rate if the price level rises to 1.1 or falls to 0.9?
5. Suppose investment spending were more sensitive to the interest rate so that the IS becomes ($Y = 5,821.43 - 60r$). What happens to the slope of the AD curve? What does this imply about the effectiveness of monetary policy?

Solutions:

1. Set real money demand equal to real money supply (equilibrium in the money market) to derive the equation for the LM curve:

   $-250 + 0.4Y - 35r = 1,800/P$
   $Y = 4,500/P + 625 + 87.5r$

2. IS equation: $Y = 5,821.43 - 28.57r$

   Therefore:
   $r = (5,821.43 - Y)/28.57$

   LM equation: $Y = 4,500/P + 625 + 87.5r$

   Replacing "r" with $(5,821.43 - Y)/28.57$:
   $Y = 4,500/P + 625 + 87.5 [(5,821.43 - Y)/28.57]$

   Solving for Y gives us:
   $Y = 1,107.69/P + 4,542.31$

3. $Y = 1,107.69/1 + 4,542.31$

   $Y = 5,650$
   $r = (5,821.43 - 5,650)/28.57 = 6\%$

4. If the price level rises to 1.1:

   $Y = 1,107.69/1.1 + 4,542.31 = 5,549.30$
   $r = (5,821.43 - 5,549.30)/28.57 = 9.53\%$

   If the price level falls to 0.9:

   $Y = 1,107.69/0.9 + 4,542.31 = 5,773.08$
   $r = (5,821.43 - 5,773.08)/28.57 = 1.69\%$

   The table below summarizes the relationship between the price level, GDP, and the interest rate:

Price Level	GDP	Interest Rate
0.9	5,773.08	1.69%
1.0	5,650.00	6.00%
1.1	5,549.30	9.53%

   VERY IMPORTANT
   - The inverse relationship between the price level and GDP is the AD curve.
   - The inverse relationship between GDP and the interest rate is the IS curve.

5. If the IS equation becomes $Y = 5,821.43 - 60r$, the equation for the AD curve will be:

   $Y = 1,829.27/P + 3,705.12$

   Comparing the new AD curve to the old one, notice that Y is now more sensitive to the price level (i.e., the AD curve is flatter). This makes monetary policy more effective. For example, if real money supply increases, the interest rate must fall and/or aggregate expenditure must increase to stimulate money demand. Since investment spending is now more sensitive to the interest rate (coefficient of r in the IS curve is –60 versus –28.57 previously) income will have to rise by more (than previously) to generate sufficient saving and maintain the S – I differential.

LESSON 4: AGGREGATE DEMAND, AGGREGATE SUPPLY, AND
EQUILIBRIUM: PART 3 (MACROECONOMIC CHANGES AND EQUILIBRIUM)

LOS 16g: Explain the aggregate supply curve in the short run and long run. Vol 2, pp 148–150

Aggregate supply (AS) represents the quantities of goods and services that domestic producers are willing and able to supply at various price levels.

The very short run is defined as the time period over which companies can only change output levels to a limited extent without changing price. The very short-run aggregate supply (VSRAS) curve is therefore represented by a horizontal line in Figure 4-1.

- If demand increases, companies will increase output (to earn higher profits) and run their operations more intensively as long as they are able to cover their variable costs.
- If demand falls, companies will decrease output and run their operations less intensively. They may also carry out efficiency-enhancing projects that were postponed during busier periods.

The short run is defined as the time period over which some more costs become variable. However, wages and prices of other inputs remain constant in the short run. Therefore, as prices increase (with no corresponding increase in input prices) companies can increase profits by raising output. This positive relationship between price and quantity supplied is represented by the upward-sloping short-run aggregate supply (SRAS) curve in Figure 4-1.

The long run is defined as the time period over which wages and prices of other inputs are also variable. As prices increase over the long run, wages and other input prices also increase proportionately, so the higher price level has no effect on quantity supplied. This is shown by the vertical long-run aggregate supply (LRAS) curve in Figure 4-1. Note that in the long run, wages, prices, and expectations can adjust, but capital and technology remain fixed. This condition is relaxed in the very long run, which we consider later in the reading.

Figure 4-1: Aggregate Supply Curve

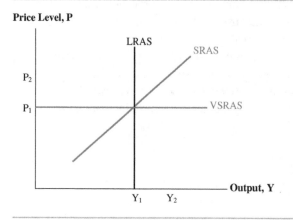

The LRAS curve basically defines the potential output of the economy (i.e., the amount that can be produced given the available quantities of capital and labor, and the current state of technology [existing technological base]). The potential output of any economy does not vary with the price level. The economy's ability to produce goods and services is limited to the output level where all its resources are fully employed.

When an economy operates at its potential output level, all its resources are fully employed and it is said to be working at full employment. At this output level, unemployment is at its natural rate.

The natural rate of unemployment includes frictional and structural unemployment.

- Structural unemployment results from structural changes in the economy, which make some skills obsolete and leave previously employed people jobless.
- Cyclical unemployment is the unemployment generated as an economy goes through the phases of a business cycle.

LOS 16h: Explain causes of movements along and shifts in aggregate demand and supply curves. Vol 2, pp 150–162

- The point of intersection of the AD curve and the LRAS curve defines the economy's long-run equilibrium position. At this point, actual real GDP equals potential GDP.
- The point of intersection of the AD curve and the SRAS curve defines the economy's short-run equilibrium position. Short-run fluctuations in equilibrium real GDP may occur due to shifts in either or both the AD and SRAS curves. Short-run equilibrium may be established at, below, or above potential output. Deviations of short-run equilibrium from potential output result in business cycles.
    - In an expansion, real GDP is increasing, the unemployment rate is falling, and capacity utilization is rising. Further, inflation tends to rise during an expansion.
    - In a contraction, real GDP is decreasing, the unemployment rate is rising, and capacity utilization is falling. Further, inflation tends to fall during a contraction.

Business cycles are covered in more detail in the next reading.

Shifts in Aggregate Demand

Changes in the price level result in movements along the AD curve. Shifts in the AD curve may be caused by changes in:

- Household wealth: An increase in household wealth will encourage households to spend a higher proportion of their disposable income in the current period, which results in an increase in aggregate demand (wealth effect).
- Consumer and business confidence: When consumers feel confident about their future incomes and job safety, they tend to spend a higher proportion of their disposable income (consumption increases). Similarly, when businesses feel confident about future profits, they tend to spend more on capital projects (investment increases).
- Capacity utilization: When companies have excess capacity, they are able to expand output by increasing capacity utilization of their current plants. If companies are operating close to full capacity they **will** need to increase investment expenditure to expand further, which would increase aggregate demand.
- Fiscal policy: Fiscal policy refers to the use of government expenditure and tax policies to affect the level of aggregate expenditures in an economy. An increase in

Note that in practice several factors may work simultaneously. For example, consumer and business confidence are likely to be influenced by other factors.

Monetary and fiscal policies are discussed in detail in Reading 18.

government expenditure (G) leads to a direct increase in aggregate demand. Lower taxes increase disposable income, resulting in an increase in consumption (C).

- **Monetary policy:** Monetary policy refers to the actions taken by a country's monetary authority (usually the central bank) to affect aggregate output and prices. An increase in money supply (a decrease in interest rates) results in an increase in consumption and investment.

- **Exchange rate:** An appreciating domestic currency will make domestic goods more expensive for the rest of the world, hurting exports. At the same time (since domestic currency appreciation implies foreign currency depreciation), it will make foreign goods more competitive in the domestic market, helping imports. Therefore, an appreciating domestic currency will reduce aggregate demand.

- **Growth in the global economy:** Faster economic growth in foreign countries encourages consumers in those countries to increase their expenditure on domestic goods, increasing domestic exports. Rapid domestic economic growth increases domestic demand for imports, reducing aggregate demand.

See Table 4-1.

Table 4-1: Impact of Factors Shifting Aggregate Demand[3]

An Increase in the Following Factors	Shifts the AD Curve	Reason
Stock prices	Rightward: Increase in AD	Higher consumption
Housing prices	Rightward: Increase in AD	Higher consumption
Consumer confidence	Rightward: Increase in AD	Higher consumption
Business confidence	Rightward: Increase in AD	Higher investment
Capacity utilization	Rightward: Increase in AD	Higher investment
Government spending	Rightward: Increase in AD	Government spending a component of AD
Taxes	Leftward: Decrease in AD	Lower consumption and investment
Bank reserves	Rightward: Increase in AD	Lower interest rate, higher investment, and possibly higher consumption
Exchange rate (foreign currency per unit domestic currency)	Leftward: Decrease in AD	Lower exports and higher imports
Global growth	Rightward: Increase in AD	Higher exports

Interest Rates and Aggregate Demand

- If the increase in aggregate demand is caused by an increase in money supply, interest rates fall. The increase in income results in an increase in saving, so rates must fall to stimulate a corresponding increase in investment (and keep the saving-interest differential constant).

- If the increase in aggregate demand is caused by any other factor mentioned above, (with real money supply, M, constant) interest rates will rise (to offset the effect of higher income on money demand and keep money demand at the same level). The increase in income (PY) implies that there must be a corresponding increase in the velocity of circulation (V).

---

3 - Exhibit 18, Volume 2, CFA Program Curriculum 2018

Shifts in Short-Run Aggregate Supply

Changes in the price level result in movements along the SRAS curve. Shifts in the SRAS curve may be caused by changes in:

- **Nominal (money) wages:** Recall that in the short run, wages and other input prices were assumed constant. Therefore, an increase in nominal wages increases costs of production and results in a fall in SRAS. The impact of labor costs on SRAS can be measured by calculating the change in unit labor cost.

  % Change in unit labor cost = % Change in nominal wages − % Change in productivity

  For example, assume that workers in a factory are paid $10/hour to produce 100 units/hour (unit labor cost = $10/$100 = $0.10/unit).
  - If wages increase by 10%, and workers' productivity also increases by 10%, unit labor cost will remain at $11/110 = $0.10, so there will be no shift in SRAS.
  - If wages increase by 10%, and workers' productivity increases by 5%, unit labor cost will rise to $11/105 = $0.105, so SRAS will shift to the left (fall).
  - If wages increase by 10%, and workers' productivity increases by 15%, unit labor cost will fall to $11/115 = $0.087, so SRAS will shift to the right (increase).
- **Input prices:** Higher (lower) prices of raw materials increase (decrease) costs of production resulting in a decrease (an increase) in SRAS.
- **Expectations about future prices:** If a company expects the price of its output to increase (decrease) relative to the general price level in the economy, it will increase (decrease) supply in anticipation of higher profit margins in the future, increasing SRAS. Further, if companies expect the general price level (and resource costs) to be higher in the future, they may decide to increase current output to build up inventories. However, such a move would also depend on the cost of carrying inventory (e.g., financing, storage, spoilage, etc.). Therefore, higher expected future prices may shift the SRAS curve to the right, but the shift may not be significant and probably will be temporary.
- **Business taxes and subsidies:** Higher business taxes increase production costs and result in a decrease in SRAS. Higher subsidies decrease production costs resulting in an increase in SRAS.
- **The exchange rate:** An appreciating domestic currency will make imports of raw materials cheaper for domestic producers and increase SRAS.
- The SRAS curve will also shift if the LRAS curve shifts.

Shifts in Long-Run Aggregate Supply

Long-run aggregate supply equals the economy's potential output. Therefore, a change in any factor that has an impact on the resource base of an economy will cause a shift in LRAS (and SRAS), including:

- **Supply of labor (and quality of labor or human capital):** As the supply of labor increases, an economy is able to produce more output.
- **Supply of natural resources:** An increase in the availability of natural resources results in an increase in the economy's potential output.

- Supply of physical capital: An increase in the supply or quality of physical capital increases labor productivity and increases potential output.
- Labor productivity and technology: An increase in labor productivity (by training workers to improve quality, increasing the capital-labor ratio, or providing more advanced technology) increases potential output.

See Table 4-2.

Memorize

Table 4-2: Impact of Factors Shifting Aggregate Supply[4]

An Increase in	Shifts SRAS	Shifts LRAS	Reason
Supply of labor	Rightward	Rightward	Increases resource base
Supply of natural resources	Rightward	Rightward	Increases resource base
Supply of human capital	Rightward	Rightward	Increases resource base
Supply of physical capital	Rightward	Rightward	Increases resource base
Productivity and technology	Rightward	Rightward	Improves efficiency of inputs
Nominal wages	Leftward	No impact	Increases labor cost
Input prices (e.g., energy)	Leftward	No impact	Increases cost of production
Expectation of future prices	Rightward	No impact	Anticipation of higher costs and/or perception of improved pricing power
Business taxes	Leftward	No impact	Increases cost of production
Subsidy	Rightward	No impact	Lowers cost of production
Exchange rate	Rightward	No impact	Lowers cost of production

LOS 16i: Describe how fluctuations in aggregate demand and aggregate supply cause short-run changes in the economy and the business cycle. Vol 2, pp 162–173

LOS 16j: Distinguish between the following types of macroeconomic equilibria: long-run full employment, short-run recessionary gap, short-run inflationary gap, and short-run stagflation. Vol 2, pp 162–173

LOS 16k: Explain how a short-run macroeconomic equilibrium may occur at a level above or below full employment. Vol 2, pp 162–173

LOS 16l: Analyze the effect of combined changes in aggregate supply and demand on the economy. Vol 2, pp 162–173

Short-Run Equilibrium

Short-run macroeconomic equilibrium is established at the point where aggregate demand equals short-run aggregate supply. Figure 4-2 illustrates short-run macroeconomic equilibrium with a price level of P_0 and real GDP level of Y_0.

4 - Exhibit 20, Volume 2, CFA Program Curriculum 2018

Figure 4-2: Short-Run Equilibrium

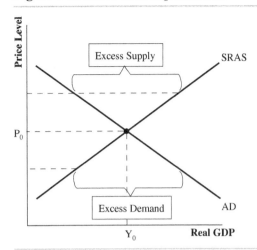

- At price levels above P_0, quantity supplied exceeds quantity demanded. As a result of excess supply, inventories pile up on store shelves forcing producers to sell their stock at lower prices. This continues until equilibrium is restored at a price level of P_0.
- At price levels below P_0, there is a shortage in the economy, which forces prices to rise until equilibrium is restored at a price level of P_0.

It is important to remember that we construct the short-run aggregate supply curve with the assumption that money wages are constant. In the short run there is no adjustment of money wages to achieve full employment. Therefore an economy can operate at a level below, above, or at full employment in the short run.

Long-Run Full Employment Equilibrium

Long-run full employment equilibrium (see Figure 4-3) is achieved when the intersection of the aggregate demand curve and the short-run aggregate supply curve occurs at a point on the long-run aggregate supply curve. At this point, actual real GDP equals potential GDP or full employment GDP. Note that unemployment equals the natural rate (does not equal 0).

Figure 4-3: Long-Run Equilibrium

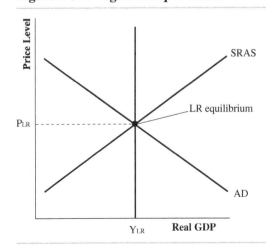

In reality however, real GDP rarely equals potential GDP. The AD and SRAS curves keep shifting, thereby causing fluctuations in short-run equilibrium real GDP. Therefore observations of real GDP cannot be used to estimate potential GDP with precision. Further, estimates of potential GDP based on production capacity estimates of all the economy's available resources tend to be inaccurate. However, economists are more confident in estimating the long-run growth rate in potential GDP. Therefore, studies of business cycles tend to focus on the growth rate of actual GDP relative to estimates of the long-run growth rate of potential GDP. Measures such as unemployment are also used to determine the extent of the economy's deviation from its potential output.

Business Cycles

Fluctuations in aggregate demand and aggregate supply in the short run explain why short-run real GDP deviates from potential GDP. These deviations of actual GDP from full-employment GDP form phases of the business cycle.

Figure 4-4a illustrates a situation where short-run equilibrium occurs short of full employment output. When actual real GDP (Y_A) is lower than potential GDP (Y_P), the output gap is known as a deflationary gap, recessionary gap, or an Okun gap. When short-run equilibrium occurs at an output level above potential output (Figure 4-4b) the output gap is known as an inflationary gap or expansionary gap.

Figure 4-4: Deflationary and Inflationary Gaps

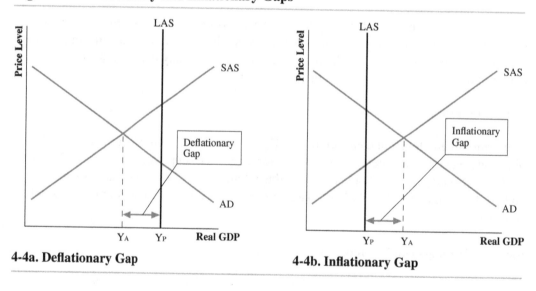

4-4a. Deflationary Gap   **4-4b. Inflationary Gap**

Note that there are several factors other than an increase in government expenditure (e.g., loosening of monetary policy, lower taxes, improvement in consumer and business confidence) that can increase AD and result in an inflationary gap.

Figure 4-5 illustrates an economy in LR equilibrium as $SRAS_0$ and AD_0 intersect at a point on the LRAS. Assume that the government increases its expenditure (G), which shifts demand to AD_1. Consequently, the price level rises to P_1 and there is an inflationary gap as real GDP expands to Y_1. Notice that the economy is only in short-run equilibrium, (aggregate demand equals short-run aggregate supply) but not in long-run equilibrium (as the point of intersection of AD and SRAS does not fall on the LRAS curve). Further, unemployment is *below* the natural rate (as the economy is operating above its potential).

Figure 4-5: LR Adjustment to an Inflationary Gap

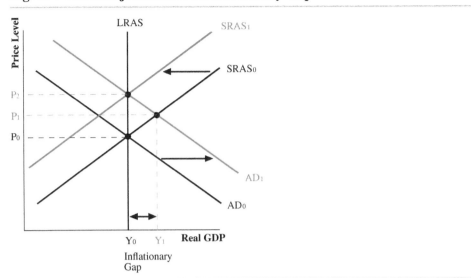

The increase in price level *reduces* real wages so workers demand an *increase* in their money wages. Producers, who are already operating above capacity, accede to the demand for higher wages because they are eager to retain workers (as the resources of the economy are already stretched) and maintain output levels given the high product prices. The increase in money wages and costs of production *reduces* SRAS to SRAS$_1$. Eventually, long-run equilibrium is restored, but at a higher price level, P$_2$.

The self-adjusting mechanism (described in the paragraph above) is how some economists would see the economy returning to its potential output (without the need for government action). The key to this adjustment process is that producers would be willing to increase nominal wages to retain workers. In practice however, this adjustment can take several years. Therefore, some economists advocate the use of monetary (by decreasing money supply and increasing interest rates to reduce AD) or fiscal (by decreasing government expenditure or raising taxes to reduce AD) measures to bring equilibrium back to the full employment level. The problem is that these policies have an impact on economic activity after significant lags.

Investment Applications of an Increase in AD Resulting in an Inflationary Gap

If economic data suggest that the economy is undergoing an expansion caused by an increase in AD, going forward:

- Corporate profits will be expected to rise.
- Commodity prices will be expected to increase.
- Interest rates will be expected to rise.
- Inflationary pressures will build in the economy.

Therefore, investors should:

- Increase investments in cyclical companies as their earnings would rise significantly in this scenario.
- Increase investments in commodities and/or commodity-oriented companies.
- Reduce investments in defensive companies, as their profits would not rise as significantly as those of cyclical companies.

Cyclical companies are companies with sales and profits that regularly expand and contract with the business cycle or state of economy (for example, automobile and chemical companies).

Defensive companies are companies with sales and profits that have little sensitivity to the business cycle or state of the economy (for example, food and pharmaceutical companies).

- Reduce investments in fixed-income securities (especially those with longer maturities), as their values would fall when interest rates go up.
- Increase investments in junk bonds, as default risk (already factored into their prices) should fall in an expansion (and result in an increase in their prices).

In Figure 4-6, a reduction in government expenditure causes the AD curve to shift to the left to AD_1, which *reduces* prices to P_1 and results in a deflationary gap. The economy is in short-run equilibrium but not in long-run equilibrium as it operates *below* its potential GDP. The lower price level equates to an increase in real wages. Producers, who are working below capacity and suffering from low prices, will try to reduce money wages. Workers (theoretically) will have to accept lower wages because there are ample (unemployed) resources in the economy. Lower wages reduce costs of production and shift the SRAS curve to the right to $SRAS_1$ bringing the economy to a new long-run equilibrium at a lower price level, P_2.

Figure 4-6: LR Adjustment to a Deflationary Gap

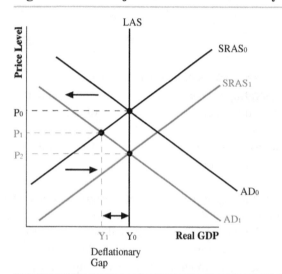

The key to this self-correcting mechanism is that workers would be willing to accept a decrease in their nominal wages. In practice, this adjustment can take several years. The government could employ expansionary monetary (by increasing money supply and decreasing interest rates to stimulate AD) or fiscal (by increasing government expenditure or reducing taxes to increase AD) measures to bring equilibrium back to the full employment level.

Investment Applications of a Decrease in AD Resulting in a Deflationary Gap

If economic data suggest that the economy is undergoing a recession caused by a decrease in AD, going forward:

- Corporate profits will be expected to fall.
- Commodity prices will be expected to decline.
- Interest rates will be expected to fall.
- Demand for credit will decrease.

Therefore, investors should:

- Reduce investments in cyclical companies.
- Reduce investments in commodities and/or commodity-oriented companies.
- Increase investments in defensive companies, as their profits would decline modestly compared to cyclical companies.

- Increase investments in investment-grade or government-issued fixed-income securities, as their values (particularly of those with longer maturities) will rise if interest rates go down.
- Decrease investments in junk bonds, as default risk should rise in a recession (and result in a decrease in their prices).

Stagflation

Shifts in the SRAS curve (due to any of the factors discussed earlier in the reading) cause structural fluctuations in real GDP. A decrease in SRAS causes stagflation (high unemployment and higher inflation), while an increase in SRAS brings about economic growth and low inflation.

Figure 4-7 illustrates the case of a decline in SRAS. A shift in the SRAS curve from $SRAS_0$ to $SRAS_1$ leads to a decline in output from Y_0 to Y_1, while the price level increases from P_0 to P_1. Over time, wages and input prices may be expected to fall, which would shift the SRAS curve outward and restore equilibrium at full employment output (Y_0). However, this self-adjustment process is typically extremely slow so the government may step in and stimulate the economy using expansionary fiscal and/or monetary measures. This will increase aggregate demand and shift the AD curve to the right (to AD_1), to bring the economy back to its potential output. However, notice that this would come at the cost of a further increase in the price level (from P_1 to P_2).

> The global economy experienced stagflation in the 1970s as unemployment and inflation soared due to an increase in oil prices. In the United States, the recession was exacerbated by the Fed's decision to increase interest rates (a contractionary monetary measure) to combat the higher inflation.

Figure 4-7: Stagflation

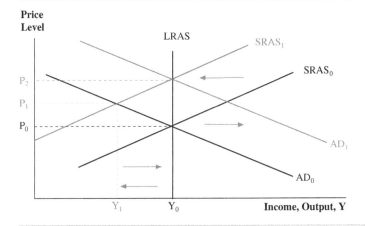

Investment Applications of a Shift in SRAS

If the SRAS curve shifts to the left (SRAS declines), investors may want to:

- Reduce investments in fixed-income securities because increasing output prices (inflation) may put upward pressure on nominal interest rates (which would decrease the value of fixed-income instruments).
- Reduce exposure to equities in anticipation of a decline in output and profit margins coming under pressure.
- Increase investments in commodities and/or commodity-oriented companies because their prices and profits are likely to rise (due to higher prices).

Tables 4-3 and 4-4 summarize the effects of shifts in the AD and AS curves.

Table 4-3: Conclusions on AD and AS

	Real GDP	Unemployment Rate	Aggregate Level of Prices
An increase in AD	Increases	Falls	Increases
A decrease in AD	Falls	Increases	Falls
An increase in AS	Increases	Falls	Falls
A decrease in AS	Falls	Increases	Increases

Table 4-4: Effect of Combined Changes in AS and AD[5]

Change in AS	Change in AD	Effect on Real GDP	Effect on Aggregate Price Level
Increase	Increase	Increase	Uncertain
Decrease	Decrease	Decrease	Uncertain
Increase	Decrease	Uncertain	Decrease
Decrease	Increase	Uncertain	Increase

LESSON 5: ECONOMIC GROWTH AND STABILITY

LOS 16m: Describe sources, measurement, and sustainability of economic growth. Vol 2, pp 173–184

LOS 16n: Describe the production function approach to analyzing the sources of economic growth. Vol 2, pp 173–184

LOS 16o: Distinguish between input growth and growth of total factor productivity as components of economic growth. Vol 2, pp 173–184

Economic growth may be calculated as:

- The annual percentage change in real GDP, which tells us how rapidly the economy is expanding as a whole; or
- The annual change in real per capita GDP: Real GDP per capita is calculated as total real GDP divided by total population. It is a useful indicator of the standard of living in a country.

A small increase in the growth rate of per capita GDP can have a large impact on an economy's standard of living if sustained over time. Rapid growth is not always sustainable and is typically associated with higher inflation, environmental damage, and high savings (low consumption). Therefore, instead of just aiming for a high economic growth rate, countries aim to make economic growth sustainable. Sustainable economic growth comes from an economy constantly adding to its productive capacity and enhancing its potential GDP.

---

5 - Exhibit 26, Volume 2, CFA Program Curriculum 2018

The Production Function and Potential GDP

The Solow (neoclassical) growth model provides a framework for identifying the underlying sources of growth in an economy. The model is based on the production function. We'll work with the following two-factor production function to identify the different sources of economic growth:

$$Y = AF(L, K)$$

Where:
Y = Aggregate output
L = Quantity of labor
K = Quantity of capital
A = Technological knowledge or total factor productivity (TFP)

Total Factor Productivity

Total factor productivity (TFP) is a scale factor that accounts for the portion of economic growth that is not explained by capital and labor quantities. The main influence on TFP is technological change.

The production function asserts that an increase in an economy's potential GDP can be caused by:

- An increase in the quantity of inputs used in the production process (e.g., capital and labor).
- An increase in the productivity of these inputs with the application of better technology. Improving technology enables an economy to produce more output using the same quantity of inputs.

In defining an economy's production function, we assume the following:

- There are constant returns to scale. If the quantities of labor and capital are doubled (holding the state of technology constant) output would also double.
- Production inputs exhibit diminishing marginal productivity.

Malthus

> Marginal product equals the extra output produced by the additional input unit holding quantities of all other inputs constant.

Traditional economists (notably Thomas Malthus) focused on labor as the only variable factor of production. Given that labor suffers from diminishing marginal returns, Malthus predicted that eventually, as the population grows and more and more units of labor work with the given quantities of fixed factors, the marginal product of labor would decline to zero. This implies that there would be zero long-term economic growth. Fortunately, this dire prediction never came true.

Subsequently, economists shifted their focus to capital. Given diminishing marginal returns to capital, if capital were to grow at a faster rate than labor, the productivity of capital would decline, resulting in slower growth. This has the following implications:

- For long-term sustainable economic growth, countries cannot rely solely on increasing the quantity of capital relative to labor.
- Given that the marginal productivity of capital is higher in developing countries (relative to developed countries) due to the lower quantities of capital used in those countries, growth in developing nations should outpace growth in developed nations. Therefore, eventually there should be a convergence in incomes across developed and developing countries.

Because of diminishing marginal returns to labor and capital, the only way to "sustain" growth in potential GDP is growth in TFP (A). Improvements in technology result in an outward shift in the production function (i.e., enable an economy to produce a larger quantity of output given the same quantities of labor and capital).

The growth accounting equation shows that the rate of growth of potential GDP equals the growth in technology plus the weighted average growth rate of capital and labor based on their relative shares in national income.

$$\text{Growth in potential GDP} = \text{Growth in technology} + W_L (\text{Growth in labor}) + W_K (\text{Growth in capital})$$

- The weight of capital equals the sum of corporate profits, net interest income, net rental income, and depreciation, divided by total GDP.
- The weight of labor equals employee compensation divided by total GDP.

This equation highlights the fact that the contribution of labor and capital to GDP growth depends on their relative shares in national income. In the United States, since the share of labor is higher (70% versus 30% for capital) an increase in the quantity of labor will have a more significant (more than twice the magnitude) impact on GDP compared to an equivalent increase in the quantity of capital.

Since standard of living is measured on a per capita basis, we can gain a deeper insight into the contribution of various sources of GDP to per capita GDP growth by expressing the growth equation in per capita terms:

$$\text{Growth in per capital potential GDP} = \text{Growth in technology} + W_K (\text{Growth in capital-labor ratio})$$

The capital-labor ratio measures the quantity of capital per unit of labor in the economy. In the equation above, it is weighted by the weight of capital in national income. What this equation shows is that advances in technology have a more significant impact on an economy's standard of living compared to capital (weight of growth in technology = 1; weight of growth in capital-labor ratio < 1).

Sources of Economic Growth

- Growth in labor supply: The potential quantity of labor in an economy is measured in terms of total hours worked.

$$\text{Total hours worked} = \text{Labor force} \times \text{Average hours worked per worker}$$

The labor force is defined as the portion of the working age population (over the age of 16) that is employed or available for work but not currently employed. Note that growth in the labor force is usually different from the population growth rate due to changes in the labor force participation rate and changes in hours worked per person. Labor supply is also affected by net immigration.
- Improvements in quality of human capital: Human capital refers to the accumulated knowledge and skill that workers acquire from education, training, and experience. Investment in health and education improves the quality of human capital in an economy.

- Growth in physical capital stock: Physical capital stock refers to the accumulated amount of buildings, machinery, and equipment used to produce goods and services. Countries with high growth rates of net investment exhibit a higher rate of economic growth.
- Improvements in technology: This is the most important factor affecting economic growth. Technology refers to the process used to transform inputs into outputs. Advancements in technology make it possible to produce more and more goods and services using the same quantity of inputs.
- Availability of natural resources: Raw materials are important inputs for growth and include everything from oil to land. There are two main types of natural resources:
    - Renewable resources can be replenished (e.g., forests).
    - Nonrenewable resources are depleted once consumed (e.g., oil).

Countries such as Brazil and Australia have recently benefited immensely from their large resource base. However, other countries, such as Japan in the 1960s and 1970s, have experienced rapid growth by acquiring the required inputs through trade.

Measures of Sustainable Growth

The growth accounting equation discussed earlier cannot be used to accurately estimate the growth rate of potential GDP as there is no observed data on potential GDP and TFP. Further, information on quantities of labor and capital is not readily available (especially in developing countries). Therefore, economists focus on labor productivity, an area where more reliable information is more readily available.

Labor productivity refers to the quantity of goods and services (real GDP) that a worker can produce in one hour of work.

$$\text{Labor productivity} = \text{Real GDP} / \text{Aggregate hours}$$

We use total hours instead of the number of workers to account for differences in the number of hours worked by each individual.

Dividing the production function by L, the number of workers in an economy allows us to identify the factors that drive labor productivity:

$$Y / L = AF(1, K / L)$$

Y/L equals output per worker (a measure of labor productivity). The equation above implies that labor productivity depends on:

- Physical capital per worker (K/L) or the mix of inputs (which is easily calculated based on input data).
- Total factor productivity or technology (A). This is a scale factor and can be estimated based on output and input data.

Therefore, labor productivity is much easier to measure directly than growth in potential GDP. Labor productivity can explain differences in living standards and long-term sustainable growth rates across countries.

Level of labor productivity: The higher the productivity of labor, the more goods and services the economy can produce given the number of workers. Labor productivity depends on the stock of human and physical capital and the state of technology. Labor productivity tends to be higher in developed countries.

Growth rate of labor productivity: This equals the percentage increase in productivity over a year and tends to be higher in developing countries (due to the relative scarcity of physical capital). Rapid productivity growth means that the same number of labor units can produce more and more goods and services, which allows companies to pay higher wages and still make high profits. Therefore, high productivity growth is a positive for stock prices. Low productivity growth would mean that businesses would have to cut wages or increase prices to improve profits. Since both of these are rather difficult, low rates of productivity growth are typically associated with flat or declining stock prices.

Measuring sustainable growth: Potential GDP is a combination of aggregate hours and productivity of labor:

$$\text{Potential GDP} = \text{Aggregate hours} \times \text{Labor productivity}$$

This equation can be expressed in terms of growth rates as:

$$\text{Potential GDP growth rate} = \text{Long-term growth rate of labor force} + \text{Long-term labor productivity growth rate}$$

Therefore, if the labor force is growing at 1% per year and productivity of workers is growing at 2% per year, then potential real GDP would be expected to grow at 3% per year.

READING 17: UNDERSTANDING BUSINESS CYCLES

LESSON 1: THE BUSINESS CYCLE

LOS 17a: Describe the business cycle and its phases. Vol 2, pp 199–204

Overview of Business Cycles
- Business cycles usually occur in economies that mainly rely on business enterprises (as opposed to agricultural or centrally planned economies).
- There is a sequence of distinct phases that comprise a business cycle. *See below*.
- Almost all sectors of the economy undergo the phases of the business cycle at about the same time. Phases of the business cycle are not restricted to certain sectors.
- Business cycles are recurrent (they occur again and again), but they are not periodic (they do not always have the same intensity and/or duration).
- Business cycles typically last between 1 and 12 years.

Phases of the Business Cycle
- The trough is the lowest point of a business cycle, as the economy comes out of a recession towards an expansion.
- An expansion occurs after the trough and before the peak. It is a period during which aggregate economic activity is increasing.
- The peak is the highest point of a business cycle, as the expansion slows down and the economy moves towards a recession.
- A contraction (or recession) occurs after the peak. It is a period during which aggregate economic activity is declining. A particularly severe recession is known as a depression.

> Notice the use of the phrase *aggregate economic activity* in defining expansions and contractions. This is because even during an expansion (contraction), some economic sectors may not be growing (contracting) so we look at aggregate economic activity.

Figure 1-1: Phases of the Business Cycle[1]

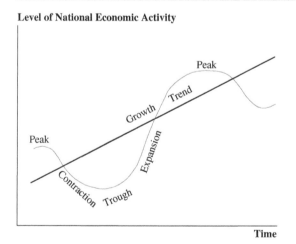

Business cycles may also be defined as fluctuations around the trend growth of an economy. Therefore, for each individual cycle, the peak and the trough occur at different levels of economic activity. See Figure 1-1.

Table 1-1 summarizes how important macroeconomic variables fluctuate through the different phases of a typical business cycle.

---

1 - Exhibit 1 Panel A, Volume 2, CFA Program Curriculum 2018

Table 1-1: Important Macroeconomic Variables[2]

	Early Expansion (Recovery)	Late Expansion	Peak	Contraction (Recession)
Economic Activity	Gross domestic product (GDP), industrial production, and other measures of economic activity stabilize and then begin to increase.	Activity measures show an accelerating rate of growth.	Activity measures show decelerating rate of growth.	Activity measures show outright declines.
Employment	Layoffs slow but new hiring does not yet occur and the unemployment rate remains high. Business turns to overtime and temporary employees to meet rising product demands.	Business begins full-time rehiring as overtime hours rise. The unemployment rate falls.	Business slows its rate of hiring. The unemployment rate continues to fall but at a decreasing rate.	Business first cuts hours and freezes hiring, followed by outright layoffs. The unemployment rate rises.
Consumer and Business Spending	Upturn in spending often most pronounced in housing, durable consumer items, and orders for light producer equipment.	Upturn becomes more broad-based. Business begins to order heavy equipment and engage in construction.	Capital spending expands rapidly, but the growth rate of spending starts to slow down.	Cutbacks appear most in industrial production, housing, consumer durable items, and orders for new business equipment, followed, with a lag, by cutbacks in other forms of capital spending.
Inflation	Inflation remains moderate and may continue to fall.	Inflation picks up modestly.	Inflation further accelerates.	Inflation decelerates, but with a lag.

Analysts should also examine other macroeconomic variables (e.g., unemployment, GDP growth, industrial production, and inflation) when identifying business cycle peaks and troughs.

In the United States, the National Bureau of Economic Research (NBER) defines a recession as two successive quarters of negative GDP growth.

During a recession, investors flock to safer assets like government securities and shares of stable companies with steady cash flows (e.g., utilities). Toward the end of a recession (at the onset of an expansion), risky assets such as corporate bonds and stocks (especially those of cyclical companies) rise in value due to improving profitability forecasts.

2 - Exhibit 1 Panel B, Volume 2, CFA Program Curriculum 2018

A boom generally occurs in the latter part of an expansion, when economic growth starts testing the limits of the economy.

- Companies face a shortage of qualified workers so they start bidding wars to tempt employees away from competitors.
- Companies (believing that the expansion will continue into the foreseeable future) borrow money to expand production capacity.
- Excessive salary growth can lead to inflation, while excessive borrowing can result in cash flow problems. During the boom, the economy is said to be overheating so typically, central banks step in to "cool down" the economy and avoid high inflation.

> Typically, the equity market hits its bottom about 3 to 6 months before the overall economy and well before economic indicators start exuding positive signals. Therefore, the equity market is classified as a leading indicator of the economy.

equity mkt) lead.

Generally speaking, during a boom:

- Risky assets witness a significant increase in value.
- Safer assets (that are in demand during a recession) usually have lower prices (high yields).

The peak occurs at the end of the expansion or boom, and signals the onset of a contraction (also known as downturn or slowdown). Contractions are characterized by rising unemployment and declining GDP growth.

Resource Use through the Business Cycle

Fluctuations in inventory, employment, and investment are linked to fluctuations in the economy. Suppose that an economy is overheating (see Figure 1-2) with short-run equilibrium occurring at a point beyond the long-run aggregate supply (LRAS) curve. Actual GDP exceeds potential GDP, so the central bank decides to cool down the economy by increasing interest rates. The rise in interest rates reduces aggregate demand (from AD_0 to AD_1), which results in a fall in price levels (from P_0 to P_1) and a decline in actual GDP (from GDP_0 to GDP_1). Due to the decrease in demand, companies end up with excess inventories so they decide to scale down production. As a consequence, workers no longer receive overtime payments, while physical capital is not used to full capacity, both of which result in a further decrease in aggregate demand (from AD_1 to AD_2), an even lower price level (P_2), and a lower real GDP (GDP_2).

Figure 1-2: Policy-Triggered Recession

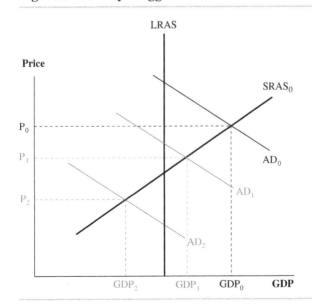

The slowdown may be worsened if:

- Workers choose to cut down consumption (even if they do not expect to be fired) and businesses choose to cut back on capital expenditure in anticipation of leaner times ahead.
- Businesses move to recession mode by cutting all nonessential costs (e.g., consultancy fees and advertising) and liquidating inventories.
- Banks grow wary of advancing credit to businesses given the gloomy economic outlook.

Note that during the downturn, businesses will typically not sell physical capital because it is difficult to find buyers. The stock of physical capital adjusts through aging of equipment and technical obsolescence.

Notice that at GDP$_2$, the economy is in a recessionary gap (actual GDP is less than potential GDP), unemployment exceeds the natural rate, and wages and other input prices are relatively low. Eventually, the central bank may move to cut interest rates to revive the economy. Low input prices along with low interest rates encourage companies to increase inventories and invest in more equipment, while low prices and interest rates induce consumption (e.g., in durable goods). This stage is the turning point of the business cycle as aggregate demand slowly starts to increase (shift to the right).

As the economic revival begins, companies will initially be cautious and look to use existing resources to build up inventory levels. This is known as the inventory rebuilding or restocking phase of an expansion. Eventually, as more concrete signs of an expansion abound from the economy, businesses will boost capital expenditure and demand for all factors of production will increase.

As aggregate demand continues to grow, the economy may boom again. During this phase two results can occur:

1. The economy may experience shortages as demand for factors of production exceeds supply; or
2. There may be excess demand caused by an overly optimistic build-up of production capacity, which implies that down the road, supply of capital will exceed demand. An example of this scenario occurred recently in many countries as overbuilding resulted in the housing bubble.

Both of these scenarios could trigger the next recession.

LOS 17b: Describe how resource use, housing sector activity, and external trade sector activity vary as an economy moves through the business cycle. Vol 2, pp 204–213

Fluctuations in Capital Spending

Changes in capital spending (spending on tangible goods, such as property, plant, and equipment) affect business cycles in three stages or phases:

During a recession, businesses focus on improving efficiency rather than enhancing capacity.

Stage 1: Spending on equipment falls off abruptly at the onset of an economic slowdown. Initially, orders for technology and light equipment are cut (or cancelled if possible) as they typically have shorter lead times. These cutbacks contribute to the economy's initial slowdown. Cutbacks in construction and installation of more complex pieces of equipment take longer. Eventually, when they do materialize, these cutbacks add to the negative momentum in the economy.

Stage 2: In the initial stages of an economic recovery, orders begin to pick up (despite low capacity utilization levels) due to the following:

A leading indicator of the future direction of capital spending is orders (not shipments) of capital equipment.

- The increase in earnings and free cash flow (due to an improving economy) encourages businesses to increase spending.
- The upturn in sales encourages managers to reverse order cancellations that were made hastily in the early stages of the preceding downturn. Orders initially reinstated tend to be for equipment to improve efficiency more than expand capacity.

Stage 3: Eventually, after an extended expansion, businesses are unable to meet consumer demand with existing capacity and, therefore, look to expand. In this stage, orders focus on heavy and complex equipment, warehouses, and factories. Businesses actually start spending on increasing capacity long before it becomes apparent that these additions are necessary. This is because they aim to be in prime position to take advantage of the boom once it arrives. Therefore, this phase of capital spending can occur very soon after the initial recovery is underway.

Fluctuation in Inventory Levels

Inventory levels tend to fluctuate dramatically over the business cycle, which results in them having a significant impact on economic growth despite their relatively small aggregate size. An important inventory indicator is the inventory-sales ratio. The interaction of this ratio with the business cycle can be broken down into three stages:

The inventory-sales ratio measures the outstanding stock of inventories relative to total sales.

Stage 1: Typically, businesses are slow to cut back on production when the economy starts to slow down. This results in an involuntary build-up of inventories and, combined with a drop in sales, results in a sharp increase in the inventory-sales ratio. Because inventories are a part of aggregate demand (investment expenditure), this initial build-up of inventories blunts any initial signs of economic weakness. Therefore, analysts also examine final sales numbers (which are not influenced by inventory swings) to determine the strength of the economy. In order to liquidate these unwanted inventories, businesses start decreasing production levels even below reduced-sales levels. These drastic production cutbacks eventually reduce final sales and worsen the downturn.

Stage 2: As businesses continue to cut back on production (to get rid of excess inventories), the inventory-sales ratio approaches normal levels. However, businesses soon start to raise production (even though there is no apparent growth in sales) just to arrest the decline in inventory levels. Here again, analysts should evaluate final sales to determine the strength of the economy. The increase in production gives an impression that the economy is improving, which may prompt businesses to end layoffs, and increase demand for other inputs. These signs mark the beginning of an upturn.

Note that if businesses did not have time to reduce inventories to acceptable levels during the contraction phase, they may not need to increase production to keep pace with the sales growth for a period of time.

Stage 3: During the upturn, as sales rise, businesses struggle to keep production on pace with sales growth, which leads to declining inventory levels. The rapidly-falling inventory-sales ratio stimulates businesses to increase production. They start hiring aggressively and the economy shows markedly exaggerated signs of strength for some time.

Consumer Behavior

Household consumption is typically the largest single sector in almost every developed economy. Two measures of household consumption are retail sales and a broad-based indicator of consumer spending that also includes nonretail purchases (e.g., utilities, household services, etc.).

Sales data is usually presented in nominal terms so it is deflated to identify trends in real sales growth. Analysts usually break up consumer spending into:

- Durable goods (e.g., autos, appliances, and furniture)
- Nondurable goods (e.g., food, medicine, cosmetics, and clothing)
- Services (e.g., medical treatment, entertainment, and communications)

Since durable goods typically have longer useful lives, households are more willing to defer purchases of durables in difficult economic times. Therefore:

- A decrease in spending on durable goods relative to nondurable goods and services is an early indication of economic weakness.
- An increase in spending on durable goods (to catch up for the delay in spending on them) relative to nondurables and services suggests that a recovery may be on the way.

Surveys are also used to evaluate consumer confidence or sentiment and to gain insights into future spending patterns. Generally speaking however, the usefulness of these surveys is limited as respondents usually answer them on the basis of their perceptions of a typical consumer, not necessarily based on their own behavior.

A better indicator of consumer spending is growth in disposable income. Another measure frequently used by analysts is permanent income, which adjusts for temporary unsustainable sources of income and estimates the income that households can rely on. Spending on durables tends to fluctuate with changes in temporary or unsustainable sources of income, which are excluded from the calculation of permanent income. Basic consumption expenditure is related to permanent income.

Unfortunately, consumer spending frequently diverges from income, making it difficult to predict consumer spending patterns based on estimates of income alone. Analysis of the savings rate can also be useful.

- Fluctuations in the savings rate capture changes in consumers' willingness to reduce spending out of current income.
- The savings rate is also a good indicator of consumers' expectations regarding future income. A rise in the savings rate may indicate that consumers are uncertain about future income, suggesting that the economy is weakening. Note that a very high savings rate contributes to future spending and, therefore, can help revive the economy even before incomes start to rise.

Housing Sector Behavior

Although the housing sector forms a relatively small part of the economy, fluctuations in the sector occur so rapidly that it makes a significant contribution to overall economic movements. Housing sector statistics (e.g., new and existing home sales, residential construction activity, inventory of unsold homes) typically follow fairly regular cyclical patterns and are therefore very important economic indicators.

- Since most home sales are usually financed by mortgage loans, housing sector activity is particularly sensitive to the level of interest rates. A rise (fall) in interest rates leads to a decline (an increase) in home purchasing and construction.
- Home sales are also affected by income levels relative to housing prices. Low housing prices relative to income, coupled with low costs of supporting an average house (when mortgage rates are low), increase demand for housing units.

Note that typically, toward the end of an expansion, the increase in house prices and mortgage rates is relatively high compared to the increase in incomes. The resulting slowdown in home sales can lead to a downturn initially in purchasing activity and later (as inventories of unsold units build up) a downturn in construction activity. Sometimes, however, rising house prices can extend an expansion if people buy houses to gain exposure to expected price increases. Such a flurry of speculative "late buying" activity can lead to overbuilding and eventually cause a more severe correction (as was the case in the United States during 2008 and 2009).

Finally, housing (more than any other economic sector) also responds to demographics (e.g., the pace of family or household formation). The proportion of the population between 25 and 40 years old can be used to evaluate how significantly the housing sector will contribute to growth going forward.

External Trade Sector Behavior

The contribution of the external sector to GDP varies considerably from country to country. For example, Singapore's economy is more reliant on international trade (for acquiring production inputs as well as for selling its output) compared to the U.S. economy.

Generally speaking:

- An increase in domestic GDP leads to an increase in demand for imports. Domestic exports usually tend to rise with an increase in GDP of major trading partners even if the domestic economy is weak. Therefore, patterns of external trade balances are not directly linked to domestic economic cycles.
- An appreciation of the domestic currency makes imports cheaper and, at the same time, makes domestic goods more expensive for trading partners, reducing net exports.
- GDP growth differentials have a more immediate and straightforward impact on the external trade balance.
- Currency movements have a more complex and gradual impact on the trade balance.

LOS 17c: Describe theories of the business cycle. Vol 2, pp 213–218

Neoclassical School of Thought

Defining assertions:
- The "invisible hand" will lead the market toward general equilibrium. Fluctuations in aggregate economic activity are short-lived as the economy will quickly readjust (e.g., via lower interest rates and lower wages if aggregate demand falls).
- Resources are allocated efficiently when MC equals MR, and there is no voluntary unemployment of labor and capital.
- All that is produced will be sold as supply creates its own demand (Say's Law). When something is produced, factors of production are compensated for their services. This creates purchasing power and stimulates demand.

Criticisms:

- The Great Depression (a prolonged downturn during the 1930s) would not have occurred if the assertions of neoclassical theory were actually true.
- The neoclassical school does not offer a theory on business cycles. It only mentions Schumpeter's creative destruction theory, which causes cycles within industries (not economy-wide fluctuations) due to technological advances. Essentially, neoclassical economics recognized that business cycles exist but treats them as temporary disequilibria.
- Treats economy-wide business cycles merely as short-term disequilibria which self-adjust.

Austrian School of Thought

Defining assertions:

- Shares some views with the neoclassical school, but focuses more on money and government.
- Money was not important in the neoclassical school (as barter could be used to achieve equilibrium), while the role of the government was limited to upholding the law and securing borders.
- The Austrian school argues that when governments try to increase employment and GDP through expansionary monetary policies, interest rates fall below their natural rate, which leads to overinvestment (an inflationary gap). Once companies realize that they have gone overboard, they cut back spending drastically, which reduces aggregate demand and causes a recession. The government only causes a "boom-and-bust" cycle. To restore equilibrium, the economy must be left alone and all prices (including wages) must decrease.
- The theory explicitly identifies "misguided government intervention" as the cause of business cycles.

Criticisms:

- The Great Depression (a prolonged downturn during the 1930s) would not have occurred if the assertions of Austrian school of thought were actually true. In the absence of government intervention, the economy did not self-adjust.
- The theory attributes the entire blame for business cycles on the government.

To summarize, the neoclassical and Austrian schools both argue that:

- If a recession occurs, no government intervention is needed.
- Problems related to unemployment and excess supply of goods will be solved by allowing prices (including wages) to decrease until markets clear.

Keynesian School of Thought

Defining assertions:

- The general price and wage reduction (required under the Austrian and neoclassical schools to bring the economy out of a recession) are hard to attain.
- Even if nominal wages were reduced, lower salary expectations would only result in a further decline in aggregate demand and actually exacerbate a recession (the domino effect).
- Lower interest rates will not necessarily reignite growth due to weak business confidence.
- The economy's self-correcting mechanism may work in the long run, but definitely should not be relied upon in the short run. It is the short run that really matters.

- The government should step in during a recession and stimulate aggregate demand (via larger fiscal deficits) to keep labor and capital employed.
- Note that Keynes did not encourage the government to be ever-present in fine-tuning the economy.

Criticisms:
- Fiscal deficits imply higher government debt, which must be serviced and repaid. The government may lose control over its finances trying to stimulate aggregate demand.
- While the government can try to fix the economy in the short run by stimulating demand, its actions may result in the economy overheating in the long run.
- There is a time lag until fiscal actions take effect in the economy. It is possible that the government's actions may only kick in once the economy is already recovering.
- Does not give any importance to money supply.

Monetarist School of Thought

Defining assertions:
- Money supply is supremely important. The government should maintain a steady growth rate of money supply.
- If money supply grows too fast, there will be an unsustainable boom and inflation. If it grows too slowly, there will be a recession.
- The government's expansionary fiscal actions may take effect once the recession is over and actually do more harm than good.
- The government should play a very limited role in the economy. Fiscal and monetary policy should be clear and consistent over time.
- Business cycles can be caused by exogenous shocks or government actions. During a recession it would be better to let the economy restore equilibrium on its own than to risk worsening the situation.

Criticism:
- If everyone knows that the government will lower interest rates in a recession, a company would not invest outside of a recession unless it had to. Companies would stop investing until they cause a recession (which otherwise would not have occurred), during which they will easily be able to obtain cheap loans from the government.

The New Classical School (RBC Theory)

This school of thought is based on new classical macroeconomics. When an economic agent faces an external shock, its behaviour is governed by the aim of maximizing utility. Further, the approach assumes that all economic agents are very similar, so they all behave in a similar manner and markets gradually adjust toward equilibrium.

Real Business Cycle (RBC) Theory

Defining assertions:
- Business cycles have real causes (e.g., changes in technology). Monetary variables (such as inflation) are assumed to have no impact on GDP and unemployment.
- The government should not intervene in the economy (through fiscal or monetary policy).

- Unemployment (apart from frictional unemployment) is only short term. A person would only be unemployed if she is asking for wages that are too high. Since markets are perfectly flexible, if the person drops her wage demands, she will find an employer who would be willing to hire her. The labor market would clear if workers avoided unrealistic wage expectations or enjoyed extra leisure combined with lower consumption.
- Aggregate supply plays a more prominent role (than in other theories) in bringing about business cycles.

Criticisms:

- During recessions, people are eagerly looking for jobs and unable to find employment despite reducing their wage demands.

Neo-Keynesian or New Keynesian Theory

Defining assertions:

- Like the New Classical School, this theory seeks to draw macroeconomic conclusions based on microeconomic (utility-maximizing) reasoning.
- Markets do not self-adjust seamlessly if they find themselves in disequilibrium. This is because:
  - Prices and wages are "downward sticky" (in contrast to the new classical view).
  - It is costly for companies to constantly update prices to clear markets (menu costs).
  - Companies need time to reorganize production in response to economic shocks.

Therefore, government intervention is useful in eliminating unemployment and restoring macroeconomic equilibrium.

LESSON 2: UNEMPLOYMENT, INFLATION, AND ECONOMIC INDICATORS

LOS 17d: Describe types of unemployment and measures of unemployment. Vol 2, pp 221–225

One of the objectives of a government is to limit the rate of unemployment in the economy. Generally speaking, unemployment is at its highest at the trough of a business cycle (when the economy is coming out of a recession), and at its lowest at the peak of the cycle.

One of the causes of a downturn in the economy is a tight labor market. When the economy is operating above its potential, inflation is relatively high and unemployment is very low. Workers ask for higher wages as they expect prices to continue to escalate, while businesses give in to these demands as there are few idle resources available. This upward pressure on wages triggers a price-wage inflationary spiral.

A key aspect to this inflationary spiral is inflation expectations. When the economy is overheating, inflation expectations are high, so the pressure to raise wages is stronger. Therefore, businesses try to increase product prices in advance to safeguard their profit margins. Hoping to arrest this upward trend in prices and wages, the central bank may attempt to bring inflationary expectations down by increasing interest rates. However, governments must beware that this contractionary measure can actually result in a deep recession. The takeaway is that whenever analysts see a price-wage inflationary spiral develop, they should consider the consequences of inflation and of a drastic rise in interest rates.

Labor market conditions can provide important insights into the condition of the economy. The following terms are used to assess the state of the labor market:

- Employed: Number of people with a job. This excludes those working in the informal sector (e.g., unlicensed cab drivers, illegal workers, etc.).
- Labor force: Number of people who either have a job, or are actively looking for one. This excludes people who are not employed and are not actively seeking employment (e.g., retirees, children, stay-at-home parents, fulltime students, etc.).
- Unemployed: People who are currently without a job, but are actively looking for one.
    - *Long-term unemployed*: People who have been out of work for a long time (more than 3–4 months) and are still looking for a job.
    - *Frictionally unemployed*: People who have just left a job and are about to start another one i.e., they already have a job waiting for them, which they have not started yet.
- Unemployment rate: Ratio of the number of people unemployed to the labor force.
- Activity (or participation) ratio: Ratio of the labor force to total working age population (usually those between 16 and 64 years of age).
- Underemployed: People who currently have jobs, but have the qualifications to do significantly higher-paying jobs. The fact that such individuals have jobs (even though they are overqualified for them) results in them being excluded from unemployment numbers. Data for part-time employment is sometimes used as a proxy for the underemployment rate.
- Discouraged worker: A person who has stopped looking for a job. These people are excluded from the labor force and therefore, not accounted for in the official unemployment rate. The official unemployment rate may actually decrease during severe recessions, as a lot of people become discouraged and stop searching for work (and are therefore, not counted as unemployed). Therefore, it is important to look at the unemployment rate in conjunction with the participation rate to determine whether a fall in the unemployment rate is actually due to an improved economy or due to an increase in the number of discouraged workers.

> Discouraged workers and underemployed people are considered examples of "hidden unemployment."

- Voluntarily unemployed: These are people who choose to remain outside the labor force (e.g., workers who retire early, or those who are unwilling to take up a vacancy because the wage offered is lower than their threshold).

The Unemployment Rate

The unemployment rate equals the ratio of the number of people who are unemployed to the total labor force. Countries around the world use different calculations to compute the unemployment rate, which makes comparisons across borders difficult. Although unemployment measures provide useful insights into the current state of an economy, they are not very useful in predicting an economy's cyclical direction as they are lagging economic indicators. This is because:

> Leading and lagging economic indicators are described later in the reading.

- The size of the labor force responds to changes in economic conditions. Further, during severe recessions, people get discouraged and stop looking for jobs, which results in them being left out of unemployment calculations and artificially lowers the unemployment rate when the economy is actually weakening. On the other hand, when the economy rebounds, a lot of people start looking for jobs, but are unable to find employment immediately. This artificially increases the unemployment rate when the economy is actually improving.
- Businesses are reluctant to lay off workers at the first sign of economic weakness (in order to retain good workers or due to their hands being tied by labor contracts). This means that unemployment measures rise relatively slowly at the onset of a recession. Also, businesses are slow to rehire previously-laid-off workers in the early stages of a recovery (until they are more confident that an expansion is underway and existing resources are fully utilized), which causes the unemployment rate to fall slowly at the onset of an expansion.

> Statistical agencies sometimes base the unemployment rate on the total working age population to avoid this bias. However, this measure may (incorrectly) include people with severe disabilities who can never seek work.

Overall Payroll Employment and Productivity Indicators

Some of the other measures that analysts use to determine the cyclical direction of an economy are:

- Size of payrolls: This measure is not biased by the number of discouraged workers. Generally speaking, payrolls tend to shrink when the economy slides into a recession and rise when a recovery is underway. The problem with this measure is that it is difficult to count employment in small businesses, which play a very important role in employment growth.
- The number of hours worked (especially overtime) and the use of temporary workers tend to increase at the first signs of a recovery and decrease at the first signs of economic weakness.
- An economy's productivity is measured by dividing total output by the number of hours worked. It measures the intensity of workflow of existing employees. Initially, as output falls, the number of hours worked does not change significantly because businesses are usually reluctant to reduce the number of workers on their payroll. As a result, productivity measures (if available promptly) can identify an economy's cyclical direction even before a change in the number of hours worked is noticed. Productivity increases during an expansion (as output rises) and decreases during a recession (as output falls).

> Note that productivity may also rise as a result of technological breakthroughs, which may negatively affect employment numbers. However, such changes occur over decades and have little relation to business cycles.

LOS 17e: Explain inflation, hyperinflation, disinflation, and deflation. Vol 2, pp 225–239

Inflation

Generally speaking, inflation is procyclical (i.e., it goes up and down with the business cycle), but with a lag of around one year. Inflation is defined as a persistent increase in the overall level of prices (aggregate price level) in an economy over a period of time. The inflation rate measures the speed of overall price movements by calculating the rate of change in a price index. The value of money decreases in an inflationary environment as the same amount of money will purchase fewer real goods and services in the future.

Investors watch the inflation rate of an economy very closely because:

- The inflation rate helps assess the state of the economy.
- It can be used to predict changes in monetary policy, which have a significant impact on asset prices.
- Very high inflation rates can lead to social unrest and political risk for investments in those economies.

Policy makers pay a lot of attention to the inflation rate in conducting monetary policy.

- If the economy is experiencing high inflation along with high economic growth and low unemployment, it is overheating so the monetary authority may take steps to cool it down.
- If an economy is experiencing high inflation along with high unemployment and slow economic growth, it is said to be suffering stagflation. Such an economy is usually left to correct itself as no short-term economic policies are thought to be effective.

Deflation

Deflation is defined as a persistent decrease in the aggregate level of prices in an economy over a period of time. The value of money actually rises in a deflationary environment. Since most debt contracts are written in fixed monetary amounts, the liability (in real terms) of the borrower rises during deflation. In a recession, as prices fall leveraged companies that are short of cash will lay off workers and cut back investments due to (1) the increase in the real value of their liabilities and (2) declining revenues as a result of lower prices. This would weaken the economy even further. Therefore, deflation is not good for the economy. The general consensus is that annual inflation of around 2% is ideal for developed countries.

Hyperinflation

Hyperinflation refers to a situation when the inflation rate is extremely high. It typically occurs when, instead of being backed by real tax revenue, large-scale government spending is supported by an increase in money supply. In other words, more money is printed to support government spending and more cash chases limited goods and services. Hyperinflation is usually triggered by a shortage of supply during or after a war, economic regime transition, or economic distress caused by political instability. People prefer to hold on to real goods instead of cash during hyperinflation, as the value of money falls very quickly. Therefore, money changes hands very quickly during hyperinflation.

Disinflation

Disinflation is defined as a fall in the inflation rate (e.g., from 15% to 5%). Disinflation is very different from deflation in the sense that deflation refers to a situation when the inflation rate is negative (aggregate price level is decreasing), while disinflation refers to a situation when the inflation rate falls, but remains positive (the aggregate price level continues to increase, but at a slower rate). During the 1990s many developed countries witnessed a decline in inflation rates as a result of high productivity growth rates.

LOS 17f: Explain the construction of indices used to measure inflation.
Vol 2, pp 227–229

LOS 17g: Compare inflation measures, including their uses and limitations.
Vol 2, pp 227–233

As mentioned previously, the inflation rate is calculated as the percentage change in a price index over a period. A price index represents the average prices of a basket of goods and services.

A price index that holds quantities of goods in the consumption basket constant is called a Laspeyres index. Most price indices around the world are Laspeyres indices, and consumption baskets are only updated after a certain number of years (typically 5). Using a fixed basket of goods and services to measure the cost of living gives rise to three biases:

1. Substitution bias: Changes in the relative prices of goods motivate consumers to replace expensive goods with cheaper substitutes. Use of a fixed basket results in an upward bias in the computed inflation rate. Use of chained price index formulas (e.g., the Fisher index) can mitigate this bias.
2. Quality bias: Improvements in product quality sometimes come at the cost of higher prices. If price indices are not adjusted for quality improvements, there will be an upward bias in the measured inflation rate. Prices can be adjusted for quality improvements through a practice known as hedonic pricing.
3. New product bias: Recently introduced products are not included in the price index if the consumption basket is fixed. This usually creates an upward bias in the measured inflation rate. In order to mitigate this bias, new products can be introduced into the basket more regularly.

Example 2-1 illustrates the use of different price index formulas in computing the change in prices of goods in a consumption basket over time.

Example 2-1: Calculating Inflation Rates

Using the consumption basket in Table 2-1, compute the inflation rate based on the Laspeyres index, the Fisher index, and the Paasche index.

Table 2-1: Consumption Basket and Prices over Two Months

Time	January 2010		February 2010	
Goods	Quantity	Price	Quantity	Price
Wheat	70 kg	$2/kg	100 kg	$3/kg
Gasoline	50 liters	$5.5/liter	60 liters	$5.6/liter

The price index in the base period is usually set to 100. If the price index in January 2010 is set to 100, then the price index in February 2010 is calculated as:

$$\text{Price index in February 2010} = \frac{\text{Value of wheat in Feb 2010} + \text{Value of gasoline in Feb 2010}}{\text{Value of wheat in Jan 2010} + \text{Value of gasoline in Jan 2010}} \times 100$$

Laspeyres Index

In computing a Laspeyres index, the quantities of wheat and gasoline in the consumption baskets will be fixed at their **base-period** levels.

$$\text{Price index in February 2010} = \frac{(70 \times 3) + (50 \times 5.6)}{(70 \times 2) + (50 \times 5.5)} \times 100 = 118.07$$

The inflation rate (change in the index over the period) therefore equals $(118.07/100) - 1 = 18.07\%$

Paasche Index

A Paasche Index is based on the **current** composition of the basket.

$$\text{Paasche index in February 2010} = \frac{(100 \times 3) + (60 \times 5.6)}{(100 \times 2) + (60 \times 5.5)} \times 100 = 120$$

Inflation rate = 20%

Fisher Index

A Fisher Index is calculated as the **geometric mean** of the Laspeyres index and the Paasche index.

Fisher index in February 2010 = $(118.07 \times 120)^{0.5} = 119.03$

Inflation rate = 19.03%

Price Indices and Their Usage

Different countries use consumer price indices with different names and different weights for different categories of goods and services. In the United States:

- The CPI only covers urban areas, which is why it is known as the CPI-U.
- The Personal Consumption Expenditures (PCE) price index uses business surveys to cover personal consumption.
- The Producer Price Index (PPI) tracks price changes experienced by domestic producers and includes items such as fuels, farm products, machinery, and equipment. Since higher production costs may eventually be passed on to consumers, the PPI is a good indicator of future changes in the CPI.
- Headline inflation is based on an index that includes all goods and services in the economy.
- Core inflation is based on an index that excludes food and energy prices from the basket. Core inflation is a better predictor of domestic inflation.

Also note that:

- Countries around the world specialize in different industries so the differences in weights of different categories of goods and services in the PPI across countries are even more significant than differences in CPI weights.
- Some countries refer to the PPI as the Wholesale Price Index (WPI) and use it to track the overall level of inflation in the domestic economy. However, WPI may not be a good indicator of the overall level of inflation since it is based on wholesale prices, which do not reflect retail margins.

LOS 17h: Distinguish between cost-push and demand-pull inflation. Vol 2, pp 233–236

Practitioners may use the unemployment rate or the participation rate to assess labor market conditions. The merits of both these measures have been discussed earlier.

Cost-Push Inflation

Cost-push inflation occurs when rising costs compel businesses to raise prices. Costs of production may rise because of an increase in money wage rates or an increase in the price of raw materials. Therefore, analysts can look for signs of cost-push inflation in the commodity and labor markets. Since labor is the biggest cost for most businesses, analysts tend to focus on the labor market.

- The higher the rate of unemployment, the lower the probability of shortages arising in the labor market.
- The lower the unemployment rate, the higher the probability of a labor shortage, which may exert an upward pressure on wages.

The natural rate of unemployment is also often referred to as the nonaccelerating inflation rate of unemployment (NAIRU). The natural rate of unemployment for an economy changes over time due to changes in technology and economic structure.

The effect of labor market constraints on wage rates is usually observed relative to the natural rate of unemployment (NARU). It is at the natural rate of unemployment (not at 0% unemployment), that the economy begins to experience bottlenecks in the labor market and feel wage-push inflationary pressures. Consider the technology sector, for example. This sector has grown so rapidly that the qualified and trained labor has been in short supply even though there is considerable unemployment in the broader economy. Until workers are trained in the new technologies, the economy may continue to experience a high NARU and feel significant wage-push pressures.

There are a variety of labor market indicators (e.g., hourly wages, weekly earnings, and overall labor costs) that indicate changes in the cost of labor for businesses, which can be used to gauge wage-push inflation pressures. However, it is preferred to combine trends in labor costs with productivity measures to evaluate the state of the labor market.

Labor productivity (output per hour) is important because it determines the number of units across which businesses can spread their labor costs. Unit labor cost (ULC) is calculated as:

$$ULC = W/O$$

where:
O = Output per hour per worker
W = Total labor compensation per hour per worker

- If wage rates grow at a faster rate than labor productivity, businesses' costs per unit of output (ULC) increase. Businesses then look to increase output prices to protect profit margins so the end result is cost-push inflation.
- If wage rates increase at a slower rate than labor productivity, ULC falls. This eases inflationary pressures.

Demand-Pull Inflation

Demand-pull inflation is caused by increasing demand, which causes higher prices and eventually results in higher wages to compensate for the rise in cost of living. Similar to the impact of labor market constraints on wage rates, demand-pull inflation may be analyzed based on the economy's capacity utilization levels:

- As the economy's actual GDP approaches its potential GDP (capacity utilization increases), there is an increase in the probability of shortages and bottlenecks occurring, so prices tend to rise.
- The further the economy operates below its potential output, the greater the probability of a slowdown in inflation (or even outright deflation).

Monetarists' Views on Inflation

Monetarists believe that inflation occurs when the growth rate of money supply in the economy outpaces growth in GDP. They explicitly place the blame for demand-pull inflation on excess money growth. Analysts may track the effect of money supply on inflation by looking at growth in money supply relative to growth in nominal GDP.

- If money growth exceeds nominal GDP growth, there is a possibility of inflation.
- If money growth is slower than nominal GDP growth, there could be disinflationary or deflationary pressures in the economy.

The ratio of nominal GDP to money supply equals the "velocity of money." The velocity of money may decline due to:

- A fall in nominal GDP (numerator). In this case the economy is more likely to soon enter an upswing than to experience inflationary pressures.
- A rise in money supply (denominator). In this case the economy is more likely to experience inflationary pressures than to witness an upturn.

While upward pressure on commodity prices can signal excess demand, economists do not use commodity prices as indicators of demand-push inflationary pressures in an economy because commodities trade in the global market and therefore reflect global conditions more than those in an individual economy.

Inflation Expectations

Inflation expectations also play an important role in policy-making. Once economic agents start expecting prices to continue to rise going forward, they change their actions in line with those expectations. This can lead to higher inflation and cause it to persist in the economy even after its real underlying cause is no longer present. Economists try to measure inflation expectations by:

- Observing past inflation trends and assuming that market participants usually set expectations about the future based on past experiences.
- Conducting surveys of inflation expectations. However, these are often biased.
- Comparing the nominal yield on government bonds to Treasury Inflation-Protection Securities (TIPS) whose yields adjust with inflation. However, this approach should be applied cautiously as yields on bonds are influenced by several other market factors.

LOS 17i: Describe economic indicators, including their uses and limitations. Vol 2, pp 239–246

An economic indicator is a variable that provides information on the state of the broader economy. A list of some U.S. economic indicators can be found in Table 2-2.

- Leading economic indicators have turning points that usually **precede** the turning points of the broader economy. Economists use them to predict the economy's **future state**.
- Coincident economic indicators have turning points that usually occur **close to** the turning points of the broader economy. Economists use them to identify the **current state** of the economy.
- Lagging economic indicators have turning points that usually occur **after** the turning points of the broader economy. Economists use them to identify the economy's **past condition**.

Practitioners take an aggregate perspective when interpreting various economic indicators. Typically aggregate measures are combined into composites known to lead the cycle, coincide with the cycle, or lag the cycle. For example, in the United States, the composite of leading economic indicators is known as the Index of Leading Economic Indicators (LEI). Note that each country's index of leading indicators is composed of different indicators based on its own historical experiences. However, the Composite Leading Indicators (CLI), which is calculated by the Organisation for Economic Co-operation and Development (OECD) is consistent across countries and can be used to compare different economies.

The timing record of various composite indices has varied considerably. For example, in the United States, the coincident indicator index has closely matched turnarounds in the economy, with 8 out of the last 13 turning points in the coincident indicator index corresponding to peaks and troughs. On the other hand, the leading indicator index has historically exhibited greater variability, leading contractions by 8 to 20 months and leading expansions by 1 to 10 months on average.

Further, the relationship between an indicator and the business cycle can be quite uncertain. For example, some leading indicators may be excellent predictors of expansions but poor predictors of recessions. This is why analysts combine different indicators with common factors among them when constructing indicator indices. This is also one of the reasons why diffusion indices are used. A diffusion index measures the proportion of the index's components that have moved in the same direction as the overall index. For example, if 7 out of the 10 indicators in the LEI point toward an expansion, the diffusion index would have a value of 70. An increase in this value would suggest that more components of the index are rising, and implies that analysts can be more confident that the index is representing broader movements in the economy.

Table 2-2: U.S. Economic Indicators[3]

Indicator and Description	
Leading	*Reason*
1. Average weekly hours, manufacturing	Because businesses will cut overtime before laying off workers in a downturn and increase it before rehiring in a cyclical upturn, these measures move up and down before the general economy.
2. Average weekly initial claims for unemployment insurance	This measure offers a very sensitive test of initial layoffs and rehiring.
3. Manufacturers' new orders for consumer goods and materials	Because businesses cannot wait too long to meet demands for consumer goods or materials without ordering, these gauges tend to lead at upturns and downturns. Indirectly, they capture changes in business sentiment as well, which also often leads the cycle.
4. ISM new order index[a]	This index is a diffusion index that reflects the month-to-month change in new orders for final sales. The weakening of demand, which can lead to a recession, is usually first reflected in the decline of new orders.
5. Manufacturers' new orders for non-defense capital goods excluding aircraft	In addition to offering a first signal of movement, up or down, in an important economic sector, movement in this area also indirectly captures business expectations.
6. Building permits for new private housing units	Because most localities require permits before new building can begin, this gauge foretells new construction activity.
7. S&P 500 Index	Because stock prices anticipate economic turning points, both up and down, their movements offer a useful early signal on economic cycles.
8. Leading Credit Index	This index aggregates the information from six leading financial indicators, which reflect the strength of the financial system to endure stress. A vulnerable financial system can amplify and propagate the effects of negative shocks, resulting in a widespread recession for the whole economy.
9. Interest rate spread between 10-year Treasury yields and overnight borrowing rates (federal funds rate)	Because long-term yields express market expectations about the direction of short-term interest rates, and rates ultimately follow the economic cycle up and down, a wider spread, by anticipating short rate increases, also anticipates an economic upswing. Conversely, a narrower spread, by anticipating short rate decreases, also anticipates an economic downturn.
10. Average consumer expectations for business and economic conditions	If consumers are optimistic about future business and economic conditions, they tend to increase spending. Because consumption is about two-thirds of the U.S. economy, its future movements offer early insight into the direction ahead for the whole economy.

(Table continued on next page...)

3 - Exhibit 5, Volume 2, CFA Program Curriculum 2018

Table 2-2: (*continued*)

Coincident	*Reason*
1. Employees on non-agricultural payrolls	Once recession or recovery is clear, businesses adjust their full-time payrolls.
2. Aggregate real personal income (less transfer payments)	By measuring the income flow from non-corporate profits and wages, this measure captures the current state of the economy.
3. Industrial Production Index	Measures industrial output, thus capturing the behavior of the most volatile part of the economy. The service sector tends to be more stable.
4. Manufacturing and trade sales	In the same way as aggregate personal income and the industrial production index, this aggregate offers a measure of the current state of business activity.

Lagging	*Reason*
1. Average duration of unemployment	Because businesses wait until downturns look genuine to lay off, and wait until recoveries look secure to rehire, this measure is important because it lags the cycle on both the way down and the way up.
2. Inventory-to-sales ratio	Because inventories accumulate as sales initially decline and then, once a business adjusts its ordering, become depleted as sales pick up, this ratio tends to lag the cycle.
3. Change in unit labor costs	Because businesses are slow to fire workers, these costs tend to rise into the early stages of recession as the existing labor force is used less intensely. Late in the recovery when the labor market gets tight, upward pressure on wages can also raise such costs. In both cases, there is a clear lag at cyclical turns.
4. Average bank prime lending rate	Because this is a bank-administered rate, it tends to lag other rates that move either before cyclical turns or with them.
5. Commercial and industrial loans outstanding	Because these loans frequently support inventory building, they lag the cycle for much the same reason that the inventory–sales ratio does.
6. Ratio of consumer installment debt to income	Because consumers only borrow heavily when confident, this measure lags the cyclical upturn, but debt also overstays cyclical downturns because households have trouble adjusting to income losses, causing it to lag in the downturn.
7. Change in consumer price index for services	Inflation generally adjusts to the cycle late, especially the more stable services area.

[a]A diffusion index usually measures the percentage of components in a series that are rising in the same period. It indicates how widespread a particular movement in the trend is among the individual components.

Example 2-2: Interpreting Different Economic Indicators

What do the following observations suggest regarding the state of the economy?

1. An increase in the ratio of consumer installment debt to income.
2. A positive change in the S&P 500.
3. A slight increase in the LEI over two consecutive months.

Solution:

1. The ratio of consumer installment debt to income is a lagging indicator. An increase in the ratio suggests that an upturn is already underway. If coincident indicators have recently been pointing to an upturn, an increase in the ratio of consumer installment debt to income would confirm that the economy has rebounded.
2. The S&P 500 is a leading indicator. An increase in the index is a positive sign for future economic growth.
3. A small increase in the LEI over two consecutive observations suggests that a modest economic expansion can be expected.

Other economic indicators typically used by analysts include reports based on surveys of industrialists (ISM polls in the United States and Tankan Report in Japan), bankers, labor associations, and households on the state of their finances, level of activity, and their confidence in the future.

STUDY SESSION 5: ECONOMICS: MONETARY AND FISCAL POLICY, INTERNATIONAL TRADE, AND CURRENCY EXCHANGE RATES

READING 18: MONETARY AND FISCAL POLICY

LESSON 1: MONETARY POLICY (PART I)

LOS 18a: Compare monetary and fiscal policy. Vol 2, pg 263

- Monetary policy refers to the government's or central bank's manipulation of the money supply to influence the quantity of money and credit in the economy.
- Fiscal policy refers to the government's use of spending and tax policies to influence various aspects of the economy, including:
  - The level of aggregate demand and, therefore, overall economic activity.
  - The distribution of wealth.
  - The allocation of resources between different subsectors and economic agents.

LOS 18b: Describe functions and definitions of money. Vol 2, pp 264–271

LOS 18c: Explain the money creation process. Vol 2, pp 266–269

Problems with a Barter Economy

- Relies on the double coincidence of wants (i.e., each party must want what the other is selling).
- It is difficult to undertake transactions involving goods that are indivisible.
- Perishable goods are not good stores of value.
- There is no common measure of value.

The Functions of Money

Medium of exchange: Money's most important function is as a medium of exchange to facilitate transactions. Money effectively eliminates the requirement of a double coincidence of wants by serving as a medium of exchange that is accepted in all transactions by all parties. In order to effectively serve as a medium of exchange, money must have the following qualities:

- It must be readily acceptable.
- It must have known value.
- It must be easily divisible.
- It must have a high value relative to its weight.
- It must be difficult to counterfeit.

Store of value: Money is more liquid than most other stores of value because, as a medium of exchange, it is readily accepted everywhere. Further, money is an easily transported store of value that is available in a number of convenient denominations. Money holds on to its value better when inflation is low.

Unit of account: Money also functions as a unit of account, providing a common measure of the value of goods and services being exchanged. Knowing the value of a good in terms of money helps us quantify the opportunity cost of consuming the good and facilitates efficient decision-making. For example, if oranges cost $6/dozen and a pair of shoes costs $12 we know that the opportunity cost of buying the pair of shoes is 2 dozen oranges.

Paper Money and the Money-Creation Process

All banks are required to hold a certain percentage of their deposits in the form of reserves (cash in its vaults plus deposits at the central bank). A required reserve ratio of 20%, when the bank's total deposits stand at $10 million, would require the bank to hold a total of at least $2 million in its vaults and its deposit account at the central bank combined.

> Required reserve ratio = Required reserves / Total deposits

Let's go through an example to see how money is created. Suppose the Fed purchases a Treasury security worth $1,000 from Warren, who banks with ABC Bank. To pay for this security, the Fed will increase the balance in ABC's deposit account at the Fed by $1,000, and ABC will increase the balance in Warren's account by $1,000. The increase in the balance of ABC's account at the Fed represents an increase in its reserves (assets), and the increase in Warren's account at ABC represents an increase in ABC's deposits (liabilities).

If the required reserve ratio is 20%, ABC must retain $200 of the $1,000 increase in its deposits in the form of reserves. Assume that it lends its excess reserves ($800) to another client, Donald. Donald uses the $800 loan to make some purchases from PQR Inc. and PQR deposits the money in its bank, XYZ Bank.

As a result of PQR's deposit, XYZ's deposits and reserves will rise by $800. XYZ will hold $160 (20% of the increase in deposits) in the form of reserves and loan out the remaining $640. The client borrowing the $640 will make some purchases and the money will eventually be deposited back into the banking system and potentially create more loans. This cycle will continue with dwindling numbers and, eventually, the total quantity of money in the economy will have increased by a multiple (5 times) of the initial increase in the monetary base (which was only $1,000). This multiple is known as the money multiplier (M) and is calculated as:

> Money multiplier $= 1 / (\text{Reserve requirement}) = 1 / (0.2) = 5$

The initial stimulus of a $1,000 increase in the monetary base will eventually increase the quantity of money in the economy by $1,000 \times 5 = \$5,000$ and result in $5,000 worth of economic transactions. Note that ABC Bank is not solely responsible for the creation of money in our example. It is the banking system as a whole that goes through the following cycle and increases the quantity of money:

1. Banks have excess reserves.
2. They lend the excess reserves.
3. Bank deposits increase.
4. Quantity of money increases.
5. Deposits in the banking system increase.
6. These deposits in turn create excess reserves which are loaned out.

Definitions of Money

Money may be defined as any medium (e.g., notes and coins) that can be used to purchase goods and services. Monetary authorities in most countries use a variety of measures of money. Generally speaking however, the stock of money consists of notes and coins in circulation, plus deposits in banks and other financial institutions that can readily be used to purchase goods and services in the economy. Economists focus on the rate of growth of narrow money and broad money.

- Narrow money refers to notes and coins in circulation plus other highly liquid deposits.
- Broad money includes narrow money plus the entire range of liquid assets that can be used to make purchases.

Checking account balances are included in measures of money because funds in them can be transferred from one person to another and can be used to make payments. Checks make this transfer possible but this does not make the check itself money.

Credit cards are not money either. Credit cards work in exactly the same way as a loan. If you purchase goods using a credit card, the credit card company will pay the seller today and you will have an obligation to pay the credit card company when you receive your bill. This obligation to the credit card company does not represent money. Money only changes hands between you and the credit card company when you pay your bill.

LOS 18d: Describe theories of the demand for and supply of money. Vol 2, pp 271–274

The Quantity Theory of Money

The quantity theory of money expresses the relationship between money and the price level. The quantity equation of exchange states that:

$$M \times V = P \times Y$$

where:
M = Quantity of money
V = Velocity of circulation
P = Price level
Y = Real output

Basically, what the equation asserts is that the amount of money used to purchase all goods and services in the economy (M × V) equals the value of these goods and services (P × Y). If velocity is assumed constant, then total spending in money terms (P × Y) is proportional to the quantity of money (M).

Money neutrality says that an increase in money supply will not result in an increase in real output (Y). Therefore, an increase in money supply will cause the aggregate price level (P) to rise. The assertions of the quantity theory of money are in line with the consequences of money neutrality (as velocity is assumed constant).

> Velocity of circulation is the number of times a unit of currency changes hands annually to purchase goods and services. If a $20 bill is used by ten people over the year, it would have been used to buy goods and services worth M × V or $200.
>
> Under the quantity theory, velocity is assumed constant.

Monetarists use the quantity theory of money to support their belief that inflation can be controlled by manipulating the money supply growth rate.

The Demand for Money

Demand for money reflects the amount of wealth that households choose to hold in the form of money (instead of bonds or equities). There are three reasons for holding money:

Transactions-related demand for money arises from the need to use money to finance transactions. Generally speaking, transactions-related demand for money is positively related to average transaction size and overall GDP. Note that the ratio of transactions balances to GDP has not changed significantly over time.

Precautionary money balances are held for use in unforeseen circumstances. Precautionary balances are positively related to average transactions size, total volume of transactions, and therefore to overall GDP as well.

Speculative or portfolio demand for money is related to perceived opportunities and risks of holding other financial instruments (such as bonds). Speculative demand for money is inversely related to the returns available on other financial assets. At the same time, it is positively related to the perceived risk in these financial assets.

Supply and Demand for Money

Money supply is assumed fixed so it is represented by a vertical line (MS). Money demand is inversely related to interest rates (speculative money demand increases as interest rates fall). Therefore, money demand is represented by a downward-sloping line (MD). The point of intersection between the money demand and supply curves (e) determines short run equilibrium nominal interest rates (i_e). At interest rates above the equilibrium rate (i_1), the quantity of money supplied exceeds the quantity of money demanded. (See Figure 1-1.) Firms and individuals purchase government securities with excess money, which increases demand for these securities. Consequently, the prices of these securities rise and interest rates fall.

Figure 1-1: Supply and Demand for Money

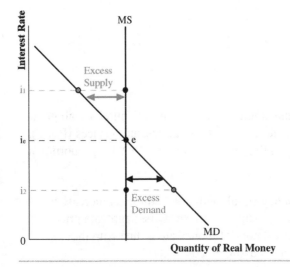

You will learn more about the relationship between fixed-income security prices and interest rates in later readings. For now just remember that prices of fixed-income securities and interest rates are inversely related.

At interest rates below the equilibrium rate (i_2), the quantity of money supplied is less than the quantity of money demanded. Facing a shortage of money, firms and individuals sell government securities. The increase in supply of these securities lowers their prices and interest rates rise.

If the central bank were to raise money supply, interest rates would fall. In this scenario, if money neutrality were assumed to hold in the long run, the price level would increase, leaving output and employment unchanged. The reason behind this line of thinking is that simply increasing money supply (or lowering the price of money) does not change the availability of factors of production that influence the economy's ability to produce *real* things. Note that:

- In practice, it is difficult to determine whether money neutrality holds in the long run.
- Central banks seem to believe that money supply does have a real impact on the economy in the short run. Otherwise, there would be almost no point to monetary policy.

LOS 18e: Describe the Fischer effect. Vol 2, pp 274–275

The Fischer effect is directly related to the concept of money neutrality. It states that the nominal interest rate (R_N) reflects the real interest rate (R_R) and the expected rate of inflation (Π^e).

$$R_N = R_R + \Pi^e$$

For example, if the real interest rate in an economy equals 3% and expected inflation rises from 4% to 5%, then nominal interest rates must rise from 7% to 8%.

According to money neutrality, money supply and/or the money growth rate should not affect R_R, but will affect inflation and inflation expectations.

One factor that does influence the nominal interest rate but is not considered by the Fischer effect is uncertainty. Investors are never certain about the future values of economic variables, so the nominal interest rate also reflects a risk premium to account for the uncertainty associated with the future. The greater the uncertainty, the higher the required risk premium.

LOS 18f: Describe roles and objectives of central banks. Vol 2, pp 277–280

The Roles of the Central Bank

- Monopoly supplier of currency: Under the gold standard, currency could be converted into a pre-specified amount of gold. Nowadays, money is not convertible by law into anything else (this is known as fiat money) but it does have legal tender (i.e., it must be accepted when offered in exchange for goods and services). Fiat money derives its value from its universal acceptability in the financial system. Central banks have the responsibility of safeguarding the value of fiat currencies and maintaining confidence in them. If central banks increase the supply of money irresponsibly, the currency will lose its value.
- Banker to the government (and to other banks) and lender of last resort: The central bank stands ready to supply funds to banks when they face reserve shortfalls. This support, along with government bank deposit insurance, promotes confidence in banks.

- In some countries, it is the central bank's responsibility (solely or in conjunction with another authority) to supervise the banking system.
- Central banks oversee, regulate, and set the standards for a country's payments system so that procedures are robust and standardized such that the system can handle the millions of financial transactions that take place daily. The central bank also coordinates payment systems internationally with other central banks.
- Most central banks also manage the country's foreign currency and gold reserves.
- Central banks are usually responsible for conducting monetary policy.

Objectives of Monetary Policy

The U.S. Federal Reserve (Fed) states that the nation's monetary policy should promote:

- Maximum employment.
- Stable prices.
- Moderate long-term interest rates.

Other central banks around the world also perform many different roles and have multiple objectives, but generally speaking the overarching objective of most central banks is to maintain price stability.

LOS 18g: Contrast the costs of expected and unexpected inflation.
Vol 2, pp 281–283

Costs of Inflation

Expected inflation is the inflation rate that economic agents expect to see in the economy in the future. Expected inflation gives rise to:

- Menu costs: Costs of repeatedly changing advertised prices of goods and services.
- Shoe leather costs: These represent the time and effort put in by people to deal with the effects of inflation, such as holding less cash on hand and making frequent trips to the bank when in need of cash.

Expected or anticipated inflation is reflected in all long-term contracts. People accept this level of inflation, and budget for it. If a 1% increase in price levels is expected in an economy currently working at full employment, aggregate demand will be expected to move up by 1%. Also, because the 1% increase in prices is expected, wages will also rise by 1%, causing aggregate supply to fall by 1%. Effectively, when inflation is expected, it becomes a self-fulfilling prophecy.

Unexpected inflation is the level of inflation that comes as a surprise to economic agents. It is arguably more costly than expected inflation. In addition to the costs of expected inflation, unexpected inflation also leads to:

- Inequitable transfers of wealth between borrowers and lenders.
    - If actual inflation is less than expected inflation (which is built into nominal interest rates), lenders benefit and borrowers lose out as the real value of payments on debts rises.
    - If actual inflation is greater than expected inflation, borrowers benefit and lenders lose out as the real value of payments on debts falls.

- Higher risk premium in borrowing rates: Higher uncertainty associated with future inflation leads to lenders demanding a higher risk premium, which inflates the nominal interest rate and hurts economic activity.
- A reduction in the information content of market prices: Businesses may attribute an increase in prices of their products to an increase in demand (or decrease in supply) when in fact the price increase may be in line with the overall level of inflation in the economy. Businesses would increase production only to find that they are struggling to sell their output and involuntarily build up inventories. As a result, they would cut back production drastically, which would hurt the economy.

LESSON 2: MONETARY POLICY (PART II)

LOS 18h: Describe tools used to implement monetary policy. Vol 2, pp 283–295

LOS 18i: Describe the monetary transmission mechanism. Vol 2, pp 285–287

LOS 18k: Explain the relationships between monetary policy and economic growth, inflation, interest, and exchange rates. Vol 2, pp 283–295

LOS 18l: Contrast the use of inflation, interest rate, and exchange rate targeting by central banks. Vol 2, pp 283–295

Monetary Policy Tools

Required reserve ratio: All banks are required to hold a certain proportion of their deposits in the form of reserves. Reserves are defined as "vault cash plus deposits at the Fed." If a bank has deposits of $100, and if the reserve requirement is 20%, it must hold a total of $20 in its account at the Fed and currency in its vaults. If the bank actually holds $30 in the form of reserves, it has excess reserves of $10, which it can use to make loans (as illustrated earlier in the reading). Note that this policy tool is not used much in developed economies anymore. However, it is still used in many developing economies, including India and China.

The central bank's policy rate: The central bank's official policy rate influences short- and long-term interest rates and eventually has an impact on the broader economy. In the United States, this rate is known as the discount rate. It is the rate at which the Fed stands ready to lend reserves to depository institutions in case their reserves fall below required levels.

The most important interest rate in the conduct of U.S. monetary policy is the Fed funds rate (FFR), which is the interest rate at which banks make overnight loans of reserves to each other. The Fed sets a target FFR by manipulating the quantity of reserves in the banking system through open market operations.

Generally speaking, the higher the policy rate, the higher the penalty that banks will have to pay the central bank if they run short of liquidity. This would make them more conservative in lending, reducing broad money supply.

> In recent years, the discount rate has been approximately a percentage point above the federal funds rate, which makes it a relatively unimportant factor in the control of money supply.

Open market operations involve the sale and purchase of government securities. They are conducted by the central bank to directly influence the level of reserves held by banks. For example, if the central bank sells securities through an open-market operation, it withdraws the required amount from the purchaser's bank's account at the central bank, which directly reduces the bank's reserves. This diminishes the bank's capacity to make loans, causing broad money growth to decline through the money multiplier mechanism.

The Transmission Mechanism

If the central bank increases its official policy rate:

- Banks respond to the increase in the official interest rate by increasing their base rates (the reference rates on which they base lending rates to customers). As a result, individuals and businesses borrow less.
- Asset prices and values of capital projects tend to fall, as present values of expected future cash flows decline.
- Economic agents' expectations regarding the economy are dampened as they associate higher interest rates with slower future economic growth and reduced profits.
- The domestic currency appreciates in value (as hot money flows in). This makes domestic goods and services more pricey (less competitive) in the international market, leading to a decline in exports.
- If the increase in interest rates is widely expected to be followed by further rate hikes, economic agents will change their behavior to reflect these revised expectations.
- Overall, the decline in consumption, borrowing, and asset prices will reduce aggregate demand.
- Weaker demand will reduce domestic prices. This, along with lower import prices (due to appreciation of the domestic currency), will put a downward pressure on actual inflation.

Important: The central bank aims to have a direct effect on inflation expectations (and asset prices and the exchange rate) by setting the official policy rate at a particular level. By resetting expectations of inflation, it hopes to eventually have a real impact on aggregate demand, which subsequently influences actual domestic inflation.

The above analysis (rather simplistically) suggests that the use of contractionary monetary policy:

- Has an impact on economic growth in the short run (which is why central bankers continue to believe in the value of monetary policy in influencing real economic variables in the short run).
- Has an impact on the rate of inflation (or the price level) in the long run (in line with money neutrality).

See Figure 2-1.

Figure 2-1: The Money Transmission Mechanism

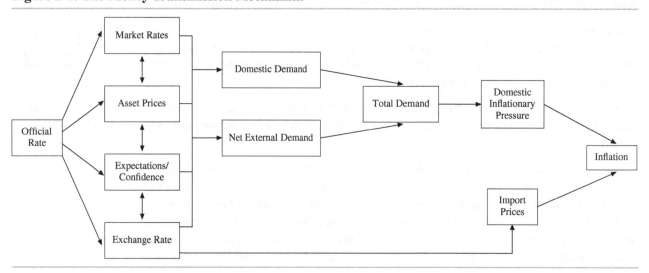

Source: Bank of England.

Monetary Policy Strategies

Inflation targeting: Under this strategy, the central bank makes a public commitment to achieving an explicit inflation target and to explaining how its actions will achieve that target. Inflation targets are specified in terms of a CPI inflation rate. The argument here is that inflationary expectations must be managed and, when everyone is aware (and believes) that the central bank will move to contain inflation within an acceptable range, spending and investing decisions will be made wisely.

Exchange rate targeting: Many developing economies choose to target their currency's exchange rate rather than an explicit level of inflation. The central bank supports the target exchange rate by buying and selling the domestic currency in the foreign exchange market. Basically, the aim here is to "import" the inflation experience of an economy with a good track record on inflation by tying the domestic currency to the currency of that economy. However, the downside is that in its efforts to maintain the exchange rate at the stated level, the central bank could lose control over domestic money supply and interest rates, which can become more volatile (especially if the inflation experience of the economy is markedly different from that of the targeted economy).

> When the central bank chooses to target a specific value for its exchange rate, conditions in the domestic economy must adapt to accommodate this target.

For example, assume that a central bank targets the exchange rate versus the USD. If inflation in the domestic economy is greater than inflation in the United States, with a floating exchange rate, the domestic currency would fall in value. The central bank would need to purchase the domestic currency (sell USD) in the foreign exchange market to maintain parity. As a result, domestic money supply would fall and short-term interest rates would rise. If this tightening is expected to bring down inflation, the domestic currency will eventually rise against the USD.

Further, if the central bank loses credibility regarding its commitment and ability to support the exchange rate, the domestic currency can come under speculative attacks and lose significant value, which can eventually lead to a full-blown crisis (e.g., Asian financial crisis of 1997–1998).

LOS 18j: Describe qualities of effective central banks. Vol 2, pp 288–293

The success of the central bank in meeting its objectives depends on its level of independence, credibility, and transparency.

- The central bank should be independent and not come under political pressures when formulating policy. For example, ruling politicians would be interested in keeping interest rates relatively low during election years in the hope that higher asset prices and a growing economy would help their reelection campaigns. The central bank should focus on its objectives and bear in mind that extended periods of low interest rates can lead to high inflation.

There are two aspects of central bank independence:

1. Operational independence is when the central bank decides the level of interest rates.
2. Target independence is when the central bank determines the inflation rate that is targeted and the horizon over which this target is to be achieved.

> The ECB is operationally and target independent, while the BOE is only operationally independent (the government determines the inflation target).

- The public should have confidence in the central bank (i.e., it must have credibility). If economic agents believe that the central bank will hit its inflation target, the belief itself could become self-fulfilling. If economic agents do not believe that the central bank is credible, they might expect high inflation (irrespective of the target). For example, if the government is heavily burdened with debt, it might have an incentive to set a high inflation target so that the real value of its borrowings falls. A high level of inflation would lower confidence in the economy and since people will not believe that the government is intent on containing inflation, the government would lack credibility. Unchecked inflation expectations would gradually be reflected in wage claims and eventually cause inflation to rise.
- There should be transparency in the central bank's decision-making. Transparency comes from the central bank clearly explaining its views on the economy and communicating its views on various economic indicators to economic agents on a regular basis. Transparency is a way of building credibility for the central bank.
- Finally (if the central bank follows an inflation targeting strategy), the central bank must have a realistic, forward-looking inflation target.
  - The target should be well above 0% so that the threat of deflation is minimized.
  - The central bank should target future inflation, not current inflation because:
    - The monetary transmission mechanism takes time to flow through the economy.
    - The current headline inflation rate reflects historical inflation (inflation over the past 12 months).

Challenges to the Effectiveness of Monetary Policy in Developing Countries

- The government bond market and interbank market are typically not sufficiently liquid or developed to facilitate the smooth conducting of monetary policy.
- The economy experiences rapid changes, which makes it difficult to identify the neutral rate.
- Rapid financial innovation results in frequently changing definitions of money supply.
- The central bank may lack credibility due to its poor historical record in controlling inflation.
- The government may be reluctant to let the central bank operate independently.

LOS 18m: Determine whether a monetary policy is expansionary or contractionary. Vol 2, pp 296–297

Contractionary and Expansionary Monetary Policies

- When the central bank believes that the current growth rate of economic activity will lead to inflation, it will look to reduce money supply and increase interest rates. Such actions are known as contractionary measures, as they are meant to rein in an overheating economy.
- When the central bank believes that the current level of economic growth is too slow and inflation is weakening, it will look to increase money supply and reduce interest rates. Such actions are known as expansionary measures, as they are meant to stimulate a receding economy.

The Neutral Rate of Interest

The neutral rate is the rate of interest that neither slows down nor spurs growth in the underlying economy. When the policy rate is below (above) the neutral rate, monetary policy is expansionary (contractionary). However, economists' estimates of the neutral rate for a given economy typically vary. What they do agree on is that the neutral rate has two components:

- Real trend of growth in the underlying economy: This corresponds to the rate of economic growth that gives rise to stable inflation in the long run.
- Long run expected inflation.

For example, in an economy with a credible inflation-targeting regime, if the inflation target is 2% and it is believed that the economy can grow sustainably over the long run at 3%, the neutral rate would be estimated at 5%. Generally speaking, central banks do communicate what they believe to be the neutral rate in the economy. However, their estimates are constantly monitored and changed to reflect evolving economic circumstances.

One final note: It is very important for the central bank to determine the source of any shock to the system before deciding on its policy response:

- If inflationary pressures build due to a demand shock (e.g., rising consumer and business confidence) the appropriate response would be to tighten monetary policy to rein in domestic demand.
- If inflationary pressures build due to a supply shock (e.g., rising oil prices) monetary tightening would take the economy further into a recession with lower consumption and higher unemployment.

LOS 18n: Describe limitations of monetary policy. Vol 2, pp 297–303

Limitations of Monetary Policy

The monetary transmission mechanism (see Figure 2-1) is not as seamless and straightforward as it appears to be in theory. Central banks do not always have strict control over money supply:

- They cannot control the amount of money that households and businesses choose to save. Some central banks (e.g., Japan in the early 2001) cut interest rates to near 0%, but this move still was not able to reduce the saving rate and stimulate consumption, nor was it able to eliminate deflation. This situation is referred to as a liquidity trap.
- While central banks can influence the ability of banks to extend loans and create credit, they cannot easily control the willingness of banks to do so. The different rounds of quantitative easing (QE) in the United States, subsequent to the credit crisis of 2008 were meant to kick start lending, causing broad money to expand and eventually lead to an increase in real economic activity. Banks however, continued to remain cautious. As far as they were concerned, it was better to hold excess reserves than lend to customers who could default.
  - There are risks involved with quantitative easing, as the central bank pumps money into the system by purchasing risky (toxic) assets. If it accumulates too many low-quality assets, economic agents could eventually lose confidence in the central bank and fiat money.

Quantitative easing involves the central bank printing money and pumping large quantities into the economy. While it is operationally similar to an open market operation, it is conducted on a much larger scale.

- If the central bank lacks credibility, there is a lower chance of its "policy message" being successfully transmitted through the economy. A credible monetary policy framework and authority typically do not require bond market vigilantes to do the work for it.

LESSON 3: FISCAL POLICY

LOS 18o: Describe roles and objectives of fiscal policy. Vol 2, pp 302–310

Fiscal Policy

Roles and Objectives of Fiscal Policy

The main aim of fiscal policy is to regulate the economy's real GDP by influencing aggregate demand. Expansionary fiscal policy involves one or more of the following:

- Reducing personal income taxes to increase disposable income.
- Reducing indirect taxes to raise real income.
- Reducing corporate taxes to boost profits.
- Reducing taxes on saving to raise disposable income.
- Increasing expenditure on social goods and infrastructure, which increases personal incomes.

Keynesians believe that fiscal policy can have a powerful impact on aggregate demand, output, and employment, while Monetarists believe that fiscal changes only have a temporary impact on the economy and that monetary policy is more effective in controlling inflation. Further, monetarists do not advocate the use of monetary policy in regulating business cycles.

Fiscal policy is an important tool for economic stabilization through its impact on output.

- In a recession, governments can increase spending and/or reduce taxes (expansionary fiscal policy) to try to raise employment and output.
- In an expansion, governments can reduce spending and/or increase taxes (contractionary fiscal policy) to try to control inflation.

The budget surplus/deficit equals the difference between the government's revenue and expenditure over a period of time. Analysts look at the change in the budgetary position to determine whether fiscal policy is getting tighter or looser:

- An increase (decrease) in a budget surplus is contractionary (expansionary).
- An increase (decrease) in a budget deficit is expansionary (contractionary).

Automatic stabilizers work in the absence of explicit action by the government to bring the economy toward full employment. There are two automatic stabilizers embedded in fiscal policy.

1. Induced taxes: Revenue from income taxes rises in an expansion and falls in a recession. In a recession, when tax revenues fall due to lower total incomes, the budget moves toward a deficit, which is exactly the budgetary stance required to deal with the demand shortfall. In an expansion, tax revenues rise and take the budget toward a surplus, which is the budgetary stance required to cool down the economy.

2. Needs-tested spending: These are government programs that pay benefits to qualified individuals and businesses (e.g., unemployment benefits). In a recession (expansion), the unemployment rate exceeds (is less than) the natural rate, and the amount of unemployment benefits paid out by the government increases (decreases). This increase (decrease) in government spending leads the budget toward a deficit (surplus), and stimulates (reduces) aggregate demand.

Empirical evidence suggests that automatic stabilizers play a significant role in mitigating deviations from potential output. They reduce the severity of both expansions and recessions.

Discretionary fiscal actions are enacted by the government and involve changing tax rates or the level of government spending. Basically, these actions are up to the government's discretion, as opposed to automatic stabilizers which act on their own to bring the economy toward full employment.

LOS 18q: Describe the arguments about whether the size of a national debt relative to GDP matters. Vol 2, pp 307–310

Deficits and National Debt

Governments finance fiscal deficits by borrowing from the private sector. Extended periods of significant deficits can result in a sizable buildup of government debt. Eventually, as the ratio of debt to GDP continues to rise, there comes a point when the country's solvency comes into question (e.g., Greece in 2011).

Following the credit crisis in 2008, several Organization for Economic Cooperation and Development (OECD) countries (e.g., Japan) saw a marked increase in the ratio of gross government financial liabilities to GDP (172.1% in 2008) as government spending was raised significantly to stimulate their economies. An important issue for these countries (and their creditors) was whether the additional spending would lead to sufficient extra tax revenues to pay interest on the debt used to finance the spending. If the real growth in the economy (which dictates the growth of tax revenues, assuming tax rates are not changed) is lower than the real interest rate on debt (which determines the dollar amount of the debt burden) the economy may have issues servicing its debt obligations going forward.

Note that within the national economy, inflation would result in a decline in the real value of outstanding debt. However, if the price level falls, the ratio of debt to GDP may remain high for a prolonged period and investors may lose confidence in the government's ability to satisfy its debt obligations.

Reasons to be concerned about national debt relative to GDP:
* High debt levels may lead to high tax rates (to service the debt) going forward. Higher expected future tax rates may serve as a disincentive for labor and entrepreneurial activity.
* If markets lose confidence in the government, the central bank may have to print money to finance the deficit. This would lead to high inflation (e.g., Zimbabwe in 2008–2009).

- Government spending may crowd out private investment. Higher demand for borrowing (to finance the deficit) by the government would raise interest rates, reducing private sector investment.

Reasons not to be concerned about national debt relative to GDP:
- The problem is not really a major issue if debt is owed to the country's own citizens. In this case the government can just print money to retire the debt. However, note that this strategy comes with the risk of high inflation.
- Some of the borrowed funds may have been used for capital investment projects, which would raise the economy's productive capacity (and tax revenues) going forward.
- The private sector may adjust to offset fiscal deficits by increasing savings in anticipation of future tax increases (to finance the deficit). This is known as Ricardian equivalence: the increase in government spending (or reduction in taxes) meant to stimulate aggregate demand will have no impact on economic activity as economic agents will save more because they expect the government to finance the deficit by increasing taxes in the future.
- If there is widespread unemployment in the economy, fiscal deficits will not be diverting any resources away from productive uses so total output will increase.
- Large fiscal deficits require tax changes, which may correct the distortions created by the current tax structure.

It is important to distinguish between short-term and long-term effects. For example, crowding out may have little effect over the short term, but over the long term it can significantly hinder capital accumulation in the economy.

LOS 18p: Describe tools of fiscal policy including their advantages and disadvantages. Vol 2, pp 310–314

Fiscal Policy Tools and the Macroeconomy

Government spending takes the following forms:

- Transfer payments are welfare payments that include unemployment benefits, job search allowances, and income support for poor families. They provide a way for the government to change the overall distribution of income in the economy. Note that these payments are not included in GDP.
- Current government spending refers to spending on goods and services that are provided on a recurring, regular basis (e.g., health, education, and defense). This type of spending has a significant impact on the quality of human capital and on labor productivity.
- Capital expenditure refers to infrastructure spending. This type of spending contributes to the economy's capital stock and adds to its productive capacity.

Justifications for Government Spending
- The government provides services such as defense that benefit all citizens equally.
- Infrastructure spending helps the country's economic growth.
- Goverment spending helps redistribute wealth in society.
- Goverment spending can be used as a tool to control inflation, unemployment, and growth.
- Goverment spending can be used to subsidize the development of innovative and high-risk new products (e.g., alternative energy).

Types of Taxes
- Direct taxes are levied on income, wealth, and corporate profits and include capital gains taxes, labor taxes, corporate taxes, and income and property taxes.
- Indirect taxes are taxes on spending on goods and services (e.g., VAT, excise duties, and taxes on fuel and tobacco).

Taxes can be justified in terms of raising revenue to finance government expenditure and in terms of income and wealth redistribution.

Desirable Properties of Tax Policy
- Simplicity: Taxpayers should find it easy to comply with tax laws and the authorities should find it easy to enforce them.
- Efficiency: Tax policy should minimize disincentives to work and invest. The aim of attaining "efficient" outcomes must be balanced against the urge to promote "good" economic activities or the urge to discourage "bad" activities (e.g., smoking).
- Fairness: While the concept of fairness remains subjective, it is generally believed that people in similar situations should pay similar taxes (horizontal equity) and richer people should pay more taxes (vertical equity).
- Revenue sufficiency: This aim may at times be in conflict with fairness and efficiency, so the government must find the right balance.

Advantages and Disadvantages of Different Fiscal Policy Tools

Advantages
- Indirect taxes can be adjusted very quickly. They are very effective in influencing spending behavior and in generating revenue at little cost to the government.
- Social objectives (e.g., reducing alcohol or cigarette consumption) can easily be met by raising indirect taxes.

Disadvantages
- Direct taxes, and welfare and other social transfers, are difficult to change without significant notice. However, they begin to have an impact on behavior soon after their announcement.
- Capital spending decisions are slow to plan, implement, and execute.

In addition to their direct effects on the economy, the above-mentioned fiscal policy tools also have strong expectational effects on the economy. For example, an announcement that income taxes will be raised next year would have an impact on spending patterns almost immediately. Also note that:

- Direct government spending has a much bigger impact on aggregate spending and output than income tax cuts or transfer increases.
- However, if transfer increases target the poorest in society (whose marginal propensity to consume is highest), they can have a relatively strong impact on spending.

LOS 18r: Explain the implementation of fiscal policy and difficulties of implementation. Vol 2, pp 316–320

The Fiscal Multiplier

- The net impact of the government sector on aggregate demand is:
  G – T + B = Budget deficit (surplus).
- Net taxes (NT = Taxes – Transfers) reduce disposable income (Y_D) relative to national income (Y) as follows:
  - $Y_D = Y - NT = (1 - t)Y$ where t is the net tax rate.
  - For example, given a net tax rate of 20%, each $1 rise in national income will increase taxes by $0.20 and disposable income by $0.80.

- When government spending increases (assume by $10), the recipients of the resulting income save a portion and spend the rest. The proportion of additional disposable income that is spent is known as marginal propensity to consume (MPC). Ignoring taxes, if MPC equals 0.9, households would spend $9 out of the total of $10 and save $1. The $9 spent by the recipients of $10 from the government would be the source of income for other households, who would then spend $8.10 (out of $9) and save $0.90. As the effect of the initial increase in government spending ($10) trickles down the economy, there will be an aggregate increase in spending of $100, which implies that the multiplier equals 10 (calculated as eventual increase in income, $100, divided by initial increase in income, $10). The multiplier can also be calculated as:
  - $1/(1 - MPC) = 1/(1 - 0.9) = 10$
- Now bringing taxes back into the frame, a $10 increase in government spending would result in taxes of $2 (assuming a tax rate of 20%). The recipients of the $10 from the government would have $8 in disposable income. They would spend $7.20 and save $0.80. The households that receive the $7.20 would pay $1.44 in taxes, spend $5.18, and save $0.58. The fiscal multiplier (assuming a 20% tax rate and an MPC of 90%) equals:
  - $$\frac{1}{[1 - MPC(1 - t)]} = \frac{1}{[1 - 0.9(1 - 0.2)]} = 3.57$$
  - The increase of $10 in government spending results in a $3.57 \times \$10 = \$35.70$ increase in aggregate spending/income.

The Balanced Budget Multiplier

An increase in government spending combined with an equivalent dollar increase in taxes leads to a higher real GDP. Consider an economy that has a GDP of $1,000 comprised entirely of consumption expenditure ($800) and investment expenditure ($200) only. Suppose that the government sets its spending at $100 financed by a tax rate of 10% (10% × $1,000 results in tax revenue of $100).

- The initial effect of the $100 increase in government spending will be an increase in income/output by $100.
- The initial effect of the $100 increase in taxes will be less than $100 as long as MPC is less than 1. This is because for every dollar less in disposable income, spending only falls by MPC.

- For example, if MPC equals 0.9, the increase in taxes will initially only reduce spending by MPC × ($100) = $90.
- The net initial effect would be an increase in spending of $100 − $90 = $10. This $10 increase would then lead to further increases in income through the multiplier effect.

Note that in the above scenario the higher government spending-higher tax combination only left the budgetary position unchanged (balanced) initially. Over time (through the multiplier effect) the induced rise in output would generate further tax revenue increases and affect the budgetary position.

Issues in Fiscal Policy Implementation

Deficits and the Fiscal Stance

The size of a fiscal deficit cannot be used to determine whether fiscal policy is expansionary or contractionary. Automatic stabilizers, for example, lead to changes in the budgetary status that are unrelated to fiscal policy changes. Therefore, economists look at the structural or cyclically adjusted budget deficit as an indicator of the government's fiscal stance. The structural deficit is the deficit that would exist were the economy working at full employment.

There is another reason why actual deficits may not be good indicators of the fiscal stance. Government expenditure includes the cash amount of payments on debt, which inflates the actual deficit. This is because the real value of outstanding debt falls with inflation. Therefore, it would be more appropriate to include real (or inflation-adjusted) interest payments in expenditure.

Difficulties in Executing Fiscal Policy

There are various reasons why governments do not use discretionary fiscal policy to stabilize aggregate demand and ensure that the economy always operates at full employment.

Recognition lag: This refers to the time that it takes the government to figure out that the economy is not functioning at potential output. A lot of data including unemployment rates, jobless claims, GDP growth, and inflation numbers must be analyzed before the state of the economy can be determined. This lag has been likened to "driving in the rear view mirror."

Action lag: Fiscal actions must be approved by Congress, and before approval there are numerous committee meetings and debates because members have different ideas regarding the most appropriate course of action. The government might have recognized the need for action, but its implementation may be delayed in obtaining the necessary approvals.

Impact lag: This refers to the time it takes for a fiscal stimulus to flow through the economy and generate the changes in spending patterns that are desired.

Macroeconomic forecasting models cannot be relied upon to aid policy-makers. A stimulus may occur at the same time as a sudden rise in domestic demand (e.g., due to a rise in investment spending). In such situations the government stimulus would do more harm than good. Further, given that mere announcements of fiscal stimuli can change consumption and investment behavior, it becomes difficult to determine the exact amount of fiscal adjustment that is needed.

Other Macroeconomic Issues

- If an economy is suffering from high unemployment and high inflation, raising aggregate demand will lead to higher prices.
- A government with a high national debt-GDP ratio may face difficulties in raising funds to further stimulate demand.
- The economy may already be operating at full employment (without the government knowing it).
- Private investment may be crowded out as government borrowing leads to high interest rates.
- The fact that there may be unused resources in the economy could be down to low labor supply (not necessarily low aggregate demand). In such a case, a fiscal stimulus will simply bring inflationary pressures to the economy.

LOS 18t: Explain the interaction of monetary and fiscal policy. Vol 2, pp 320–324

The Relationships Between Monetary and Fiscal Policy

Fiscal and monetary policies both affect aggregate demand, but use different channels. The following scenarios illustrate this (assume that wages and prices are rigid).

Easy fiscal policy/tight monetary policy: A decrease in taxes or an increase in government spending would increase aggregate demand. If money supply was reduced and interest rates increased, private sector demand would fall. The end result would be higher output, higher interest rates, and government expenditure would form a larger component of national income.

Tight fiscal policy/easy monetary policy: The private sector's share of overall GDP would rise (as a result of low interest rates), while the public sector's share would fall.

Easy fiscal policy/easy monetary policy: This would lead to a sharp increase in aggregate demand, lowering interest rates, and growing private and public sectors.

Tight fiscal policy/tight monetary policy: This would lead to a sharp decrease in aggregate demand, higher interest rates, and a decrease in demand from both private and public sectors.

Fiscal and monetary policies are not interchangeable. Further, they can work against each other unless the government and central bank coordinate their objectives.

Factors Influencing the Mix of Fiscal and Monetary Policy

- If the government is primarily concerned with growing the economy's potential output, it should aim to keep interest rates low and keep fiscal policy relatively tight to ensure that free resources are available in the growing economy.
- If the government's main concern is to build infrastructure and develop high-quality human capital, it should focus on spending in those areas. If monetary policy is kept loose during this time, inflation may result.

An IMF study concluded that:

When not accompanied by monetary accommodation:

- Increases in government spending have a much larger effect on GDP than similar-sized social transfers because transfers are not believed to be permanent. This is despite the fact that real interest rates rise as monetary authorities react to the increase in aggregate demand and inflation.
- Social transfers to the poorest citizens have more of an impact than nontargeted transfers.
- Labor tax reductions have a slightly greater impact than nontargeted transfers.

When accompanied by monetary accommodation:

- Fiscal multipliers are larger than when there is no monetary accommodation.
- These larger multipliers result from falling real interest rates, which in turn lead to additional private sector spending.

Further, credibility and commitment on the part of the government remain very important to the effectiveness of fiscal stimuli. Persistent high deficits raise real interest rates and crowd out private investment, limiting the economy's productive potential. As economic agents realize that these deficits are persistent, inflation expectations and long-term interest rates rise. This reduces the effectiveness of any stimulus. Further, if the ratio of government debt to GDP is allowed to rise, real interest rates would rise, reducing GDP.

One final note: We mentioned quantitative easing earlier, where the central bank purchases government or private securities from economic agents with the ultimate aim of stimulating spending in the economy. If the central bank purchases government securities on a large scale, it is essentially lending to the government. Stated differently, the central bank is funding the government's fiscal deficit, making central bank independence an "illusion."

READING 19: INTERNATIONAL TRADE AND CAPITAL FLOWS

LESSON 1: BASIC TERMINOLOGY: ABSOLUTE AND COMPARATIVE
ADVANTAGE

LOS 19a: Compare gross domestic product and gross national product.
Vol 2, pp 336–337

Gross Domestic Product (GDP) measures the market value of all **final** goods and services
produced by factors of production (e.g., labor, capital, etc.) located **within** a country/
economy during a period of time.

- GDP *includes* goods and services produced by foreigners within the country.
- GDP *excludes* goods and services produced by citizens outside the country.

Gross National Product (GNP) measures the market value of all **final** goods and services
produced by factors of production (e.g., labor, capital, etc.) supplied by the citizens of the
country, regardless of whether production takes place within or outside of the country.

- GNP *includes* goods and services produced by citizens outside the country.
- GNP *excludes* goods and services produced by foreigners within the country.

Analysts prefer to use GDP over GNP because it measures the value of goods and services
produced *within* the country, which have an impact on employment, growth, and the
investment environment in the domestic economy.

Imports refer to purchases of goods and services from other countries by the domestic
economy. Exports refer to sales of goods and services by the domestic economy to other
countries. The difference between the value of a country's exports and imports (exports
minus imports) is referred to as net exports.

- If the value of a country's exports equals the value of its imports, the country's
  trade is balanced.
- If the value of a country's exports is greater than the value of its imports, the country
  has a trade surplus. When a country has a trade surplus, it finances the trade deficits
  of its trading partners by lending to them or purchasing assets from them.
- If the value of a country's exports is less than the value of its imports, the country
  has a trade deficit. In such a situation, the country must borrow from foreigners or
  sell assets to them.

Terms of trade refer to the ratio of the price of exports to the price of imports. Export
and import prices are typically represented by price indices. The terms of trade measure
the relative cost of imports in terms of exports. If export prices improve relative to import
prices, the terms of trade are said to have "improved," as the country will be able to purchase
more imports with the same amount of exports. Since each country exports and imports a
wide variety of goods and services, the terms of trade are measured as an index number that
represents the ratio of the average price of exports to the average price of imports.

If a country does not participate in international trade, all goods and services are produced
and consumed domestically. Such an economy is referred to as an autarkic economy
or a closed economy and the price of a good or service in such an economy is called its
autarkic price. An open economy is one that does participate in international trade.

In the absence of trade restrictions, countries can trade freely with each other at prices prevailing in the world market (also called the world price). Under free trade, equilibrium quantities and prices of goods and services are determined by global aggregate demand and supply.

Trade restrictions (e.g., tariffs and quotas) imposed by governments are known as trade protection. Protectionist policies prevent free market forces from determining equilibrium quantity and price. Over the years, the increased role of multinational corporations (MNCs) and international institutions (like the WTO) in economies around the world has led to global integration of markets for goods, services, and capital.

When a firm in the source country makes an investment in the productive assets of the host country, it is referred to as foreign direct investment (FDI). The firm making the investment becomes an MNC, as it now operates in more than one geographical location. On the other hand, foreign portfolio investment (FPI) refers to shorter-term investments in foreign financial instruments (e.g., foreign stocks, foreign government bonds, etc.).

LOS 19b: Describe benefits and costs of international trade. Vol 2, pp 343–347

The fact that trade increases overall welfare does not mean that each individual in a country is better off as a result of international trade. What it means is that, on the whole, economies are better off and (in theory at least) winners can compensate losers and still be better off.

Benefits:
- Countries gain from exchange and specialization as trade enables them to receive a higher price for their exports (which increases profits) and pay a lower price (relative to the cost of goods produced domestically) for their imports. International trade results in more efficient resource allocation as countries can reduce domestic production of goods that they cannot produce efficiently (and instead import them) and increase production of goods that they are more efficient at producing (and export them). Specialization enables production and consumption of larger quantities of goods, which increases welfare.
- Domestic companies gain access to global markets and customers, which leads to increased exchange of ideas and greater awareness of changing consumer tastes and preferences.

Gains from specialization based on comparative advantage are described later in the reading.

- Capital-intensive industries gain access to much larger markets, enabling them to reap the benefits of economies of scale.
- Domestic households are able to choose from a wider variety of goods and services.
- Increased foreign competition reduces monopoly power of domestic firms and forces them to continuously strive to become more efficient.
- Trade liberalization can lead to higher inflation-adjusted GDP as a result of a more efficient allocation of resources, learning by doing, knowledge spillovers, and improved productivity.

Costs:
- Companies that are less efficient than international firms may go out of business if foreign firms are allowed to enter the market. This will lead to higher (structural) unemployment. These unemployed workers would need to be retrained for jobs in expanding industries.
- The counter argument is that despite the short- and medium-term costs and unemployment, these resources will eventually be reemployed in more efficient industries.

LOS 19c: Distinguish between comparative advantage and absolute advantage. Vol 2, pp 347–352

Absolute advantage refers to a country's ability to produce a good at a **lower cost** or using fewer resources than its trading partners. On the other hand, comparative advantage refers to a country's ability to produce a particular good at a **lower opportunity cost** than its trading partners. Example 1-1 should help clarify these concepts.

Example 1-1: Absolute and Comparative Advantages

Suppose there are only two countries, Germany and Bangladesh. These countries trade regularly with each other. Output per worker per day for cars and cloth is shown below:

Table 1-1: Output per Worker per Day

	Cars	Cloth (yards)
Germany	8	16
Bangladesh	4	32

Based only on the information given, answer the following questions:

1. Which country has an absolute advantage in the production of:
   a. Cars
   b. Cloth
2. Which country has a comparative advantage in the production of:
   a. Cars
   b. Cloth
3. Illustrate the gains for each country from trading based on comparative advantage.

Solutions:

1a. A worker in Germany is able to produce 8 cars per day, while a worker in Bangladesh is only able to produce 4 cars per day. Therefore, Germany has an absolute advantage in the production of cars.
1b. A worker in Bangladesh is able to produce 32 yards of cloth per day, while a worker in Germany is only able to produce 16 yards of cloth per day. Therefore, Bangladesh has an absolute advantage in the production of cloth.
2. On any given day, a German worker can produce either 16 yards of cloth or 8 cars. Therefore, the opportunity cost to Germany of producing a car is the $16/8 = 2$ yards of cloth sacrificed. Similarly, the opportunity cost to Germany of producing a yard of cloth is $8/16 =$ half a car. The opportunity costs of producing cars and cloth for both countries are shown in Table 1-2.

Table 1-2: Opportunity Costs

	Germany	Bangladesh
Opportunity cost of producing cars (in terms of cloth)	16/8 = 2	32/4 = 8
Opportunity cost of producing cloth (in terms of cars)	8/16 = 0.5	4/32 = 0.125

2a. Germany's opportunity cost of producing 1 car is 2 yards of cloth. On the other hand, Bangladesh's opportunity cost of producing 1 car is 8 yards of cloth. Since Germany has a lower opportunity cost of producing cars, it has a comparative advantage in the production of cars.

2b. Germany's opportunity cost of producing 1 yard of cloth is 0.5 cars. On the other hand, Bangladesh's opportunity cost of producing 1 yard of cloth is 0.125 cars. Since Bangladesh has a lower opportunity cost of producing cloth, it has a comparative advantage in the production of cloth.

3. If Germany is able to sell 1 car for more than 2 yards of cloth (which represents its opportunity cost of producing cars), and if Bangladesh is able to purchase 1 car for less than 8 yards of cloth (which represents its opportunity cost of producing cars), both countries would benefit from trade. Therefore, the world price for a car in terms of cloth should be between the autarkic prices of the trading partners (i.e., between 2 and 8 yards of cloth for one car).

The further away the world price of a good or service is from its autarkic price in a given country, the more that country benefits from trade. For example:

- If Germany were able to sell 1 car for 6 yards of cloth (closer to Bangladesh's autarkic price) it would gain an additional 4 yards of cloth per car sold to Bangladesh compared to its own autarkic price of 1 car for 2 yards of cloth.
- If Germany were able to sell 1 car for only 4 yards of cloth (closer to Germany's autarkic price) it would only gain an additional 2 yards of cloth per car sold to Bangladesh compared to its own autarkic price of 1 car for 2 yards of cloth.

Table 1-3 presents the total production and consumption of cars and cloth in Germany and Bangladesh, assuming that they are both autarkic economies.

Table 1-3: Production and Consumption in an Autarky

	Production	Consumption
Germany		
Cars	100	100
Cloth	200	200
Bangladesh		
Cars	50	50
Cloth	400	400
Global aggregates		
Cars	150	150
Cloth	600	600

In the absence of international trade:

- Domestic consumption of a good equals domestic production.
- Germany produces and consumes 100 cars and 200 yards of cloth.
- Bangladesh produces and consumes 50 cars and 400 yards of cloth.
- Global output equals 150 cars and 600 yards of cloth.

Now assume that Germany and Bangladesh start trading at a world price of 1 car = 4 yards of cloth. Note that this price is within the acceptable price range for both countries to benefit from trade (it lies between the autarkic prices of 1 car = 2 yards of cloth in Germany and 1 car = 8 yards of cloth in Bangladesh). Germany specializes in producing cars while Bangladesh specializes in producing cloth. Table 1-4 shows the production and consumption of cars and cloth in the two countries.

Table 1-4: Gains from Trade

	Production	Consumption
Germany		
Cars	200	130
Cloth	0	280
Bangladesh		
Cars	0	70
Cloth	800	520
Global aggregates		
Cars	200	200
Cloth	800	800

We assume that Germany exports 70 cars to Bangladesh in return for 280 yards of cloth (world price: 1 car = 4 yards of cloth). Once the economies open up, notice that:

- German consumption of cars equals 130 and its consumption of cloth equals 280.
  - Relative to autarkic levels, its consumption of cars rises by 30 units, while its consumption of cloth rises by 80 yards.
- Bangladesh's consumption of cars equals 70 and its consumption of cloth equals 520.
  - Relative to autarkic levels, its consumption of cars rises by 20 units, while its consumption of cloth rises by 120 yards.
- Global consumption of cars equals 200 and consumption of cloth equals 800.
  - Relative to autarkic levels, global consumption of cars rises by 50 units, while consumption of cloth rises by 200 yards.

Bottom Line: Total welfare has increased and both economies are better off with international trade than without.

We should point out here that even if a country does not have an absolute advantage in the production of a good or service, it (and its trading partners) can still gain from trade if it produces and exports goods in which it has a comparative advantage. For instance, if Bangladesh were only able to produce 10 yards of cloth per day instead of 32 yards of cloth (as stated in Table 1-1), Germany would have an absolute advantage in the production of both cars and cloth. However, Bangladesh would still have a comparative advantage in the production of cloth because its opportunity cost of producing 1 yard of cloth would be 4/10 = 0.4 cars, while Germany's opportunity cost of producing 1 yard of cloth would be 0.5 cars.

It is important for analysts to be able to examine the sources of a country's comparative and absolute advantages (e.g., government policy and regulations, demographics, human capital, and demand conditions) and to analyze changes in them. This information can help analysts identify sectors, industries, and companies that stand to benefit from these changes.

LOS 19d: Explain the Ricardian and Heckscher–Ohlin models of trade and the source(s) of comparative advantage in each model. Vol 2, pp 354–355

The Ricardian Model and the Heckscher–Ohlin Model attempt to explain the sources of comparative advantage for countries. The Ricardian Model focuses on differences in technology across countries, while the Heckscher–Ohlin Model focuses on differences in factor endowments.

Ricardian Model

- Assumes that labor is the only variable factor of production.
- A country gains a comparative advantage in the production of a good based on differences in labor productivity, which reflect underlying differences in technology.
- Differences in technology are the key source of comparative advantage.
- Even if the country is very small compared to the size of its trading partner, it will continue to produce the good that it holds a comparative advantage in and trade some of it to obtain other goods. Its trading partner will specialize in production of the good that it holds a comparative advantage in producing, but still continue to produce some of the good that the small country specializes in (due to the small quantities that it can import from its smaller trading partner).
- Technological gaps between countries can decrease over time, leading to shifts in comparative advantage.

Heckscher–Ohlin Model (also referred to as the factor-proportions theory)

- Assumes that both capital and labor are variable factors of production, so a good can be produced with varying combinations of the two.
- Technology is the same in each industry across countries, but it varies across different industries.
- Differences in factor endowments are the primary source of comparative advantage.
- A country has a comparative advantage in a good whose production requires intensive use of a factor with which it is relatively abundantly endowed.
  - For example, if a country has large quantities of labor (relative to capital), it would specialize in goods whose production is more labor-intensive and export them.
- Allows for redistribution of income through trade as it assumes that more than one factor of production is variable.
  - Specialization and trade increase demand for the factor that is used in the production of goods that the country exports and decrease demand for factors used in the production of goods that the country imports. For an economy with abundant labor, increased demand for labor-intensive goods results in an increase in wages. Over time, income is redistributed from capital to labor in such economies.
- Theoretically, free trade should eventually result in equal prices of goods and services and equal prices of factors of production across countries.
  - However, in the real world trade only results in a tendency for factor prices to converge in the long run.

Note that differences in technology and differences in factor endowments are both important drivers of trade so the two theories are complementary, not mutually exclusive.

LESSON 2: TRADE AND CAPITAL FLOWS: RESTRICTIONS AND AGREEMENTS

LOS 19e: Compare types of trade and capital restrictions and their economic implications. Vol 2, pp 356–361

Trade Restrictions

Arguments for Trade Restrictions
- Protection of established domestic industries from foreign competition.
- Protection of new (infant) industries from foreign competition until they mature.
- Protection of employment in the country.
- Generation of revenue from tariffs.
- Retaliation against trade restrictions imposed by trading partners.

Tariffs

Tariffs are taxes levied on imports. Figure 2-1 illustrates the impact of a tariff. With free trade, at the world price (P_W) domestic demand equals Q_{D0} and domestic supply equals Q_{S0}. The shortage in supply is met by imports ($Q_{D0} - Q_{S0}$). When the government imposes a tariff on imports, the price effectively rises to P_T. Domestic demand falls to Q_{D1}, domestic supply rises to Q_{S1}, and the volume of imports falls to $Q_{D1} - Q_{S1}$.

Figure 2-1: Welfare Effects of Tariffs and Import Quotas

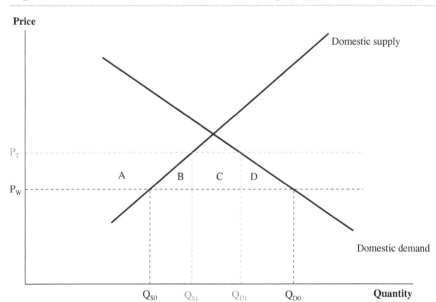

- The government managed to lower the trade deficit (by decreasing imports) but it has also managed to earn some revenue for itself (Region C).
- There is an increase in producer surplus (Region A) as domestic suppliers now get a higher price (P_T versus P_W earlier) and sell higher output (Q_{S1} versus Q_{S0} earlier).

Consumer surplus, producer surplus, and deadweight loss are defined and discussed in the prerequisite reading "Demand and Supply Analysis: Introduction" available in your online platform.

- Consumer surplus falls (Regions B, C, and D) as domestic consumers pay a higher price (PT versus PW earlier) and consume lower quantities (Q_{D1} versus Q_{D0} earlier).
- The overall effect is a net decrease in welfare equal to the area of Regions B and D.

Tariffs result in deadweight losses because they give rise to inefficiencies on the consumption and production front.

- On the production front, inefficient domestic producers whose cost of production is greater than P_W (but less than P_T) are also allowed to operate.
- On the consumption front, buyers who are willing to pay more than P_W but less than P_T are no longer able to consume.

The above analysis focused on a country that was relatively small, or a price-taker in the world market. When a large country (that is a large consumer) imposes a tariff on imports, the exporting country may lower its price in order to retain its share of the market in the importing country. This reduction in price represents a redistribution of income from the exporting country to the importing country. A large country can increase its own welfare if the improvement in terms of trade from the imposition of the tariff outweighs the associated deadweight loss and if its trading partners do not retaliate. However, there will always be an overall reduction in welfare as the increase in welfare in the large country cannot outweigh the welfare loss to its trading partner.

Quotas

Quotas are restrictions on the quantity of a good that can be imported into a country for a specified period. When a quota is in place, each importing firm receives an import license, which specifies the quantity that it can import.

The main difference between tariffs and quotas is that the government earns direct revenue through tariffs, but this is not the case with quotas. With a quota, foreign producers may raise their prices to earn higher profits than they would in the absence of the quota. These profits are known as quota rents.

Quota rents arising from a quota can be captured by the exporting country or the importing country.

In Figure 1-1, if the quota equals $Q_{D1} - Q_{S1}$, the price after quota would equal P_T (which is the same as the after-tariff price). However, Region C (previously government revenue from the tariff) is now more likely to be captured by foreign producers (quota rents), increasing the welfare loss for the importing country to Regions B + C + D (relative to just Regions B + D under a tariff). If the importing country can generate an amount equal to Area C by auctioning import licenses for a fee, then its welfare loss can be limited to just Regions B + D (as is the case with tariffs).

Voluntary Export Restraints

Voluntary Export Restraints (VERs) are restrictions on the quantity of a good that can be exported. While quotas are imposed by the importing country, VERs are imposed by the exporting country. Under VERs, the exporting country captures the quota rent (Region C), but the welfare loss to the importing country equals (Regions B + C + D).

Export Subsidies

Export subsidies refer to payments made by the government to domestic exporters of certain goods. While they aim to stimulate exports, export subsidies interfere with the free market mechanism and may result in trade patterns that diverge from those dictated by comparative advantage. Further, domestic producers would be more inclined to export their output rather than selling it in the domestic market.

- If the exporting country is a large country (or price searcher), export subsidies will result in a reduction in the world price as global supply increases. The local economy will incur a welfare loss, but the decline in world price will increase welfare in other countries (a part of the subsidy will be transferred abroad).
- If the exporting country is a small country (or price taker), the domestic price will rise by the per-unit amount of the subsidy.
  ○ However, the total loss in welfare in the exporting country will be less than the loss that would occur were the country a price searcher.

Table 2-1 summarizes some of these effects.

Table 2-1: Effects of Alternative Trade Policies[1]

Panel A: Effects of Alternative Trade Policies

	Tariff	Import Quota	Export Subsidy	VER
Impact on	Importing country	Importing country	Exporting country	Importing country
Producer surplus	Increases	Increases	Increases	Increases
Consumer surplus	Decreases	Decreases	Decreases	Decreases
Government revenue	Increases	Mixed (depends on whether the quota rents are captured by the importing country through sale of licenses or by the exporters)	Falls (government spending rises)	No change (rent to foreigners)
National welfare	Decreases in small country	Decreases in small country	Decreases	Decreases
	Could increase in large country	Could increase in large country		

Panel B: Effects of Alternative Trade Policies on Price, Production, Consumption, and Trade

	Tariff	Import Quota	Export Subsidy	VER
Impact on	Importing country	Importing country	Exporting country	Importing country
Price	Increases	Increases	Increases	Increases
Domestic consumption	Decreases	Decreases	Decreases	Decreases
Domestic production	Increases	Increases	Increases	Increases
Trade	Imports decrease	Imports decrease	Exports increase	Imports decrease

1 - Exhibit 13, Volume 2, CFA Program Curriculum 2018

LOS 19g: Describe common objectives of capital restrictions imposed by governments. Vol 2, pp 366–369

CAPITAL RESTRICTIONS

Capital restrictions are defined as controls placed on foreigners' ability to own domestic assets and/or domestic citizens' ability to own foreign assets.

Common Objectives
- The government may place restrictions on inward investment by foreigners relating to how much can be invested, and in which industries.
  - The government may impose ownership restrictions on strategic industries such as defense and telecommunications.
  - The government may forbid foreign investment into certain industries to protect domestic companies from foreign competition, and to protect jobs.
- The government may place restrictions on outflow of capital from repatriation of capital, interest, profits, royalty payments, and license fees, and on foreign investments by its citizens in order to conserve scarce foreign exchange reserves.
- Capital restrictions are often used in conjunction with other policy instruments, such as fixed exchange rate targets to achieve policy objectives in times of macroeconomic crises.
  - Capital controls are used to control the economy's external balance, while other, more traditional policy tools are used to pursue other objectives.
  - For example, consider China, who pegs its currency to the USD and imposes restrictions on capital inflows and outflows. Capital controls allow China to maintain the exchange rate peg, while at the same time shielding domestic interest rates from external market forces.

Forms of Capital Controls
- Taxes.
- Price controls, which can take the form of:
  - Special taxes on returns on international investments.
  - Taxes on certain types of transactions.
  - Mandatory reserve requirements (i.e., foreign parties wishing to deposit money in a domestic bank must first deposit a certain amount at the central bank at zero interest for a minimum period).
- Quantity controls, which can take the form of:
  - Ceilings on borrowings from foreign creditors.
  - Requiring special authorization for borrowings from foreign creditors.
  - Requiring government approval for certain transactions.
- Outright prohibitions on international trade in assets.

Benefits of Free Movement of Financial Capital
- Allows capital to be invested wherever it will earn the highest return.
- The economy's productive capacity can grow at a higher rate than possible based on domestic savings alone.

- Foreign firms may enter domestic industries, bringing competition to local firms, which may:
    - Encourage local firms to improve the quality of their goods and services.
    - Lead to better prices.
    - Bring new technologies into the country.

Effectiveness of Capital Controls

An IMF study found that:

- Effective controls on capital inflows entail significant administrative costs.
- Imposition of controls on capital outflows during times of financial crisis have produced mixed results.
- They have only provided temporary relief to some countries, but offered others (e.g., Malaysia in 1997) enough time to restructure their economies.
- If the government is wary of capital leaving the country, capital controls (when combined with fixed exchange rates) afford the central bank a degree of monetary policy independence that would not be possible without capital controls.

Costs of Capital Controls
- Administrative costs.
- Controls may give rise to negative market perceptions and make it more costly for the country to raise foreign funds.
- Protection of domestic financial markets may delay necessary policy adjustments or impede private-sector adaptation to changing international circumstances.

LOS 19f: Explain motivations for and advantages of trading blocs, common markets, and economic unions. Vol 2, pp 362–366

Members of a regional trading agreement (RTA) agree to eliminate barriers to trade and movement of factors of production among the members of the bloc. Members may or may not have similar policies regarding trade restrictions against nonmember countries. Depending on the level of integration, there are different types of trade agreements.

Members of a free trade area (FTA), for example NAFTA, eliminate almost all barriers to free trade with each other. However, each member still maintains its own policies regarding trade with nonmember countries.

A customs union (e.g., Benelux) is very similar to an FTA, but all member countries have similar policies regarding trade with nonmember countries.

A common market (e.g., MERCOSUR) incorporates all the provisions of a customs union and also allows free movement of factors of production among the member countries.

An economic union (e.g., EU) incorporates all the aspects of a common market and also requires common economic institutions and coordination of economic policies among member countries. If the members of the economic union decide to adopt a common currency, it is also referred to as a monetary union.

Countries usually prefer regional integration over multilateral trade negotiations under the World Trade Organization (WTO) because regional integration is:

- Easier to achieve.
- Takes less time.
- Politically less contentious.

It is generally believed that, by reducing barriers to trade, member countries are able to allocate resources more efficiently. However, this is not always the case. Regional integration usually results in trade creation and trade diversion, and only if trade creation is larger than trade diversion is there a positive net effect on welfare from forming the trade bloc.

- Trade creation occurs when higher-cost domestic production is replaced with lower-cost imports from fellow members of a trade bloc.
- Trade diversion occurs when lower-cost imports from nonmember countries are replaced with higher-cost imports from member countries (because tariffs are imposed on imports from nonmember countries but not on imports from member countries).

Advantages of Trade Blocs

All the benefits of free trade (greater specialization, reduction in monopoly power due to competition, economies of scale, learning by doing, knowledge spillovers, technology transfers, better quality intermediate inputs, etc.) apply to trade blocs as well. Aside from these benefits, trade blocs also offer the following benefits to their members:

- Reduce the potential for conflict among members.
- Give members greater bargaining power in the global economy as they form a united front.
- Offer new opportunities for trade and investment.
- Typically, growth in a member country tends to spill over into other members as well.

Challenges in the Formation of an RTA

- Cultural differences and historical conflicts may complicate the process of integration.
- Free trade and mobility of labor limit the extent to which member countries can pursue independent economic and social policies.

The balance of payments (BOP) is a double entry bookkeeping system that summarizes a country's economic transactions with the rest of the world over a period of time. Table 2-2 summarizes basic debit and credit entries in the BOP context.

Table 2-2: Basic Entries in a BOP Context[2]

Debits (Increase in Assets, Decrease in Liabilities)	Credits (Decrease in Assets, Increase in Liabilities)
Value of imported goods and services	Payments for imports of goods and services
Purchases of foreign financial assets	Payments for foreign financial assets
Receipt of payments from foreigners	Value of exported goods and services
Increase in debt owed by foreigners	Payment of debt by foreigners
Payment of debt owed to foreigners	Increase in debt owed to foreigners

> While you would expect the net balance of all BOP entries to equal 0, this is rarely the case in practice because the data used to record BOP transactions are compiled from different sources so there are always statistical discrepancies.

Balance of Payment Components

A country's balance of payments is composed of three main accounts:

1. The current account balance largely reflects trade in goods and services.
2. The capital account balance mainly consists of capital transfers and net sales of nonproduced, nonfinancial assets.
3. The financial account measures net capital flows based on sales and purchases of domestic and foreign financial assets.

The current account can be decomposed into the following subaccounts:

- Merchandise trade consists of all commodities and manufactured goods bought, sold, or given away.
- Services include tourism, transportation, engineering, and business services.
- Income receipts include income from ownership of foreign assets (e.g., interest and dividends).
- Unilateral transfers represent one-way transfers of assets (e.g., worker remittances, foreign aid, and gifts).

The capital account can be decomposed into the following subaccounts:

- Capital transfers include debt forgiveness and migrants' transfers. They also include:
  - Transfer of ownership of fixed assets.
  - Transfer of funds received for the sale or acquisition of fixed assets.
  - Gift and inheritance taxes.

---

2 - Exhibit 14 Panel A, Volume 2, CFA Program Curriculum 2018

- ○ Death duties.
- ○ Uninsured damage to fixed assets.
- Sales and purchases of nonproduced, nonfinancial assets such as rights to natural resources, intangible assets (e.g., patents, copyrights, etc.).

The financial account can be decomposed into the following subaccounts:

- Financial assets abroad are composed of:
    - ○ Official reserve assets.
    - ○ Government assets.
    - ○ Private assets.
  These assets include gold, foreign currencies, foreign securities, the government's reserve position at the IMF, direct foreign investment, and claims reported by resident banks.
- Foreign owned financial assets in the reporting country are composed of:
    - ○ Official assets.
    - ○ Other foreign assets.
  These assets include securities issued by the reporting country's government and private sectors, direct investment, and foreign liabilities reported by the reporting country's banking sector.

LESSON 3: THE BALANCE OF PAYMENTS AND TRADE ORGANIZATIONS

LOS 19h: Describe the balance of payments accounts including their components. Vol 2, pp 369–376

LOS 19i: Explain how decisions by consumers, firms, and governments affect the balance of payments. Vol 2, pp 377–381

National Economic Accounts and the Balance of Payments

The national income identity for an open economy is:

$$Y = C + I + G + X - M \quad \text{... Equation 1}$$

The current account balance is important because it measures the size and direction of international borrowing. A current account balance must be offset by an opposite balance in the capital and financial accounts. Therefore:

- A current account deficit must be financed by foreign direct investment, loans by foreign banks, or the sale of domestic debt and equity securities to foreign investors.
- A current account surplus is used to finance the current account deficit of trading partners (through loans and investments in real and financial assets).

Equation 1 can be rearranged into the following form:

$$CA = X - M = Y - (C + I + G) \quad \text{... Equation 2}$$

- A country can have a current account deficit and consume more than it produces (C + I + G greater than Y) if it borrows the shortfall from foreigners.
- A country can have a current account surplus and consume less than it produces (C + I + G less than Y) if it lends the excess to foreigners.

Also note that a current account deficit occurs when spending in the economy (C + I + G) is relatively high. In such times, demand for credit is also high, which increases interest rates. These higher interest rates lead to net capital inflows and result in an appreciating currency. With persistent current account deficits in the long run however, an increase in net borrowing from foreigners results in significant risk being associated with the country's debt, leading to currency depreciation.

> It would help you immensely if you were to readily associate a current account deficit with net borrowing from foreigners or net capital inflows from abroad. Similarly, current account surpluses are associated with net lending to foreigners or net capital outflows from the domestic economy.

International capital flows reflect intertemporal trades. An economy with a current account deficit is essentially importing current consumption and exporting future consumption.

Now we turn to the relationship between output, Y, and disposable income, Y_D (which equals output + Transfers (R) – Taxes)

$$\boxed{Y_D = Y + R - T} \quad \text{... Equation 3}$$

Disposable income is allocated between consumption and saving (private sector saving, S_P)

$$\boxed{Y_D = C + S_P} \quad \text{... Equation 4}$$

Combining Equations 3 and 4, we can express consumption as:

$$\boxed{C = Y_D - S_P = Y + R - T - S_P} \quad \text{... Equation 5}$$

Now substituting the right side of Equation 5 for C in Equation 2:

$$\boxed{\begin{aligned} CA &= X - M = Y - (C + I + G) = Y - (Y + R - T - S_P + I + G) \\ CA &= S_P - I + (T - G - R) \end{aligned}} \quad \text{... Equation 6}$$

(T – G – R) equals the government's budget surplus or government saving (S_G). Therefore, Equation 6 can be expressed as:

> You do not need to know how to derive these equations, but do make sure you understand their implications.

$$\boxed{S_P + S_G = I + CA} \quad \text{... Equation 7}$$

Equation 7 highlights an important difference between open and closed economies.

- In a closed economy, savings can only be used for domestic investment.
- In an open economy, savings can be used for domestic and foreign investment.

The point here is that an open country with tremendous opportunities for growth will not have its potential to invest in the economy (to avail those opportunities) limited by domestic savings. The country can raise investment by attracting foreign saving (running a current account deficit) without having to increase domestic saving.

Equation 7 can be rearranged into the following form:

$$\boxed{S_P = I + CA - S_G} \quad \text{... Equation 8}$$

This equation clearly shows that an economy's private savings can be used for:

- Domestic investment.
- Foreign investment (purchasing assets from foreigners).
- Purchasing government debt.

Finally, if we make CA the subject in Equation 8:

$$CA = S_P + S_G - I \quad \text{... Equation 9}$$

We can see that a current account deficit results from:

- Low private savings.
- A government deficit.
- High private investment.

If a country running a trade deficit mainly borrows to finance consumption, then eventually it must reduce consumption to repay its debts. If the borrowings are mainly used to finance investment, then future economic growth is likely to provide the means to repay its liabilities.

LOS 19j: Describe functions and objectives of the international organizations that facilitate trade, including the World Bank, the International Monetary Fund, and the World Trade Organization. Vol 2, pp 381–388

World Bank Group

The World Bank's main objective is to fight poverty and enhance environmentally sound economic growth. The World Bank and its affiliated entities:

- Provide cheap loans and grants to countries that have limited or no access to international financial markets.
- Provide analysis, advice, and information to countries to encourage social and economic development.
- Share knowledge and promote dialogue to increase the capabilities of their partners and members.
- Help members create the basic economic infrastructure that is essential for the development of domestic financial markets.

World Trade Organization (WTO)

The WTO's primary objective is to enhance and liberalize international trade.

- The WTO's important functions include the implementation, administration, and operation of individual agreements, providing a platform for negotiations and settling trade disputes.
- It also provides technical cooperation and training to developing, under developed, and poor countries to bring them in compliance with WTO rules.
- It reviews members trade policies on a regular basis and ensures coherence and transparency of trade policies through surveillance.

- It is a major source of economic research and analysis.
- Its framework of global trade rules provides a major institutional and regulatory base, without which large multinationals would not be able to operate on such a large scale.

International Monetary Fund

The main objective of the IMF is to ensure the stability of the international monetary system, the system of exchange rates and international payments that enables countries to participate in international trade. More specifically, the IMF:

- Provides a forum for cooperation on international monetary problems.
- Facilitates the growth of international trade, thereby promoting job creation, economic growth, and poverty reduction.
- Promotes exchange rate stability and an open system of international payments.
- Lends foreign exchange to member countries when needed, on a temporary basis and under adequate safeguards, to help them address balance of payments problems.

In the aftermath of the global financial crisis of 2007 to 2009, the IMF has redefined its operations by:

- Enhancing its lending facilities.
- Strengthening the monitoring of global, regional, and country economies.
- Helping to resolve global economic imbalances.
- Analyzing capital market developments.
- Assessing financial sector vulnerabilities.
- Working to cut poverty.

From an investment perspective the IMF helps to keep country-specific market risk and global systematic risk under control.

READING 20: CURRENCY EXCHANGE RATES

LESSON 1: THE FOREIGN EXCHANGE MARKET

LOS 20a: Define an exchange rate and distinguish between nominal and real exchange rates and spot and forward exchange rates. Vol 2, pp 401–406

An exchange rate represents the price of one currency in terms of another currency. It is stated in terms of the number of units of a particular currency (price currency) required to purchase a unit of another currency (base currency). Stated differently, it is the cost of one unit of the base currency in terms of the price currency.

In this reading, we will refer to exchange rates using the convention "A/B," that is, number of units of Currency A (price currency) required to purchase one unit of Currency B (base currency). For example, suppose that the USD/GBP exchange rate is currently 1.5125. From this exchange rate quote we can infer that:

- The GBP is the base currency and USD is the price currency.
- It will take 1.5125 USD to purchase 1 GBP.
- 1 GBP will buy 1.5125 USD or 1 GBP costs 1.5125 USD.
- A decrease in this exchange rate (e.g., to 1.5120) means that 1 GBP will be able to purchase fewer USD.
- Alternatively, less USD will now be required to purchase 1 GBP (the cost of a GBP has fallen).
- This decrease in the exchange rate means that the GBP has depreciated (lost value) against the USD, or equivalently, the USD has appreciated (gained value) against the GBP.
- It would help you to think of exchange rates in the following manner: An increase in the quoted exchange rate (price/base) means an increase (appreciation) in the value of the currency in the denominator (base currency) and a decrease (depreciation) in the value of the currency in the numerator (price currency).
- The numerical value of the exchange rate and the value of the base currency are positively related.
- The numerical value of the exchange rate and the value of the price currency are negatively related.

Nominal and Real Exchange Rates
- When the value of a currency is stated in terms of units of another currency (as in the example above), it is referred to as a nominal exchange rate.
- On the other hand, real exchange rates measure changes in the relative purchasing power of one currency compared with another.

If all goods around the world were homogeneous, markets were frictionless, and there were no trade barriers, the relative purchasing power of consumers across countries would be equal. A consumer would not be willing to pay a higher price in real terms for a cell phone in her home country if she could import an identical cell phone from overseas at a cheaper price. This concept is the basis for purchasing power parity (PPP), which asserts that nominal exchange rates adjust to ensure that identical goods (or baskets of goods) have the same price in different countries. Another way of saying this is that the purchasing power of all currencies (in terms of a standardized basket of goods) should be the same. For example, if a basket of goods costs 2 GBP in the U.K. and 3 USD in the United States, the nominal exchange rate should be 1.5 USD/GBP. A consumer would be

> Just like the price of any product, an exchange rate reflects the price of the currency in the denominator. For example, a price of $5/bag of chips reflects the price of a bag of chips (base or denominator) in terms of the price currency (USD). Similarly, a price (exchange rate) of $2/GBP is the price of GBP (base currency) in terms of USD (price currency). An increase in the price of chips (e.g., to $6/bag) means that the value of a bag of chips (the item in the denominator) in terms of USD has risen. Similarly, an increase in the exchange rate to $3/GBP implies an increase in the value of GBP (currency in the denominator).

> Note that real exchange rates are only indices created by analysts to understand the real purchasing power of a currency; they are not quoted or traded in global FX markets.

indifferent between purchasing the basket from either country. Whether she purchases it from the U.K. or the United States, the exchange rate ensures that it costs her the same (2 GBP × 1.5 USD/GBP = 3 USD).

Due to a number of reasons (e.g., the existence of trade barriers and transaction costs, differences in consumption baskets across countries, etc.) nominal exchange rates persistently deviate from PPP. Therefore, in order to evaluate changes in relative purchasing power across countries, analysts look at movements in real exchange rates. Before we dive into factors that affect the real exchange rate, let's look at purchasing power.

Suppose you live in the United States and earn income in USD. As a consumer, you always want to see an increase in your purchasing power, as it makes you better off in real terms. The purchasing power of your USD is influenced by the following factors:

- The nominal exchange rate: An increase in the nominal exchange rate (quoted in terms of units of domestic currency per unit of foreign currency: DC/FC), means that the foreign currency has become more costly in terms of the domestic currency or the foreign currency has gained value (appreciated). This means that your ability to purchase goods from the foreign country has fallen (as your currency, the USD, has declined in value). Therefore, the nominal exchange rate and relative purchasing power are **inversely** related.
- The price level in the foreign country (or foreign inflation): An increase in the price level in the foreign country will mean that you will be able to purchase fewer foreign goods (decreases your purchasing power). Therefore, the foreign price level and relative purchasing power are **inversely** related.
- The price level in the home country (or domestic inflation): An increase in domestic prices (assuming that domestic price level is directly proportional to your income) means that you will now be able to purchase more foreign goods (increases your purchasing power). Therefore, the domestic price level and relative purchasing power are **positively** related.

> The real exchange rate can be seen as the real price an individual faces when purchasing foreign goods and services. The higher the real exchange rate, the lower will be an individual's relative purchasing power.

An increase in purchasing power implies a decrease in the real exchange rate (in terms of DC/FC) (i.e., purchasing power and the real exchange rate are **inversely** related). A *decrease* in the real exchange rate implies that in real terms, fewer units of DC are needed to purchase a unit of FC, which means that domestic currency has *increased* in real value relative to the foreign currency (which makes domestic consumers better off). Therefore, we can say that the real exchange rate is:

- An increasing function of the nominal exchange rate (in terms of DC/FC).
- An increasing function of the foreign price level.
- A decreasing function of the domestic price level.

The real exchange rate may be calculated as:

$$\text{Real exchange rate}_{DC/FC} = S_{DC/FC} \times (P_{FC} / P_{DC})$$

where:
$S_{DC/FC}$ = Nominal spot exchange rate
P_{FC} = Foreign price level quoted in terms of the foreign currency
P_{DC} = Domestic price level quoted in terms of the domestic currency

> **Example 1-1: Nominal and Real Exchange Rates**
>
> Over a period of time, Alexis (a U.S. resident) notes that the nominal exchange rate (USD/EUR) has decreased by 3%, the price level in the Eurozone has increased by 5%, while the price level in the United States has increased by 6%. Compute the change in the real exchange rate and interpret your results.
>
> **Solutions:**
>
> $$\text{Change in real exchange rate} = (1 - 3\%) \times \left(\frac{1 + 5\%}{1 + 6\%} \right) - 1 = -3.92\%$$
>
> $$\text{Change in real exchange rate} \approx \Delta S_{DC/FC} + \Delta P_{FC} - \Delta P_{DC}$$
>
> $$\text{Change in real exchange rate} \approx -3\% + 5\% - 6\% \approx -4\%$$

The real exchange rate (in terms of USD/EUR) has *declined* by about 4%, which means that it now costs Alexis *less* in real terms to buy European goods. Alexis's purchasing power relative to the Eurozone has *increased*.

> Think of the real exchange rate as the real price of the currency in the denominator in terms of the currency in the numerator. If the real price of the currency in the denominator, the real exchange rate, falls, it implies higher purchasing power for the currency in the numerator.

- Because U.S. inflation was higher than the Eurozone's (6% versus 5%), the real exchange rate has declined more rapidly than the nominal exchange rate (4% versus 3%). The formula: Change in real ER = $\Delta S_{DC/FC} + \Delta P_{FC} - \Delta P_{DC}$ will help you understand this relationship.
- The combination of the stronger USD (weaker Euro) and higher U.S. inflation have resulted in a decline in the real exchange rate, *increasing* U.S. purchasing power in Euro terms.

Movements in real and nominal exchange rates affect relative prices and trade flows. Even if the nominal exchange rate remains unchanged, differences in inflation rates across countries affect relative purchasing power and hence, relative competitiveness of countries. Note that real exchange rates are just one of several factors that have an effect on nominal exchange rates, which is why changes in real exchange rates are generally poor predictors of changes in nominal exchange rates.

Some important points:

- An increase in the USD/EUR exchange rate increases the USD-denominated value of Alexis's investments in the Eurozone.
- If Alexis were to use income generated in the Eurozone to meet certain expenses in Europe, changes in the USD/EUR spot rate would not be relevant.

Spot and Forward Exchange Rates

Spot exchange rates (S) are quotes for transactions that call for immediate delivery. For most currencies, immediate delivery means "T + 2" delivery (i.e., the transaction is actually settled 2 days after the trade is agreed upon by the parties). The spot exchange rate is the rate that we hear about on the news. However, spot transactions make up a relatively small portion of total turnover in the global FX market.

Forward exchange rates (F) are quotes for transactions that are contracted (agreed upon) today, but settled at a pre-specified date in the future (settlement occurs after a longer period than the two days for spot transactions). For example, assume that a Chinese company will receive €100,000 in 70 days. One option for the company is to enter into a spot transaction after 68 days (with T+2 settlement) to sell €100,000 at the then-current spot rate. This future spot rate is currently unknown and gives rise to foreign exchange risk for the company. Specifically, the company is worried about a decline in the CNY/EUR exchange rate (depreciation of the Euro) as it would reduce the CNY-denominated value of its Euro receipts. The company can hedge this risk by entering into a forward contract today to sell €100,000 in 70 days at the forward exchange rate (which would be agreed upon today).

Several other types of contracts are used for trading currencies:

FX swaps and FX options are dealt with in more detail at Level II.

- **Futures contracts** are *standardized* contracts that trade on *exchanges* (e.g., Chicago Mercantile Exchange), in contrast to forward contracts that are *customized* and are traded on *over-the-counter (OTC) markets*. Although there are technical differences between forward and futures contracts, the underlying concept is the same: the price is agreed upon today for settlement at a specified future date. Forwards and futures are described in more detail in later readings.
- An **FX swap** consists of simultaneous spot and forward transactions. FX swap transactions are undertaken for the purpose of extending (rolling) an existing forward position to a new future date. Note that the process of rolling the position (on to a new future date) leads to a cash flow on the settlement date, which effectively serves as a mark-to-market on the forward position. FX swaps may also be used by companies that need to borrow in some other currency (swap funding). Use of FX swaps is illustrated in the Derivatives section.
- **FX options**: These are contracts that, in return for an upfront premium or fee, give the purchaser the right, but not the obligation, to make an FX transaction (buy or sell) at some pre-specified future date at an exchange rate agreed upon today. Options are only exercised if it is advantageous for the holder to do so (i.e., the exchange rate specified in the option contract is better than the exchange rate prevailing in the market at option expiration).

Market participants typically use a combination of spot, forward, swap, and option contracts to manage their specific FX risk exposures. Further, FX transactions are also frequently used in conjunction with transactions in other financial markets (e.g., equities, fixed income, etc.).

LOS 20b: Describe functions of and participants in the foreign exchange market. Vol 2, pp 406–418

Functions of the Foreign Exchange Market
- FX markets facilitate international trade in goods and services, allowing individuals and companies to purchase items produced in foreign countries.
- FX markets allow investors to convert between currencies in order to move funds into (or out of) foreign assets. The bulk of FX market volume comes from capital market transactions, which include direct investments (e.g., investments in fixed assets in other countries) and portfolio investments (e.g., the purchase of stocks, bonds, and other financial assets denominated in foreign currencies).

- Market participants who face exchange rate risk hedge their risks through a variety of FX instruments.
- Other market participants undertake FX transactions to speculate on currency values. They aim to profit from their views regarding future changes in exchange rates.

Market Participants

FX market participants can be broadly categorized as buy side and sell side. The sell side includes large FX trading banks, while the buy side consists of clients who use these banks to undertake FX transactions (buy FX products).

Sell Side

- The very largest dealing banks: Maintaining a competitive advantage in the FX market requires large investments in the technology that connects the FX market, as well as a broad, global client base. Only the largest FX trading banks (e.g., Deutsche Bank, Citigroup, UBS, HSBC) are able to compete successfully and provide competitive price quotes across a wide range of financial products. These institutions are also able to cross a large proportion of their business internally (i.e., connect buyers and sellers from within their customer base to execute transactions).
- All other regional and local banks fall into the second and third tier of the FX market sell-side. These financial institutions may have well-developed business relationships, but they lack the economies of scale and global client base required to compete successfully in the global FX market on their own. As a result, they outsource FX services to the larger tier-one banks.

Buy Side

Corporate accounts: Corporations enter into FX transactions for:

- Cross-border purchases and sales of goods and services.
- Cross-border investment flows (e.g., international M&A transactions, investments in foreign assets, and foreign currency borrowings).

Real money accounts: These are investment funds managed by insurance companies, mutual funds, pension funds, endowments, exchange-traded funds (ETFs), and other institutional investors. The term real money is used to refer to these accounts because they typically face restrictions on their use of leverage and financial derivatives.

Leveraged accounts: Often referred to as the professional trading community, leveraged accounts include hedge funds, proprietary trading shops, and all trading accounts that accept and manage FX for profit. These trading accounts vary widely in terms of their trading styles and form a growing proportion of daily FX market turnover.

Retail accounts: These include individuals, such as tourists, who exchange currencies from retail outlets. Note that with the advent of online trading technology there has been quite a surge in speculative trading by retail accounts.

Governments: Public entities may enter FX markets for transactional purposes or to achieve public policy goals of the government. Governments (both at the federal and state level) also issue debt in foreign currencies, which results in FX flows.

Central banks: These entities may enter FX markets to influence the level or trend in the domestic exchange rate. Central bank intervention may occur when:

- The domestic currency has become too weak or too strong such that it no longer reflects underlying economic fundamentals.
- Appreciation of the domestic currency is hurting the country's exports (e.g., Bank of Japan [BOJ] in late 2010).
- The exchange rate has become too volatile for businesses to transact in the FX market. The central bank also manages a country's foreign exchange reserves. Countries that have significant foreign exchange reserves (e.g., China) can have a very significant impact on exchange rates even if they are not intervening for public policy purposes.

Sovereign wealth funds (SWFs): Countries with large persistent capital account surpluses have recently started investing their capital flows into SWFs (that are managed for pure investment purposes), rather than hold them as FX reserves (that are managed by the central bank very conservatively).

To summarize, there is a wide variety of FX market participants with different trading motives and strategies. This makes it very difficult to analyze and accurately predict movements in FX rates.

Market Size and Composition
- Investment pools and professional traders account for a large (and growing) proportion of FX market volumes. Portfolio flows and speculative activities dominate FX market volumes.
- High-frequency algorithmic traders are accounting for a growing proportion of FX market volumes.
- Purchases and sales of foreign goods and services by individuals and corporations form a relatively small proportion of FX market volumes.
- London, New York, and Tokyo account for the highest FX market volumes.
- The majority of FX market transactions occur in the FX swap market.

LESSON 2: CURRENCY EXCHANGE RATE CALCULATIONS: PART 1

LOS 20c: Calculate and interpret the percentage change in a currency relative to another currency. Vol 2, pp 418–421

Exchange Rate Quotations

Recap: Exchange rates are quoted in terms of the number of units of a currency that are required to purchase one unit of another currency. An exchange rate quote of A/B represents the number of units of Currency A (price currency) that are required to purchase one unit of Currency B (base currency).

- In a direct currency quote (DC/FC), the *domestic* currency is stated as the *price* currency and *foreign* currency is stated as the *base* currency. For example, for a trader in the United States, an exchange rate quote of 1.5 USD/GBP is a direct currency quote.

> Note that the base currency is always set to a quantity of one.

- In an indirect currency quote (FC/DC), the *foreign* currency is stated as the *price* currency and *domestic* currency is stated as the *base* currency. For example, for a trader in the United States, an exchange rate quote of 0.67 GBP/USD is an indirect currency quote.

Note that direct and indirect quotes are just the inverse (reciprocal) of each other (1/1.5 = 0.67).

It is often confusing to describe exchange rate quotes as direct or indirect quotes because domestic and foreign currencies depend on where one is located. To overcome this confusion, the professional FX market has developed a set of FX market conventions, which are listed in Table 2-1.

Table 2-1: Exchange Rate Quote Conventions[1]

FX Rate Quote Convention	Name Convention	Actual Ratio (Price Currency/Base Currency)
EUR	Euro	USD/EUR
JPY	Dollar–yen	JPY/USD
GBP	Pound Sterling	USD/GBP
CAD	Dollar–Canada	CAD/USD
AUD	Aussie	USD/AUD
NZD	Kiwi	USD/NZD
CHF	Swiss franc	CHF/USD
EURJPY	Euro–yen	JPY/EUR
EURGBP	Euro–sterling	GBP/EUR
EURCHF	Euro–Swiss	CHF/EUR
GBPJPY	Pound Sterling–yen	JPY/GBP
EURCAD	Euro–Canada	CAD/EUR
CADJPY	Canada–yen	JPY/CAD

Note that most major spot exchange rates are usually quoted to four decimal places, with one exception among the major currencies being the Japanese yen, for which spot exchange rates are usually quoted to two decimal places.

Please note:

- The three-letter codes (e.g., EUR) refer to the major exchange rates. An exchange rate, which always involves 2 currencies, is different from referring to a single currency in its own right. For example, we do refer to Euro (EUR) as a single currency, but when referring to the EUR *exchange rate*, we are talking about the EUR-USD exchange rate in terms of USD/EUR (USD as **price** currency). In contrast, when referring to the JPY exchange rate, we are talking about the USD-JPY exchange rate in terms of JPY/USD (USD as **base** currency).
- The six-letter codes (e.g., EURJPY) refer to the major cross rates. These are secondary exchange rates, which are not as commonly used as the main exchange rates.
- When both currencies are mentioned in the code or the name convention, the first currency is the base currency and the second currency is the price currency. For example, dollar-yen refers to the exchange rate of JPY/USD (i.e., USD is the base currency and JPY is the price currency). Note that dollar-yen (quote: JPY) may also be written as USDJPY, USD:JPY, or USD-JPY. They all mean the same thing (i.e., JPY/USD).

Note that the three-letter codes always refer to an exchange rate involving the USD, whereas this is not the case with the six-letter codes.

1 - Exhibit 6, Volume 2, CFA Program Curriculum 2018

- Regardless of where she is located, a trader always faces a mix of direct and indirect quotes. For example, a Canadian trader may be quoted a rate of Euro-Canada (CAD/EUR), based on market convention, which is a direct quote for her. At the same time, based on market convention, she might be quoted a rate of Canada-yen (JPY/CAD), which is an indirect quote for her. As a result, traders need to familiarize themselves with market conventions.

In professional FX markets, an exchange rate is usually quoted as a two-sided price. Dealers usually quote a bid-price (the price at which they are willing to buy), and an ask-price or offer price (the price at which they are willing to sell). Bid-ask prices are always quoted in terms of buying and selling the *base* currency. For example, a EUR:USD (or USD/EUR) quote of 1.3802–1.3806 means that the dealer is willing to buy EUR for 1.3802 USD and is willing to sell EUR for 1.3806 USD. From the client's perspective, she will receive 1.3802 USD for selling 1 EUR, but will have to pay 1.3806 USD to purchase 1 EUR.

The bid-price is always lower than the ask-price and the difference between the two represents dealer revenues. Since the introduction of electronic dealing systems, FX markets have become quite efficient in linking traders across different countries. This has led to increased global competition between dealers, shrinking observed bid-ask spreads.

Suppose that the JPY/USD exchange rate increases from 77.58 to 78.45. An increase in the JPY/USD exchange rate means that USD has now become more costly in terms of JPY (it now takes more units of JPY to purchase 1 unit of USD). Stated differently, USD has appreciated against JPY, and JPY has depreciated against USD.

The unannualized percentage increase in the value of the USD against JPY can be calculated as:

$$(78.45 / 77.58) - 1 = 1.12\%$$

We can only calculate the change in value of JPY when we work with exchange rates that show us the change in value or price of JPY in terms of USD. This requires us to make JPY the base currency in our exchange rate quotes.

Please note that the percentage increase in the value of the USD against JPY does not equal the percentage decrease in the value of JPY against USD. In order to determine the percentage decrease in the value of JPY against USD, we must make JPY the *base* currency in the exchange rates that we use in the calculation. The USD/JPY exchange rate *decreases* from 1/77.58 = 0.0129 to 1/78.45 = 0.0127.

Therefore, the unannualized percentage decrease in JPY against USD is calculated as:

$$(0.0127 / 0.0129) - 1 = -1.55\%$$

LOS 20d: Calculate and interpret currency cross-rates. Vol 2, pp 421–425

A cross rate is an exchange rate between two currencies that is derived from each currency's relationship with a third currency. For example, notice from Table 2-1 that two of the major exchange rates quoted in the market are EUR (which represents USD/EUR) and JPY (which represents JPY/USD). Using these two exchange rates, we can calculate the cross rate between the Euro and the yen (EURJPY or JPY/EUR) as follows:

$$\frac{JPY}{EUR} = \frac{\cancel{USD}}{EUR} \times \frac{JPY}{\cancel{USD}}$$

The given exchange rates should be multiplied such that the third currency (common currency) disappears (or mathematically cancels out as it forms the numerator of one quote and the denominator of the other). In order to cancel out the third currency, you might sometimes need to invert one of the exchange rate quotes. For example, consider the EUR (which represents USD/EUR) and GBP (which represents USD/GBP) exchange rates. A trader who wants to calculate the cross rate between the Euro and the British pound cannot do so by simply multiplying these two exchange rates in their presented forms (because the USD will not cancel out). One of the exchange rates must be inverted. The Euro-sterling exchange rate (which represents GBP/EUR) can be calculated as:

$$\frac{GBP}{EUR} = \frac{USD}{EUR} \times \left(\frac{USD}{GBP}\right)^{-1} = \frac{USD}{EUR} \times \frac{GBP}{USD}$$

Example 2-1: Cross Exchange Rates and Percentage Changes

A trader is quoted the following exchange rates:

Table 2-2

	Spot Rate	Expected Spot Rate in One Year
EUR-USD	1.3804	1.3720
GBP-USD	1.5784	1.5698
USD-JPY	76.83	76.70

Calculate the following:

1. Spot EUR-JPY cross rate.
2. Spot EUR-GBP cross rate.
3. By what percentage is the USD expected to appreciate/depreciate against the GBP?
4. By what percentage is the USD expected to appreciate/depreciate against the JPY?
5. List the currencies from strongest to weakest based on their expected performance over the coming year.

Solutions:

1. $$\frac{JPY}{EUR} = \frac{USD}{EUR} \times \frac{JPY}{USD}$$

    $$1.3804 \times 76.83 = 106.0561$$

2. $$\frac{GBP}{EUR} = \frac{USD}{EUR} \times \left(\frac{USD}{GBP}\right)^{-1} = \frac{USD}{EUR} \times \frac{GBP}{USD}$$

    $$1.3804 \times (1.5784)^{-1} = 0.8746$$

3. Over the next year, GBP-USD is expected to decrease from 1.5784 to 1.5698. This means that the base currency (i.e., the GBP) is expected to depreciate against the USD (USD is expected to appreciate versus the GBP).

    In order to calculate the expected change in the value of the USD, we need the exchange rates to represent the price of USD (USD should be the base currency). The expected percentage appreciation in the USD against the GBP is calculated as:

    $$(1/1.5698) / (1/1.5784) - 1 = 0.55\%$$

4. Over the next year, USD-JPY is expected to decrease from 76.83 to 76.70. This means that the base currency (i.e., the USD) is expected to depreciate against the JPY.

    The expected percentage depreciation in the USD against the JPY is calculated as:

    $$(76.70 / 76.83) - 1 = -0.17\%$$

5. EUR-USD is expected to decline from 1.3804 to 1.3720. This means that EUR is expected to depreciate against USD.

    GBP-USD is expected to decline from 1.5784 to 1.5698. This means that GBP is also expected to depreciate against USD.

    Therefore, we can say that the USD is expected to be stronger than EUR and GBP over the next year.

    EUR-GBP is expected to decline from 0.8746 to $1.3720 \times (1.5698)^{-1} = 0.8740$. This means that EUR is expected to depreciate against GBP.

    USD-JPY is expected to decline from 76.83 to 76.70, which means that USD is expected to depreciate against JPY.

    Therefore, the list of currencies from strongest to weakest based on their expected performance over the next year is:

    JPY, USD, GBP, EUR

Cross currency calculations are usually performed automatically by electronic dealing machines and provided to traders. Since market participants can obtain both the underlying exchange rates as well as cross rates, it is important for cross rates to be consistent with the underlying exchange rates. Any disparities will give rise to arbitrage opportunities.

For instance, in Example 2-1, based on the EUR-USD and USD-JPY exchange rates, we determined that the EUR-JPY cross rate equals 106.0561. If a dealer quotes a EUR-JPY exchange rate of 107, then a trader would purchase Euros at JPY106.0561/Euro and sell them for JPY107/Euro, earning a riskless profit of JPY0.9439 per Euro. This type of arbitrage is referred to as triangular arbitrage since it involves three currencies. Practically speaking however, traders and automatic trading algorithms ensure that such price discrepancies almost never occur.

LESSON 3: CURRENCY EXCHANGE RATE CALCULATIONS: PART 2

LOS 20e: Convert forward quotations expressed on a points basis or in percentage terms into an outright forward quotation. Vol 2, pp 425–432

LOS 20g: Calculate and interpret a forward discount or premium. Vol 2, pp 425–432

In professional FX markets, forward exchange rates are quoted in terms of points (pips), which simply represent the difference between the forward rate and the spot rate. Note that these points (pips) are scaled so that they can be related to the last digit in the spot quote (usually the fourth decimal place).

- • If the forward rate is higher than the spot rate, the points are positive and the base currency is said to be trading at a forward premium because it is expected to appreciate in the future. At the same time, the price currency would be trading at a forward discount, which means it is expected to depreciate.
- • If the forward rate is lower than the spot rate, the points are negative and the base currency is trading at a forward discount, as it is expected to depreciate. At the same time, the price currency would be trading at a forward premium and is expected to appreciate.

> Since most exchange rates are quoted to four decimal places, the points are usually scaled up by four decimal places by multiplying them by 10,000.

For example, assume that a trader is quoted a spot CAD/USD exchange rate of 1.0155 and a one-year forward CAD/USD exchange rate of 1.0183. The forward rate is higher than the spot rate, which means that the USD (base currency) is trading at a forward premium and is expected to appreciate. The one-year forward points will be quoted as 28, calculated as follows:

$$\text{Forward points:} (1.0183 - 1.0155) \times 10,000 = 28 \text{ points}$$

Dealers typically quote forward rates in terms of the number of forward points. Forward point quotes may be converted into forward rates by dividing the number of points by 10,000 and adding the result to the spot rate quote (assuming that the quote has 4 decimal places). Continuing with our CAD/USD example, the one-year forward rate may be computed based on forward points as:

$$1.0155 + (28/10,000) = 1.0155 + 0.0028 = 1.0183$$

Sometimes forward rates or points may be quoted as a percentage of the spot rate rather than in terms of an absolute number of points. Continuing with our CAD/USD example, the one year forward rate for the USD can be quoted as:

$$[(1.0155 + 0.0028)/1.0155] - 1 = (1.0183/1.0155) - 1 = 0.2757\%$$

The base currency (USD) is said to be trading at a forward premium of 0.2757%.

When the forward premium is presented in terms of a percentage, the forward rate may be calculated by multiplying the spot rate by one plus (minus) the percentage premium (discount). Continuing with the CAD/USD example, the forward premium of 0.2757% can be used to calculate the forward rate as:

$$1.0155 \times (1 + 0.002757) = 1.0183$$

If the number of points were −28 (if the base currency were trading at a forward discount) the forward rate would be expressed in terms of a percentage as:

$$[(1.0155 - 0.0028)/1.0155] - 1 = -0.2757\%$$

In this case, the forward exchange rate would be calculated as:

$$1.0155 \times (1 - 0..2757) = 1.0127; \text{or}$$
$$1.0155 - 0.0028 = 1.0127$$

LOS 20f: Explain the arbitrage relationship between spot rates, forward rates, and interest rates. Vol 2, pp 425–432

LOS 20h: Calculate and interpret the forward rate consistent with the spot rate and the interest rate in each currency. Vol 2, pp 425–432

Forward exchange rates are calculated in a manner that ensures that traders are not able to earn arbitrage profits. This means that a trader with a specific amount of domestic currency should be able to earn the exact same amount from both of the following investment options:

Option 1: She invests the funds at the domestic risk-free rate (r_{DC}) for a particular period of time.

- If she invests 1 unit of DC at r_{DC} for 1 year, the value of her investment after 1 year would equal $(1 + r_{DC})$.

Option 2: She converts the funds into a foreign currency (at the current spot rate, $S_{FC/DC}$), invests them at the foreign risk-free rate (r_{FC}) for the same period of time (as in Option 1), and then converts them back to the domestic currency at the forward exchange rate ($F_{DC/FC}$), which she locks in today.

- When she converts her 1 unit of DC into FC, she receives $1DC \times S_{FC/DC}$. We use $S_{FC/DC}$ (an indirect exchange rate quote) because it allows us to multiply the investment amount in DC by the exchange rate quote to determine the FC investment amount.
- She invests S_{FC} units of FC at the foreign risk-free rate (r_{FC}). After one year, she receives $S_{FC/DC} \times (1 + r_{FC})$.
- This amount is converted back into DC at the 1 year forward rate (which was decided at the time of initial investment) given by $F_{DC/FC}$ (a direct quote). We use a direct quote for the forward rate because it allows us to multiply the FC amount of investment proceeds by the exchange rate quote to determine the DC value of the investment. After 1 year, the value of her investment (in DC terms) equals $S_{FC/DC} \times (1 + r_{FC}) \times F_{DC/FC}$.

Both these investment options are risk free because they require the money to be invested at risk-free interest rates. Further, the exchange rate risk in the second option is eliminated (hedged) by locking in the forward rate at the time of investment. Since these two investments have identical risk characteristics, it follows that they must have the same return (to preclude arbitrage profits), leading to the following equality:

> The CFA Program curriculum presents this equation in the following form:
> $$(1 + i_d) = \cfrac{S_{f/d}(1 + i_f)\cfrac{1}{}}{F_{f/d}}$$
> We believe that our approach is easier and more intuitive. Both the formulas will of course give you the same answer.

$$(1 + r_{DC}) = S_{FC/DC}(1 + r_{FC}) F_{DC/FC}$$

The above equality can be used to derive the formula for the forward rate:

$$F_{DC/FC} = \frac{1}{S_{FC/DC}} \times \frac{(1 + r_{DC})}{(1 + r_{FC})} \quad \text{or} \quad F_{DC/FC} = S_{DC/FC} \times \frac{(1 + r_{DC})}{(1 + r_{FC})}$$

> This version of the formula is perhaps easiest to remember because it contains the DC term in the numerator for all three components:
> $F_{DC/FC}, S_{DC/FC},$ and $(1 + r_{DC})$

Example 3-1: Calculation of Forward Exchange Rates

A trader is provided with the following information:

Spot AUD-USD = 1.0240
12-month risk-free interest rate in the United States = 2%
12-month risk-free interest rate in Australia = 4%

Calculate the one-year forward AUD-USD exchange rate.

Solution:

First of all, note that the AUD-USD exchange rate is presented in terms of USD/AUD, so it represents the price of AUD in terms of USD.

$F_{USD/AUD} = S_{USD/AUD} [(1 + i_{USD}) / (1 + i_{AUD})]$

$F_{USD/AUD} = 1.0240 \times [(1 + 0.02) / (1 + 0.04)]$

$F_{USD/AUD} = 1.0043$

Note that the price of AUD is expected to fall from 1.024USD/AUD to 1.0043USD/AUD. This implies that the AUD is trading at a forward discount of (1.0043 − 1.0240) × 10,000 = 197 pips. The currency with the higher (lower) interest rate will always trade at a forward discount (premium). The additional interest rate earned in the higher-interest-rate country will be offset by depreciation of that country's currency over the investment horizon.

Forward rates are sometimes interpreted as expected future spot rates.

$$F_t = S_{t+1}$$

$$\frac{(S_{t+1})}{S} - 1 = \Delta\%S(DC/FC)_{t+1} = \frac{(r_{DC} - r_{FC})}{(1 + r_{FC})}$$

Under this interpretation, the expected percentage change in the spot rate is proportional to the interest rate differential ($r_{DC} - r_{FC}$). However, such an interpretation should be used cautiously. Forward rates are unbiased predictors of future spot rates, but this does not make them accurate predictors of future spot rates:

> When we say that forward rates are unbiased predictors of expected future spot rates, we mean that they do not systematically over or underestimate the future spot rate. However, their predictive value is extremely limited because the margin for error in these forecasts is very significant.

- The direction of the predicted change in spot rates is counterintuitive. All other factors constant, an increase in domestic interest rates would be expected to lead to an appreciation of the domestic currency. The equation above suggests otherwise. Using the numbers in Example 3-1, the risk-free rate in Australia is higher than the risk-free rate in the United States, but the forward rate (expected future spot rate) is lower than the current spot rate (1.0043 versus 1.0240), which implies that the AUD is expected to depreciate versus the USD.
- Historical data show that forward rates are poor predictors of future spot rates. Aside from interest rate differentials, exchange rates are influenced by several other factors.

Therefore, for the purposes of the exam it is best to remember the formula for the forward rate based on the underlying no-arbitrage relationship between the two investment options outlined earlier.

We have shown that forward rates are linked to the interest rate differentials between countries. Now we illustrate why forward points (and forward rates) are related to time-scaled interest rate differentials between countries.

Table 3-1 presents a sample spot rate and forward points for the Euro-dollar (USD/EUR) exchange rate.

Table 3-1: Sample Spot and Forward Quotes[2]

Maturity	Spot Rate or Forward Points
Spot	1.2875
One week	−0.3
One month	−1.1
Three months	−5.5
Six months	−13.3
Twelve months	−26.5

2 - Exhibit 7, Volume 2, CFA Program Curriculum 2018

Notice that the absolute number of points increases with maturity. This is because the number of forward points is proportional to the yield differential between the two countries *scaled by the term to maturity.*

- Given the interest rate differential, the longer the term to maturity, the greater the absolute number of forward points.
- Given the term to maturity, the higher the interest rate differential, the greater the absolute number of forward points.

Example 3-2 illustrates the points listed in the two bullets above.

Example 3-2: Calculation of Forward Exchange Rates

Spot AUD-USD = 1.0240

Calculate:

1. The 30-day forward AUD-USD exchange rate given that the:
   - 30-day risk-free interest rate in the United States = 2%
   - 30-day risk-free interest rate in Australia = 3%
2. The 180-day forward AUD-USD exchange rate given that the:
   - 180-day risk-free interest rate in the United States = 2%
   - 180-day risk-free interest rate in Australia = 3%
3. The 180-day forward AUD-USD exchange rate given that the:
   - 180-day risk-free interest rate in the United States = 2%
   - 180-day risk-free interest rate in Australia = 4%

Solutions:

1. $$F(30)_{USD/AUD} = 1.0240 \times \frac{[1+0.02\,(30/360)]}{[1+0.03\,(30/360)]} = 1.02315$$

   The AUD is trading at a discount of approximately
   $(1.02315 - 1.0240) \times 10,000 = 8.5 \text{ pips}$

2. $$F(180)_{USD/AUD} = 1.0240 \times \frac{[1+0.02\,(180/360)]}{[1+0.03\,(180/360)]} = 1.0190$$

   The AUD is trading at a discount of approximately
   $(1.0190 - 1.0240) \times 10,000 = 50 \text{ pips}$

3. $$F(180)_{USD/AUD} = 1.0240 \times \frac{[1+0.02\,(180/360)]}{[1+0.04\,(180/360)]} = 1.0140$$

   The AUD is trading at a discount of approximately
   $(1.0140 - 1.0240) \times 10,000 = 100 \text{ pips}$

Important takeaways:

- Given the same interest rate differential (in Questions 1 and 2), the longer the term to maturity (180 versus 30 days), the higher the absolute number of forward points (50 versus 8.5 points).
    - However, note that the number of forward points is not exactly proportional to the horizon of the forward contract.
    - A six-fold increase in the horizon (from 30 to 180 days) results in the number of forward points being 50/8.5 = 5.88 times larger.
- Given the same term to maturity (in Questions 2 and 3), the higher the interest rate differential (2% versus 1%), the higher the absolute number of forward points (100 versus 50 points).
    - The number of forward points is exactly proportional to the interest rate differential.
    - A two-fold increase in the interest rate differential (from 1% to 2%) resulted in a two-fold increase in the number of forward points (from 50 to 100 points).

LESSON 4: EXCHANGE RATE REGIMES AND THE IMPACT OF EXCHANGE RATES ON TRADE AND CAPITAL FLOWS

LOS 20i: Describe exchange rate regimes. Vol 2, pp 432–443

The policy framework adopted by a country's central bank to manage its currency's exchange rate is called an **exchange rate regime**. An ideal currency regime should have the following properties:

- The exchange rate between any two currencies should be credibly fixed in order to eliminate currency-related uncertainty regarding the prices of goods and services and values of real and financial assets.
- All currencies should be fully convertible to ensure unrestricted flow of capital.
- Each country should be able to undertake fully independent monetary policy in pursuit of domestic objectives, such as growth and inflation targets.

Unfortunately, these conditions are not consistent. For example, if a country's central bank reduces interest rates (undertakes independent monetary policy), investors would seek higher returns elsewhere and sell the domestic currency. Consequently, the central bank would be forced to purchase domestic currency and sell foreign currency in order to keep the exchange rate at its previous level. The reduction in domestic money supply would eventually put upward pressure on domestic interest rates until they go back to previous levels, basically negating the initial expansionary monetary policy.

Generally speaking, the more freely the currency is allowed to float and the more tightly convertibility is controlled, the greater the effectiveness of monetary policy.

Types of Exchange Rate Regimes

Arrangements with No Separate Legal Tender
- Dollarization: A country uses the currency of another nation (usually the U.S. dollar) as its medium of exchange and unit of account.
    - The country inherits that currency's (e.g., the USD) credibility, but not its credit-worthiness.

- ○ Interest rates on U.S. dollars in a dollarized economy are usually not the same as those on dollar deposits in the United States.
  - ○ Pros:
    - ■ Central banks are not able to print their way out of high national debt.
    - ■ Can facilitate growth of trade and international capital flows, as it creates an expectation of economic stability.
  - ○ Cons:
    - ■ Countries lose their ability to conduct independent monetary policy.
- Monetary union: Member countries share the same legal tender (e.g., the European Economic and Monetary Union (EMU) whose members use the Euro as their currency).
  - ○ Monetary policy is conducted by the ECB for the entire region.
  - ○ Pros:
    - ■ Gives credibility to economies that have a history of fiscal excess and monetary indiscipline.
  - ○ Cons:
    - ■ Members do not gain creditworthiness (e.g., Greece in 2010).
    - ■ Members cannot conduct their own independent monetary policy.

Arrangements Where Countries Have Their Own Currency

Currency Board System

The IMF defines a currency board system (CBS) as "A monetary regime based on an explicit legislative commitment to exchange domestic currency for a specified foreign currency at a fixed exchange rate, combined with restrictions on the issuing authority to ensure fulfillment of its legal obligation. This implies that domestic currency will be issued only against foreign exchange and it remains fully backed by foreign assets."

- The central bank holds foreign currency reserves to cover, at the fixed parity, the entire monetary base of a country (e.g., Hong Kong).
- Expansion and contraction of the monetary base are directly linked to trade and capital flows.
- The exchange rate is essentially fixed, but it is allowed to fluctuate within a narrow band.
- The central bank cannot act as the lender of last resort, but can provide short-term liquidity.
- The system works best when:
  - ○ Domestic prices and wages are very flexible;
  - ○ Nontraded sectors of the domestic economy are relatively small; and
  - ○ Global supply of the reserve asset grows at a slow, steady rate consistent with long-run real growth with stable prices.
- The monetary authority can earn a profit by paying little or no interest on its liabilities (the monetary base), and earning a market rate on its assets (foreign currency reserves). This profit is referred to as seigniorage. Under dollarization, seigniorage goes to the country whose currency is used.

Fixed Parity

- The exchange rate is either pegged to a single currency or to a basket of currencies of major trading partners. The monetary authority stands ready to buy or sell foreign currency reserves to maintain the exchange rate within a narrow band.
- Although monetary independence is limited, the central bank can act as a lender of last resort.
- The success of this system depends on both the country's willingness as well as its ability to maintain the fixed exchange rate.
  - A certain level of foreign exchange reserves are required to maintain credibility. Otherwise, the currency is susceptible to speculative attacks and devaluation.
- Differs from a CBS in the following two ways:
  - The country can choose to adjust or abandon the parity since there is no legislative commitment to maintaining the specified parity.
  - The target level of foreign exchange reserves is discretionary and is not linked to domestic monetary aggregates.

Target Zone

- Similar to a fixed-rate system.
- The only difference is that the monetary authority aims to maintain the exchange rate within a slightly broader range.
  - This gives the central bank greater ability to conduct discretionary policy.

Active and Passive Crawling Pegs

- Under a passive crawling peg system, the exchange rate is adjusted frequently in line with the rate of inflation.
  - Used in Brazil during periods of high inflation.
  - The aim here is to prevent a run on foreign currency reserves.
- Under an active crawling peg system, the exchange rate is pre-announced for the coming weeks and changes are made in small steps.
  - Used in Argentina, Chile, and Uruguay.
  - The aim here is to manipulate inflationary expectations.

Fixed Parity with Crawling Bands

- The country initially fixes its exchange rate to a foreign currency, but gradually moves toward a more flexible system by pre-announcing the widening of bands around the central parity. This allows the country greater flexibility in determining its monetary policy.

Managed Float

- The country does not explicitly state its exchange rate target, but intervenes in the FX markets to meet its policy objectives (regarding balance of trade, price stability, or unemployment).
- Such intervention (also called dirty floating) typically also causes the country's trading partners to retaliate in a similar fashion and leads to instability in FX markets as a whole.

Independently Floating Rates

- The central bank rarely intervenes in the determination of its exchange rate, which is left to be determined by market supply and demand factors.
- Enables the central bank to engage in independent monetary policy aimed at achieving price stability and full employment.
- Also allows it to act as a lender of last resort to troubled institutions.

Note that the concepts of floating, managed, crawling, or target zone are not strict rules. Central banks do occasionally (implicitly or explicitly) switch their exchange rate regimes to meet policy objectives.

LOS 20j: Explain the impact of exchange rates on countries' international trade and capital flows. Vol 2, pp 443–453

Recap from Reading 16:

$$(X - M) = (S - I) + (T - G)$$

Classifying $(T - G)$ a government saving:

Trade surplus = Government saving + Private saving – Investment

- A trade surplus means that the economy as whole (government saving and private saving combined) saves enough to fund its investment needs. The excess saving is used to accumulate financial claims against the rest of the world. Recall that countries with a trade surplus must finance the deficits of their trading partners, which gives rise to financial claims against those countries.
- A trade deficit means that the country must borrow from the rest of the world to meet its investment needs.

Now we bring exchange rates and assets prices into the discussion.

If investors expect a significant change in the exchange rate, they will buy the currency that is expected to appreciate and sell the currency that is expected to depreciate. This implies that capital may flow from one country to another. This potential flow of capital must either:

- Be accompanied by a change in the trade balance (as the capital account and trade balances must always offset); or
- Be discouraged by changes in asset prices and exchange rates.

Because expenditure/saving decisions and prices of goods and services (which affect the trade balance) occur more slowly than changes in the exchange rate and asset prices (which affect the capital account), most of the adjustments occur in financial markets. The flow of capital is limited and actual capital flows remain consistent with trade flows.

- In a fixed exchange rate regime, the central bank absorbs the private capital flows to maintain the exchange rate. The adjustment occurs in other asset prices (typically interest rates) unless than bank is forced to let the exchange rate adjust.
- In a floating exchange rate regime, the exchange rate adjustment is very quick, which diminishes the prospects for any further movement.

The point is that (potential and actual) capital flows are the main determinants of exchange rate movements in the short and medium terms. Trade flows are more important in the long term, as saving/spending decisions are made and the prices of goods and services adjust.

Exchange Rates and the Trade Balance

The Elasticities Approach

Recap from Reading 14:

- If demand is relatively price elastic (elasticity > 1) a decrease (increase) in the price of a good will result in an increase (decrease) in total expenditure on the good.
- If demand is relatively price inelastic (elasticity < 1) a decrease (increase) in the price of a good will result in a decrease (increase) in total expenditure on the good.

A **devaluation** or depreciation of the domestic currency makes domestic goods relatively cheaper for foreigners (**reduces** the price of domestic goods in terms of foreign currency). At the same time it implies an **appreciation** of foreign currencies, which makes foreign goods relatively **more expensive** for domestic citizens (in terms of domestic currency).

Assume that a country is running a trade deficit that it wants to reduce. Given that the currency is expected to depreciate, would the country prefer that demand for imports and exports be elastic or inelastic?

- If demand for **imports** is relatively **elastic**, the **increase** in price of foreign goods (due to domestic currency depreciation) will result in a **decrease** in **total expenditure** on imports.
- If demand for **imports** is relatively **inelastic**, the **increase** in price of imports (due to domestic currency depreciation) will result in an **increase** in **total expenditure** on imports.
- If demand for **exports** is relatively **elastic**, the **decrease** in price of exports (due to domestic currency depreciation) will result in an **increase** in **total revenue** from exports.
- If demand for **exports** is relatively **inelastic**, the **decrease** in price of exports (due to domestic currency depreciation) will result in a **decrease** in **total revenue** from exports.

Therefore, the ideal combination for a country that wants to reduce its trade deficit and expects its currency to depreciate is that its imports and exports both be relatively elastic. This is the basic idea behind the Marshall-Lerner condition. Demand for imports and exports must be sufficiently price sensitive such that increasing the price of imports increases the difference between export revenue and import expenditures.

> Marshall-Lerner condition: $\omega_X \varepsilon_X + \omega_M (\varepsilon_M - 1) > 0$
>
> where:
> ω_X = Share of exports in total trade
> ω_M = Share of imports in total trade
> ε_X = Price elasticity of demand for exports
> ε_M = Price elasticity of demand for imports

If this condition is satisfied, devaluation/depreciation in the domestic currency will lead the trade balance toward a surplus.

- The first term represents the change in export revenues assuming that the domestic currency price of exports remains unchanged.
    - Export revenues (in domestic currency terms) will increase as the domestic currency falls in value (as long as demand is not perfectly inelastic) since quantity demanded will increase.
- The second term represents the change in import expenditure.
    - Assuming that imports are billed in foreign currency, the increase in price (caused by the devaluation) in domestic currency terms increases import expenditure.
    - The decrease in quantity demanded (caused by the increase in price) reduces import expenditure.
    - The net effect depends on the elasticity of import demand. If elasticity > 1, import expenditure declines.

The more elastic the demand for imports and exports, the more likely that a depreciation of the domestic currency will lead the trade balance toward a surplus. In fact, if the elasticity of demand for imports is greater than 1, the trade balance will definitely improve. Note that the elasticity of demand for imports becomes more important (and export elasticity less important) as the trade deficit gets larger. This is because a larger trade deficit means that w_M increases relative to w_E.

Generally speaking, exchange rates will be more effective in adjusting trade imbalances if the countries' imports and exports are composed of items that have relatively elastic demand, for example:

- Goods that have viable substitutes
- Goods that trade in competitive markets
- Luxury goods (rather than necessities)
- Goods that represent a larger proportion of a consumer's expenditures
- Goods that represent a larger proportion of total input costs for a final product.

A J-curve pattern will also arise if short-term elasticities do not satisfy the Marshall-Lerner condition but long-term elasticities do.

Finally, note that the impact of exchange rates on the trade balance may not always be immediate due to the fact that there is a time lag between the initial depreciation and the eventual impact on **quantities** of imports and exports. The increase in import **prices** will lead to an increase in total expenditure on imports over the short run (leading to a worsening of the deficit). However, as the currency stabilizes at the new (lower) levels, economic agents adapt and eventually the trade balance improves (toward a surplus) as **quantities** of imports and exports respond to the change in price. Overall, the trade deficit makes a "*J*-like" formation.

The Absorption Approach

Recall that an economy's trade balance equals its total savings (including the fiscal balance) minus investment expenditure. Equivalently, the trade balance equals the difference between national income/output and domestic expenditure (or absorption). This implies that devaluation of the exchange rate can direct the trade balance toward a surplus if it increases:

- National income relative to expenditure; or equivalently
- National saving relative to investment in physical capital.

If an economy is operating below full employment, then, by diverting demand toward domestically produced goods (as foreign goods become more expensive in domestic currency terms), devaluation can increase income/output. A portion of this additional income will be saved so expenditure will rise by less than income, resulting in an improvement in the trade balance.

If the economy is operating at full employment (potential GDP), output/income cannot be increased further. As a result, expenditure must decline for there to be an improvement in the trade balance.

> For a more permanent improvement in the trade balance, there must be fundamental changes in expenditure and saving behavior.

- Expenditure may decline, but the improvement in the trade balance would only be temporary. Initially, a devaluation would hurt households' real wealth. This would prompt a reduction in spending and an increase in saving, improving the trade balance. Eventually however, once real wealth is rebuilt, there will be a decrease in saving. For a more permanent improvement in the trade balance, there must be fundamental changes in expenditure and saving behavior.
- Expenditure may not decline. All other things remaining the same, domestic currency depreciation makes domestic goods cheaper for foreigners and should improve the trade balance. In this case however, depreciation of the domestic currency also causes domestic prices to rise, such that the increase in domestic prices offsets the stimulative impact of the currency depreciation, and the trade balance reverts to its original level.

206
202-
1507

Taryn
Rawlings

Lauren
Lavoro

Not
Lavy